The Artist's Workshop

STUDIES IN THE HISTORY OF ART · 38 ·
Center for Advanced Study in the Visual Arts
Symposium Papers XXII

The Artist's Workshop

Edited by Peter M. Lukehart

National Gallery of Art, Washington
Distributed by the University Press of New England
Hanover and London

Editorial Board
FRANKLIN KELLY, *Chairman*
SUSAN ARENSBERG
EDGAR PETERS BOWRON
SARAH FISHER
THERESE O'MALLEY
ELIZABETH P. STREICHER

Managing Editor
CAROL ERON

Designer
PHYLLIS HECHT

Editorial Assistant
MARIA TOUSIMIS

This publication was produced by the Editors
Office, National Gallery of Art, Washington
Editor-in-Chief, Frances P. Smyth

The type is Trump Medieval, set by
BG Composition, Baltimore, Maryland

The text paper is 80 pound LOE Dull

Printed by Schneidereith & Sons,
Baltimore, Maryland

Distributed by the University Press of
New England, 23 South Main Street,
Hanover, New Hampshire 03755

Abstracted by RILA (International Repertory
of the Literature of Art), Williamstown,
Massachusetts 01267

Proceedings of the symposium "The Artist's
Workshop" sponsored by the Center for
Advanced Study in the Visual Arts and Johns
Hopkins University Department of the History
of Art, Washington, D.C., 10–11 March 1989

ISSN 0091-7338
ISBN 089468-190-7

Contents

HENRY A. MILLON, *Dean*
Center for Advanced Study in the Visual Arts

Preface

In 1989 the Center for Advanced Study in the Visual Arts and the Department of the History of Art at Johns Hopkins University jointly sponsored the eighth and final symposium of an annual series initiated in 1982. This gathering sought to explore the varying character, uses, and practices of the artist's workshop. Among the issues investigated by the speakers and addressed in the present volume are the pedagogical responsibilities of the workshop; the workshop as a center of production and power; the workshop as a locus of aesthetic creation; and the workshop as a corporate enterprise.

The practices, traditions, and products of the workshop are examined within wide geographical and temporal contexts. In this volume are essays which focus on the artist's workshop from the trecento through the nineteenth century, from Italy and England to Iran and Japan.

The organizers are grateful to the Arthur Vining Davis Foundations for helping to make this gathering possible. More-over, the Center for Advanced Study and Johns Hopkins express their appreciation to Peter Lukehart for preparing the papers for publication and for writing the introduction to this volume.

The Center for Advanced Study was founded in 1979, as part of the National Gallery of Art, to promote study of the history, theory, and criticism of art, architecture, and urbanism through programs of fellowships, meetings, research, and publication. This publication forms part of a separate series of *Studies in the History of Art* designed to document scholarly meetings held under the auspices of the Center and to stimulate further research. A complete listing of published titles may be found on the opening leaf of this volume. A number of these publications are the result of collaborations between the Center for Advanced Study and sister institutions, such as Johns Hopkins University for this volume, and other universities, museums, and research institutes.

PETER M. LUKEHART

Trout Gallery, Dickinson College

Introduction

*Quisquam vereri potest quem inridet?
quisquam dicto oboeddiret cuius verba con-
tempserit. Quom in officina Apellis Alexander
Magnus de picturae arte dissereret, "Tace
quae nescis," inquit, "ne te pueri illi, qui
purpurissimum subterunt, contemnant" . . . .
Nemo tanta auctoritate est, qui non, ubi
peritia deficitur, ab eo qui peritior est,
despiciatur. . . .*

*Can anyone fear him whom he laughs at, or
could anyone obey his order, whose words he
despised? When Alexander the Great was discussing the art of painting in the studio of
Apelles, the painter said, "Hold your tongue
about what you don't understand, that those
boys yonder who are mixing the purple paint
may not despise you". . . . There is no one,
however authoritative, who when his skill is
at fault is not looked down upon by him who
has greater skill. . . .*[1]

Throughout history this story has been
retold by artists, theoreticians, and
rhetoricians. This version of the anecdote,
which has its immediate source in Pliny's
Natural History, is from the correspondence of Marcus Cornelius Fronto (c. 90–
166/167). In this letter, Fronto wishes to
instruct Marcus Aurelius about the appro-
priateness of content, word choice, and
presentation to the audience for whom a
particular oration is intended. Fronto chose
to illustrate his lesson with this image of
the redoubtable Alexander embarrassing
himself in the company of experts by

broaching a subject of which he had only
the most cursory knowledge; worse still,
even the young boys (*pueri*) in the studio
knew more about the métier of painting
than Alexander did.

Fronto, following Pliny, chose to describe
the space in which Apelles worked as
officina. According to the *Oxford Latin
Dictionary*, *officina* means "a place where
something is made, a workshop, manufactory, etc. *b* (applied to a hen-house) *c* an
artist's studio *d* (transf., esp. applied to a
training-school) *e* the process or act of
manufacturing."[2] Even in the definition of
the word, the editors, undoubtedly following the elusiveness of its meaning in classical Latin, elide workshop, studio, and
manufactory. In the case of Fronto, who
was so careful about the choice of words,
however, one must assume that a very
specific connotation was intended. Would
Apelles conceivably have produced his art
in a workshop? And would Alexander
have deigned to pass so many hours in the
company of an artisan? If so, Fronto could
have chosen the more precise term of *fabrica*, which always implies a craftsman's
space where something is made with the
hands.[3] The distinction between artist's
studio and artist's workshop is at least as
old as the Greco-Roman sources from
which the majority of our information
concerning the arts of antiquity derives.
Yet throughout that history, contemporary perceptions about the space in which

1. Salvator Rosa, *Alexander
in the Studio of Apelles*,
c. 1662, etching with
drypoint
Calcografia Nazionale, Rome

an artist worked corresponded both to one's experience of a studio or a workshop and to one's estimation of an artist's worth or status.

When Salvator Rosa gave physical form to the Alexandrian anecdote around 1662 (fig. 1), he was dependent on Pliny's version and not Fronto's, as is evident in the inscription at the base of the etching: "Alexandro M[agno] multa imperite in officina disserenti/silentium comiter suadebat Apelles, rideri eum dicens/a pueris, qui colores tererent (Alexander the Great used to discuss a great deal [about painting] in the studio, and Apelles would politely advise him to be silent, saying that the boys who were grinding colors were laughing at him)."[4] Rosa, who was manifestly interested in inventing an artistic persona, chose to locate the action within a studio in which the *pueri* were not grinding colors as both Pliny and Fronto tell us, but drawing.[5] Rosa's transformation of the narrative, though the figures are classically garbed, tells us more about seventeenth-century conceptions of the status of the artist and the spaces in which art was then created than it does about the conditions of Athenian artists in the fourth century B.C. Like Pliny and Fronto, Rosa made certain assumptions about the working space of the artist and about the type of work that was undertaken there, which accorded with his own view of what was appropriate for the emperor and the preeminent artist of an earlier time.[6]

Even within the title of this volume, "The Artist's Workshop," there are certain assumptions concerning the place in which art is made and the product that results from the artist's creative processes (which are challenged, reevaluated, and clarified in these papers). On the basis of artists' intentions from period to period or culture to culture, one could equally have argued that our subject should have been the artist's studio or the artists' academy. Furthermore, in the past two decades the discipline of art history has divided scholars on the significance of the relationship between artists and their environments. Whereas the contextualists insist on the intertwined nature of the artist's familial, social, cultural, and intellectual experi-

ences, post-structuralists and semioticians at least since Roland Barthes assert that the artist is merely the second-to-the-last link in the metonymic chain that results in the creation of a work of art.[7]

It is precisely the plurality of the conception of the artist's working space that remains to be dissected and interpreted with the following questions in mind. What is the artist's workshop and what does it imply? Is it a geographical locus of creation (creativity)?[8] A center of power from which a chain of command is established from master through apprentice, or in the case of court art, from patron to master (to assistants)?[9] A corporate enterprise, the individual identities of which must be posited or reconstructed in order to assign attributions?[10] Or, is it a pedagogical center in which the artist receives or completes his education, possibly after having attended other schools?[11]

The diverse studies presented here share an interest in workshop practices. The contributors tend to isolate individual artists or studios and workshops from a larger framework in order to illuminate idiosyncracies or uniqueness, placing the object of their inquiry in relief against overall trends or traditional conceptions of the terms. Contributors were requested to define their use of terms such as studio, workshop, assistants, and students. Clearly differentiated terminology might provide testing grounds for the efficacy of the common language of art-historical discourse regarding workshops and the kinds of activity that take place within them, especially important in a publication that treats a variety of cultures and periods.

We begin with trecento Italy and the question of authorship for undocumented or partially documented panel paintings. For the past three decades Mojmír Frinta has been publishing the results of his diligent studies of the punch work on gold-ground paintings, especially those of the Sienese school. Using visual comparisons to the large corpus of paintings he has studied, Frinta assigns hitherto incorrectly or unattributed panels to specific artists or workshops on the basis of punches that belonged to them. Where possible, he also refers to commissions that name the artist's workshop.

New archival evidence is examined in my own contribution regarding the roles played by members of Genoese artists' workshops and studios in the late sixteenth and early seventeenth centuries in relation to larger educational trends and to the distribution of labor in Italian workshops and studios. This documentation provides a glimpse into the division of the students within the master's *bottega* (workshop) or studio. It is argued that young Genoese artists who belonged to the bourgeoisie and the nobility were still under the care and support of their fathers (*sotto padre*) and thus did not perform the menial tasks normally associated with an apprenticeship; rather, they were taught exclusively how to draw and paint, as though members of an academy. It was, instead, the students under contract (*accartati*) to the masters and other hired helpers who cleaned the shop, prepared the paints and other materials, and provided physical assistance.

At about the time that Genoese painters were caught up in a major struggle (1590–1591) between the artists who practiced in open shops and those who practiced privately within studios in their own homes, some of the most gifted artists in Bologna were frequenting the Accademia degli Incamminati, founded in 1582 by Ludovico, Agostino, and Annibale Carracci. In "Practice in the Carracci Academy," Gail Feigenbaum treats the Carracci teaching program as well as the problems surrounding attributions to individual members of their academy. She proposes that the difficulties scholars and connoisseurs now have in identifying individual hands of the Carracci in fact may be traced to a deliberate attempt on their part to create a collective identity, one that effaces particularized styles.

In Eastern cultures within the same general period, the situation for artists could not have been more different. John Rosenfield examines the dynastic schools of painting that developed both at the courts and in aristocratic urban centers of Japan in "Japanese Studio Practice: The Tosa Family and the Imperial Painting Office in the Seventeenth Century." On the basis of biographical and visual evidence, Rosenfield posits a symbiotic rela-

tionship between court taste and the stylistic response of the studios, and in particular he traces the lineage of one of the most significant schools established in imperial Japan: that of Tosa Mitsuoki. Yet even as he accommodated the demands of his patrons, Mitsuoki responded also to his own inner struggle with artistic traditions, not only generally those of China and Japan, but also specifically those of his forebear Tosa Mitsunobu.

From the pluralistic tastes of the courts and artists of seventeenth-century Japan Marianna Shreve Simpson turns the discussion to the production of Islamic manuscripts in "The Making of Manuscripts and the Workings of the *Kitab-khana* in Safavid Iran." In an effort to clarify our conception of the division of labor in the workshop and the relationships between artists, artisans, and patrons, Simpson seeks to redefine the *kitab-khana*—which was formerly understood either as a library or book house in the Western sense, or as a locus of production to be identified as a scriptorium, atelier, studio, or workshop—as a multilayered and highly organized enterprise that is more elusive than has been assumed previously. Colophonic inscriptions and other internal evidence suggest that rather than indicating a geographical center for all facets of production, the *kitab-khana* may in some cases refer to a collecting point where the materials of calligraphers, illuminators, painters, and binders were compiled into luxury manuscripts.

Architectural practices and pedagogy in Italian and British studios, which might more properly be called ateliers, especially in the case of the latter, are addressed in the three following papers. Hellmut Hager brings the fruit of a life's study on seicento Roman architecture to bear in "Carlo Fontana: Pupil, Partner, Principal, Preceptor." The title alludes to the far-ranging influence of Fontana, not only on his own school but also on Roman architecture and urban planning in general. Drawing on primary and secondary sources, Hager traces Fontana's development from an architect-engineer, the career for which he was initially trained, into an artist-architect, as his skills were refined under the tutelage of Cortona and Bernini. When he was matriculated as an *architetto di merito* in the Accademia di San Luca in 1667, Fontana established both his professional independence and his official capacity as teacher. From this moment forward, Fontana himself directed his *giovani* (which Hager apparently defines, as I do, as students and not servants of the architect) to carry out the more mundane tasks of site drawings and preliminary drawings. Fontana's method of training, which led from the making of simple measurements and surveys to increasingly demanding collaborative efforts, was to shape the destiny of his legacy through the beginning of the eighteenth century, including the career of his son, Francesco. This educational model was to have an impact of equal proportion to that of his constructed oeuvre.

David Brownlee's essay on "Victorian Office Practice and Victorian Architecture: The Case of Sir Gilbert Scott," suggests that the Italian paradigm, if not specifically Carlo Fontana's own example, still held sway well into the nineteenth century. The English architectural offices continued to employ clerks, draftsmen, articled pupils, and designers—seemingly literal translations of the Italian terms—as well as the expected architects. Yet with all the baggage of an inherited and looming tradition, British architecture and architectural practice were transformed just when one would expect stasis or stagnation. In the absence of telling written documentation, Brownlee posits a visual and intellectual dialogue between Scott and his most gifted pupils—George Edmond Street, William White, and George Frederick Bodley—that led to the development of modern office practices. Even within a tradition-bound hierarchical arrangement, these students demonstrated individual talents that were both cultivated and esteemed.

The gradual elevation of the status of European artists from the fifteenth through the eighteenth centuries and their concomitant attempts to deny the centrality of manual labor and craftsmanship to the artist's enterprise stand in sharp contrast to the situation at the time of the Industrial Revolution and the incipient rise of Marxism and socialism. In "The

British Arts and Crafts Workshop between Tradition and Reform," we have come full circle. Larry Lutchmansingh takes up the argument of John Ruskin, William Morris, William Lethaby, and Charles Ashbee, among others, that manual labor should instead be exalted as it was, at least in the minds of the members of the Arts and Crafts Movement, in the Middle Ages.[12] The emphasis on the handmade object and the reorganization of artists into guilds and workshops—as opposed to architectural offices and academies—opened new avenues for the practice of art and architecture; additionally, it marked a significant moment in the reevaluation and valorization of the formerly disparaged decorative arts.

NOTES

I am deeply indebted to my colleagues Eric Garberson and Melinda Schlitt for their useful suggestions. I would like also to thank Diane De Grazia and Luigi Ficacci for their assistance in obtaining a photograph of Rosa's print.

1. Marcus Cornelius Fronto, *The Correspondence of Marcus Cornelius Fronto*, trans. C.R. Haines, 2 vols. (London and New York, 1920), 2:58–61.

2. P.G.W. Glare, ed., *Oxford Latin Dictionary* (Oxford, 1982), 1243. The word can apply to anything from a metalsmith's shop to an artist's studio, from a hen-house to a trade school. The use as painter's studio is noted in Vitruvius, *De architectura*, 6.4.2, as well as in Pliny, *Naturalis historia*, 35.81.

3. Glare, 665: Fabrica: "1 A craft, art. (spec.) **b** the craft of metal working; of building. . . . 2 The action or process of making, building, construction. **b** the manner of construction, workmanship. . . . 3 A workshop. . . ."

4. The full account can be found in Pliny's *Naturalis historia*, Book 35.36.12: "fuit enim et comitas illi, propter quam gratior Alexandro Magno frequenter in officinam ventitanti—nam, ut diximus, ab alio se pingi vetuerat edicto—, sed in officina imperite suadebat, rideri eum dicens a pueris, qui colores tererent. Tantum erat auctoritati iuris in regem alioqui iracundum." H. Rackham, who served as translator and editor for the Loeb edition of the *Natural History* (Cambridge, Mass., 1952), 324–325, rendered the word *officina* as "studio." My translation of Rosa's paraphrase follows Rackham's with some minor modifications.

For a discussion of the date of the print, see Mario Rotili, *Salvator Rosa Incisore* (Naples, 1974), cat. 102, 220–221. See also Richard Wallace in Richard Wallace et al., *Salvator Rosa* [exh. cat., Hayward Gallery] (London, 1973), 61–62. For the iconography of the etching and its relation to other works in Rosa's oeuvre, see Wallace, "The Genius of Salvator Rosa," *Art Bulletin* 47 (1965), 471–480, and Wendy Wassyng Roworth, *Pictor successor: A Study of Salvator Rosa as Satirist, Cynic, and Painter* (New York and London, 1978), esp. 303–328. Roworth (303) argues that *Alexander in the Studio of Apelles* should not be paired, as Wallace suggests, with *Il genio di Salvator Rosa* as a variation on personal allegory, but rather seen as a historical anecdote more convincingly related to Rosa's print of *Alexander and Diogenes*. Whereas I agree, in general, with her interpretation of the prints, I take issue with Roworth's assertion that Rosa "explicity illustrated" Apelles' *pueri* as Pliny described them "grind[ing] the colors." Clearly, none of the boys hold any of the tools that are associated with color grinding.

5. For further discussion of the status of color grinding, see my study of the studio practices of Italian artists in the late sixteenth and early seventeeth centuries elsewhere in this volume.

6. There is a vast and interesting literature on Apelles and Alexander, from which I would like to single out the works most important to the present discussion: Henry Houssaye, *Histoire d'Apelles* (Paris, 1868), though he passes over this anecdote and focuses on Alexander and Campaspe; David Cast, *The Calumny of Apelles: A Study in the Humanist Tradition* (New Haven and London, 1981); and Pierre Georgel and Ann-Marie Lecoq, *La peinture dans la peinture* [exh. cat., Musée des Beaux-Arts] (Dijon, 1982). Cast (165–166) cites the Alexander and Apelles incident as evidence of Lorenzo Valla's dictum that every discipline has its proper "rules" and "dignity," which Renaissance artists used to help aggrandize their own status. I must also give credit to Cast for his discovery of the only two illustrations of the "impolitic" passage; that is, Rosa's print reproduced here as figure 1 and a drawing by the eighteenth-century Venetian artist, Antonio Novelli (for which, see A. Bettaglio *Le dessin vénitien au XVIIIe siècle* [Venice, 1971], no. 165). Searches through Pigler's *Barockthemen* and Iconclass have been futile. Georgel and Lecoq (51–53), who depend very much on Cast's research, rightfully link the various anecdotes concerning Apelles' arrogance, including those of the shoemaker in the studio ("Let the cobbler look no higher than the shoe!") and Alexander's visit to Apelles' studio.

7. The bibliography on the subject has grown enormously since the publication of Roland Barthes' "The Death of the Author" in 1968 (reprinted in English in Barthes, *Image-Music-Text*, trans. and ed. Stephen Heath [Glasgow, 1977], 142–146). Among the many studies available, see Michel Foucault, "What Is an Author?" (reprinted in *Language, Counter-Memory, Practice: Selected Essays and Interviews*, ed. D.F. Bouchard [Ithaca, 1977]); Nikos Hadjinicolaou, *Art History and Class Struggle* (London, 1978); and, most recently, Mieke Bal and Norman Bryson, "Semiotics and Art History," *Art Bulletin* 73 (June 1991), 174–208. The problematic reception of critical theory continues to polarize the field, as evidenced by the lengthy exchange that followed the publication of Bal and Bryson's manifesto, "Some Thoughts on 'Semiotics and Art History,'" *Art Bulletin* 74 (September 1992), 522–531.

8. A far-ranging and carefully researched collection of essays on Western artists' studios throughout history was recently edited by Eduard Hüttinger, *Künstlerhäuser von der Renaissance bis zur Gegenwart* (Zürich, 1985). For an overview of the contents, see Hüttinger's introduction, "Künstlerhaus und Künstlerkult," 9–50. See also the general study of nineteenth-century German artists' studios by Christine Hoh-Slodczyk, *Das Haus des Künstlers im 19. Jahrhundert* (Munich, 1985); and the lavishly illustrated volume on Parisian studios by Alexander Liberman, *The Artist in His Studio* (New York, 1988).

There have also been a number of important exhibition catalogues concerning artists' studios and artists' self-portraits, including Rüdiger Klessman, *Selbstbildnisse und Künstlerporträts von Lucas von Leyden bis Anton Raphael Mengs* [exh. cat., Herzog Anton Ulrich-Museum] (Brunswick, 1980); Roberta Etro and Alessandro Morandotti, *I luoghi dell'arte* [exh. cat., Galleria Roberta Etro] (Milan, 1989);

Torsten Gunnarson et al., *I Konstnårens ateljé. Konstnåren i arbete under tre hundra år* [exh. cat., Nationalmuseum] (Stockholm, 1991); and John T. Spike, Elvire Perego, and Evelyn Saez, *Portrait de l'artiste. Images des peintres 1600–1890* [exh. cat., Haboldt & Co.] (Paris, 1991).

Psychoanalytic studies of artists concentrate on the workshop or studio as a reflection of, or perhaps boundary to, the artist's imagination and creativity. In this sense the people and objects surrounding the artist are implicated in the product that results from their interaction; nothing in the artist's environment or experience is meaningless.

The best-known of psychoanalytic studies of an artist is Sigmund Freud's *Leonardo da Vinci, a Psychosexual Study of an Infantile Reminiscence*, trans. A.A. Brill (New York, 1916); reprinted in numerous editions. The fundamental general study of art and psychoanalysis is Ernst Kris and Otto Kurz, *Legend, Myth, and Magic in the Image of the Artist*, trans. Alastair Laing, rev. Lottie M. Newman (New Haven and London, 1979). Many of the principles initially outlined in their joint work, first published in 1934, were later expanded by Kris in "The Image of the Artist: A Psychological Study of the Role of Tradition in Ancient Biographies," in *Psychoanalytic Explorations in Art* (New York, 1952), 64–84. See also the contributions of Rudolf and Margot Wittkower, *Born under Saturn: The Character and Conduct of Artists: A Documented History from Antiquity to the French Revolution* (London [1963]); Leo Steinberg, *The Sexuality of Christ in the Renaissance and in Modern Oblivion* (New York, c. 1983); and the very uneven study by Michael Peppiatt and Alice Bellony-Rewald, *Imagination's Chamber: Artists and Their Studios* (Boston, c. 1982).

Many feminists also employ psychoanalytical methodologies in their revisionist readings of artists and images. Of the myriad publications of the last several decades, two useful overviews are Norma Broude and Mary Garrard, eds., *Feminism and Art History* (New York, 1982); and Griselda Pollock, *Vision and Difference: Feminism, Femininity, and the Histories of Art* (London, 1988).

9. Scholars have studied the social and political implications of studio or workshop hierarchies, extending even to the economic motivations of the artist. Again there is a vast literature, but see especially the important early contribution of Arnold Hauser, *The Social History of Art*, 4 vols., trans. Stanley Goodman, New York, 1958–1962; and the review by Ernst H. Gombrich, "The Social History of Art," in *Meditations on a Hobby Horse* (London, 1965), 86–94. More recently, see T. J. Clark, "On the Social History of Art," in *Image of the People: Gustave Courbet and the 1848 Revolution* (Greenwich, Conn., 1973), 9–34; and O.K. Werkmeister, "Radical Art History," *Art Journal* 42 (Winter 1982), 284–291.

The limits of the field have been tested in the study of Dutch art, where, on the one hand, John Michael Montias has attempted to plumb the depths of the Delft archives to uncover all available personal and financial documentation on Vermeer and his compatriots, which he then interprets in *Artists and Artisans in Delft: A Socio-economic Study of the Seventeenth Century* (Princeton, c. 1982), and in *Vermeer and His Milieu: A Web of Social History* (Princeton, 1989); and, on the other hand, Gary Schwartz has undertaken a biographical study of Rembrandt that places the artist squarely within a recuperable historical moment in *Rembrandt, His Life, His Paintings: A New Biography with All Accessible Paintings Illustrated in Colour* (New York, 1985). Svetlana Alpers responded to Schwartz's characterization of Rembrandt with her own diametrically opposed interpretation in *Rembrandt's Enterprise: The Studio and the Market* (Chicago, 1988). See especially Alpers' introduction in which she sets out her argument in relation to the current state of Rembrandt studies.

Two other directions arose out of contextual or social historical studies that are best exemplified by Michael Baxandall's *Patterns of Intention: On the Historical Explanation of Pictures* (New Haven and London, 1985) and by Thomas Crow's seminal study of art, audience, and reception, *Painters and Public Life in Eighteenth-Century Paris* (New Haven, 1985).

10. See the important critical studies of connoisseurship by Carol Gibson-Wood, *Studies in the Theory of Connoisseurship from Vasari to Morelli* (New York, 1988). Much attention is also given to the history of connoisseurship in R.H. Marijnissen, *Paintings: Genuine-Fake-Fraud: Modern Methods of Examining Paintings* (Brussels, 1985).

The connoisseur's (or collector's) interest in questions of authorship or attribution does not require lengthy documentation; however, the complexity and the fragmentation implicit within the current state of indexing the production of an artist's studio or workshop are worth highlighting. Sotheby's, for example, routinely includes an exhaustive glossary at the beginning of each sales catalogue that serves as both explanation and disclaimer: "**Giovanni Bellini**. . . . Followed under the heading 'Authorship,' by the words 'ascribed to the named artist.' In our opinion, *a work by the artist*. . . . **Attributed to Giovanni Bellini** In our opinion *probably* a work by the artist. . . . **Studio of Giovanni Bellini** In our opinion, a work by *an unknown hand in the studio*. . . . **Circle of Giovanni Bellini** In our opinion, a work by an *as yet unidentified but distinct hand* closely associated with the named artist. . . . **Style of**. . . . **Follower of Giovanni Bellini** In our opinion, a work by a painter working *in the artist's style*, contemporary . . . but not necessarily a pupil. . . . **Manner of Giovanni Bellini** In our opinion, a work in the style of the artist *and of a later date*. . . . **After Giovanni Bellini** In our opinion *a copy* of a known work. . . ." (In all cases the emphasis is theirs.)

The practice of scientific conservation has in recent decades led to new means of ascertaining and verifying authorship, which some scholars have been quick to accept as incontrovertible evidence. The limits of the field are clearly established in Marijnissen's text in which he addresses not only issues of authorship and authenticity, but also originality and reproducibility from the Renaissance through the post-Walter Benjamin (and perhaps post-Warholian) era. His advocacy of scientific methods as aids to the connoisseur is thus tempered both by a sense of the relativity of his theory and, if only implicitly, by a sense of the place of his study within the continuum of the argument. Nonetheless, he promotes scientific methods as a means of making more informed judgments about matters of age, authenticity, condition, and quality: "While the appreciation of quality is subjective, this does not mean it is useless. The lens of scholarship and, *a fortiori*, the apparatus of technology allow us to see more, but we must be careful lest they interfere with the art of seeing (Marijnissen 1985, 54)."

Indeed, Marijnissen is correct in sensing a tendency to place too much credence in any one methodology. He is equally correct in seeing that much can be learned in the laboratory. Stunning proof of this is provided by the series of exhibitions at the National Gallery, London: David Bomford, Christopher Brown, and Ashok Roy, *Art in the Making: Rembrandt* (exh. cat., 12 October 1988–17 January 1989); David Bomford, Jill Dunkerton, Dillian Gordon, Ashok Roy, *Art in the Making: Italian Painting before 1400* (exh. cat., 29 November 1989–28 February 1990); and David Bomford, Raymond White, Louise Williams, *Art in the Making: Impressionism* (exh. cat., 28 November 1990–21 April 1991).

11. Many of the sources cited in notes 8–10 will yield important information concerning the education of artists. In addition to those already mentioned, I would single out as essential overviews Nikolaus Pevsner's *Academies of Art Past and Present* (Cambridge, 1940); Anton W.A. Boschloo, ed., *Academies of Art between Renaissance and Romanticism*, Leids Kunsthistorisch Jaarboek, 5–6 (1986–1987) ('S-Gravenhage, 1989); Gordon Sutton, *Artisan or Artist? A History of Teaching of Arts and Crafts in English Schools* (New York, 1967); Alessandro Conte, "L'evoluzione dell'artista," in *Storia dell'arte italiana*, 3 vols., ed. Giovanni Previtali (Turin, 1979), vol. 1, pt. 2, 117–263; as well as James Ayre's very useful *The Artist's Handbook of Materials and Techniques* (Oxford, 1982).

12. Mojmír Frinta provides an important caveat in his study of the practices of trecento workshops, elsewhere in this volume, where he dismisses as romantic the commonly held notion of the artist as master of all aspects of panel painting. Already in the fourteenth century (if not before), artists and artisans specialized.

MOJMÍR S. FRINTA
State University of New York at Albany

Observations on the Trecento and Early Quattrocento Workshop

I do not wish to bring owls to Athens and thus shall limit myself to observations culled from the investigation of punched decoration on Italian fourteenth- and fifteenth-century panel paintings insofar as they shed light on workshop practices. I also shall consider two altarpiece commissions with respect to the division of responsibility for various tasks between persons partaking of the commission. Of specific interest here is the extent to which the master carpenter made a creative contribution to the work of art.

Early fourteenth-century Tuscany, and especially Siena, was swept by a pervasive fashion for adorning the gilded surfaces of panel paintings, mainly the halos, with impressions of punches in various shapes that may be called "motif punches."[1] Formalized clusters of motif punches are characteristic innovations of great figures of the Sienese trecento, Simone Martini and Pietro and Ambrogio Lorenzetti.

Comprehensive scrutiny of the entire production of Tuscan fourteenth- and fifteenth-century panel painting makes it possible to identify sets of punches that were used in individual workshops, and their presence on problematic pictures provides clues about the relationships between pictures and about their possible creators. The presumption that the rather menial task of punching would be delegated to an assistant is not supported by the only contemporaneous writing we

have on this decorative procedure. Cennino d'Andrea Cennini in his *Il libro dell'arte* comments affectionately on the pleasure of working designs with *stampe minute*.[2] Regardless of whether it was the master or his assistant who actually executed the decoration, it is quite likely that the choice of the design should be credited to the taste of the master.

None of the punches of the period seem to have survived, and we can only speculate on the materials of which they were made. We may infer from Renaissance punches used to decorate leather bookbindings that they were metal.[3] Because authorization to work in various materials was traditionally required, in the framework of guilds, and for practical reasons, it is unlikely that the painter himself would have fashioned these metallic tools, which required engraving, carving, drilling, and filing. That would have been the domain of the fine metalworker whose specialty was cutting dies for seals, coins, and medals; however, the choice of shape and design was likely left to the painter. For example, Simone Martini must have requested the tiny fleur-de-lys from a Neapolitan silversmith for his commission from the Anjou king Robert of the panel with Saint Louis of Toulouse (fig. 1). The whimsical monster punch used by a follower of Bernardo Daddi is also finely engraved, presumably in metal (for example, appearing in the Coronation altarpiece

19

from Santa Maria Novella, Florence; fig. 2).[4] In contrast to the fleur-de-lys, the motive for creating this rare punch image remains unknown. Perhaps it was fashioned for a commission, now lost, in which it had meaning. Subsequently the painter would have used the punch with less discrimination.[5] I found this two-legged creature painted into one of the quadrilobes in the zone separating the upper and main levels of a large polyptych commissioned from Ugolino di Nerio for the church of Santa Croce, Florence (fig. 3). This same monster was also carved amid a row of birdlike creatures by Goro di Gregorio in 1324 on the marble *Arca di San Cerbone* in the crypt of the cathedral of Massa Marittima.[6] It, too, was chiseled, along with other creatures, by a Sienese goldsmith on a portable crucifix in the church of Santa Vittoria in Mantenano (near Ascoli Piceno). Variants of such two-legged monsters occasionally were painted onto the spandrels of altar panels, such as on a now-dispersed altarpiece ascribed to a follower of Pietro Lorenzetti (perhaps

Francesco di Segna) and on the Madonna pentaptych from Orvieto by Simone Martini and shop (Isabella Stewart Gardner Museum, Boston). Possibly a clue for its meaning comes from its representation in the brooch of Saint Augustine attributed to Giovanni del Biondo on the composite main altarpiece in Santa Croce in Florence (fig. 4).

There is a distinct possibility, although difficult to prove, that punched decoration had another purpose beyond the embellishment of gilded surfaces with sparkling reflections of light: it might have been a subtle attestation of the master's responsibility for a commission. The early punch marks invariably are too small to have had any decorative impact and are merely addi-

4. Giovanni del Biondo, detail of Saint Augustine, main altar, Santa Croce, Florence

tions to the elaborate free-hand decoration done by incising or stippling.[7] These secondary "signatures" of the workshop may have served as declaration of the master's autograph for some specific purpose such as appraisal of the work by an appointed body of fellow artists or, more generally, to signify to a curious public the oeuvre of a specific workshop.

The existence of specific punch repertories can be taken as a sign of an estab-

lished workshop—at least, most likely, in the first generation of users. The situation becomes less clear in the second half of the trecento. At times original repertories were then dispersed, often among former pupils of the masters. The notion of workshop continuity, which can be ascertained by the transfer of punches from older to younger painters, may help us to localize the artistic training of painters about whose beginnings nothing is known. What makes this assertion problematic is that a few of the distinctive punches were, exceptionally, not restricted to a single production and distinctive style; some sharing or borrowing may have taken place. This also may have been the result of several masters using the facilities of a single workshop. Good examples are the punch work of Andrea di Vanni and Paolo di Giovanni Fei, as well as the work from a specific phase of Bartolo di Fredi's production. We know that in 1353 Bartolo and Andrea shared a shop; a similar arrangement seems to have existed later between Andrea and Paolo. Their mutual contact can be ascertained from the evidence both of sharing the punches and of stylistic affinity (figs. 5, 6). Larger commissions in particular would be an occasion for collaboration.

5. Paolo di Giovanni Fei, Nursing Madonna of Humility, Duomo, Siena

6. Andrea di Vanni, fragmentary Enthroned Nursing Madonna San Donato, Siena

7. Here ascribed to a member of the Simone Martini-Lippo Memmi workshop, Saints Thaddeus and Bartholomew, from upper tier of Carmelite altarpiece, 1329, by Pietro Lorenzetti
Pinacoteca, Siena (62)

The inscription on the Madonna pentaptych of 1362 in the Siena Pinacoteca tells us that Niccolò di Ser Sozzo and Luca di Tommè collaborated on this altarpiece (NICCHOLAUS SER SOCII ET LUCAS THOMAS DE SENIS HOC OPUS PINXERUNT ANNI MCCCLXII). During their careers both painters assembled their own sets of punches; the predominance of Niccolò's punches on this altarpiece points to the leading role he must have played in this commission.

Among families of painters, it is natural that the son would acquire his father's punches. Andrea di Bartolo added only a few new punches to those inherited from his father, Bartolo di Fredi. The same was true for Taddeo di Bartolo and his adopted son, Gregorio di Cecco. Sometimes a son would acquire only the later punches of his father, such as Agnolo Gaddi had from Taddeo Gaddi. This could mean that Taddeo's early punches already had been discarded or lost. Moreover, relatives who

were themselves masters occasionally shared punches. With the exception of Simone Martini's early punches, his repertory also appears in the paintings of his brother-in-law Lippo Memmi. Still, it seems that Martini and Memmi each reserved a few distinctive punches for his personal use.

A contrary situation is found among the Lorenzetti brothers. Pietro and Ambrogio each had his own large and highly distinctive punch repertory, which quite likely indicates the existence of two separate workshops. Yet we know that the two brothers occasionally collaborated, as it was formerly stated in an inscription on the now-lost frescoes of 1335 on the façade of Santa Maria della Scala. It seems that Ambrogio joined Pietro for the execution of a large altarpiece for the Carmelites in 1329, because several of Ambrogio's punches appear there, side by side with Pietro's punches.

8a. Detail of a halo in Niccolò di Ser Sozzo and Luca di Tommè, Enthroned Madonna, 1362, pentaptych
Pinacoteca, Siena (51)

8b. Detail of a halo in Ambrogio Lorenzetti, Saint Michael, retable
Museo di Arte Sacra, Asciano

Some years later, another situation can be observed. A few of Pietro's punches appear alongside Ambrogio's own, in the latter's *Maestà* in Massa Marittima. Ambrogio certainly did not paint all the figures, as can be seen from the inferior quality of those at the upper left. An assistant from Pietro's shop might have joined Ambrogio, bringing along a few punches. In addition we can postulate, on the basis of anomalous punches that are seen in none of Pietro's or Ambrogio's known works, that an alien hand intervened in Pietro's earlier large commission for the Carmelites. In an upper portion of this polyptych, with Saints Thaddeus and Bartholomew (Pinacoteca, Siena, no. 62), there is a large trefoil punch which seems to occur only in the paintings of Lippo Memmi (fig. 7).

A second non-Lorenzettian punch in this top-tier panel is a larger hexa-rosette that also appears in the dismantled altarpiece from Sant'Agostino in San Gimignano (Fitzwilliam Museum, Cambridge; Wallraf Richartz Museum, Cologne; private collection, Italy) generally ascribed to Simone Martini.[8] These dispersed panels feature a few Simone-Lippo punches while others, including the hexa-rosette, are not identical (although very similar) and point to a deliberate intention to duplicate the Simone-Lippo originals. This evidence as well as stylistic considerations led me to the conclusion that the painter of the San Gimignano altarpiece was a semi-independent member of the Simone-Lippo workshop (perhaps Federigho Memmi?). This same painter may have been the person who temporarily joined the Lorenzetti in the production of the Carmine altarpiece. There are subtle stylistic differences between Siena no. 62 and other apostles in the top tier (Siena no. 64 and Yale University, 1959.15.1). I see greater similarity between Saints Thaddeus and Bartholomew and the busts of Jeremiah and Ezekiel in the medallions in the gables of the 1333 *Annunciation* from the Siena Cathedral signed by Simone Martini and Lippo Memmi (Uffizi, Florence).[9] It is most unusual to find a working relationship between the two most important and significant Sienese workshops of the early trecento.

Puzzling, too, are the channels through which several of Pietro Lorenzetti's punches were transferred to Catalonia after his death. They appear in the workshop of the Barcelonese painters, the Serra.[10] The earliest dated appearances are in the altarpieces Jaume Serra painted in Zaragoza in 1363. Did Jaume or his older brother Francesc visit Siena some time after the Black Death, or was it another Barcelonese painter, Ramón Destorrents, who brought the punches from Siena to Barcelona? In any case, neither of them can be viewed as pupils of Pietro.

A potentially meaningful line of inquiry would be to examine the phenomenon of imitating certain distinctive punches of the major masters. For instance, a slightly larger rendering of Ambrogio's curling acanthus leaf can be recognized in Niccolò di Ser Sozzo's altarpiece of 1362 mentioned above (figs. 8a, 8b). However, Niccolò also owned a dozen punches originating from the individual repertories of both Lorenzetti. This, combined with their marked stylistic influence, suggests that Niccolò initially was quite close to them, probably as a pupil of one of the brothers.

A similar situation is reflected in the paintings of the Marchigian painter Allegretto Nuzi. His schooling in Florence, which took place prior to his return to Fabriano, is stressed in the literature. A pentaptych in the Johnson Collection, Philadelphia—which, in view of the

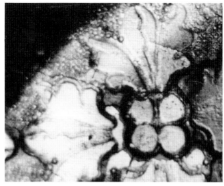

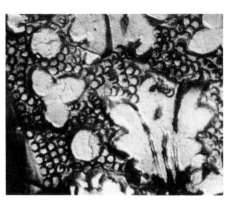

9. Here attributed to Allegretto Nuzi, detail of the Madonna in a pentaptych
John G. Johnson Collection, Philadelphia (5)

10a. Detail of a halo in Pietro Lorenzetti, Enthroned Madonna with Angels, 1340, from San Francesco in Pistoia
Uffizi, Florence

10b. Detail of a halo in Allegretto Nuzi, Coronation of the Virgin, altarpiece
Southampton Art Gallery, England

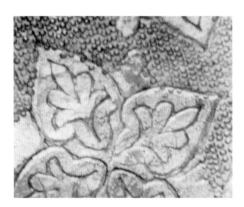

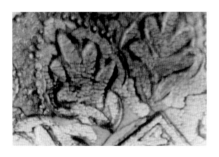

massive appearance of typical Allegretto punches, I believe is by Allegretto—was generally classified as belonging to the circle of Maso di Banco.[11] Yet Allegretto's punch work and style show that he received his first training, before 1346, in Siena (fig. 9). Several of his punches were clearly inspired by those of Pietro Lorenzetti. The rare shape of a flower punch is a copy of Pietro's punch (figs. 10a, 10b). This is also true of another floral punch, a sort of palmette (figs. 11a, 11b). Additionally, Allegretto liked to group his punches in typical Lorenzettian clusters—a formal arrangement of several punches (fig. 9). Allegretto's and Niccolò's duplicates represent, I submit, a visual expression of their admiration and indebtedness to their masters. An imitation of a highly personal punch shape may thus be interpreted as testimony to the great prestige enjoyed by the prototype's owner, as, for example, Simone Martini, even by painters rooted in the Duccesque tradition. For example, an associate of Ugolino di Nerio used his version of Simone's leaf in the Ricasoli altarpiece (figs. 12a, 12b) and in the Saint Anne in the National Gallery, Ottawa.

11a. Detail of a halo in Pietro Lorenzetti, center panel of Carmelite altarpiece
Pinacoteca, Siena

11b. Detail of a halo in Allegretto Nuzi, Enthroned Madonna
Musée du Petit Palais, Avignon (Campagna Collection, ex-Agen)

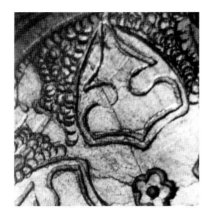

12a. Detail of a halo in
Ugolino di Nerio and
workshop, Madonna
pentaptych
Castello Ricasoli, Brolio

12b. Detail of a halo in
Simone Martini, Madonna
polyptych, 1319, from Santa
Caterina
Museo di San Matteo, Pisa

Ugolino was influenced in the twenties by the new practice of motif punches and shifted from Duccio's style of engraved patterning of the halos to the fully punched halos in his Santa Croce altarpiece (now mostly in Berlin and London).

An interesting problem arises when a master is displaced from his native city. To cite one example, although Simone Martini shared punches with Lippo Memmi while in Siena, he does not seem

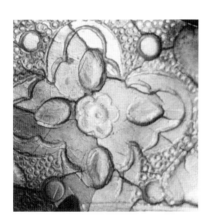

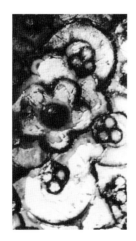

13a. Detail of a halo in
Simone Martini and Lippo
Memmi, Annunciation,
1333
Uffizi, Florence

13b. Detail of a halo in
Francesco Traini, Saint
Anne with the Virgin Mary
Princeton University Art Museum

to have taken them to Avignon. They appear in Lippo's later production, which, unfortunately, is not dated. One of them, a round-arch punch, made its way into Pisan painting (fig. 13a). The first user there was Giovanni di Nicola, who likely is the Giovanni who was an early disciple of Lippo.[12] The chief rival of Giovanni in Pisa, Francesco Traini, a better artist, made imitations of this and other Sienese punch shapes (fig. 13b).

A remarkable phenomenon in the history of "motif punch" technique is a massive transfer of Sienese punches to Florence. Most of these punches were in the possession of Bartolomeo Bulgarini, alias the Master of Ovile. The early users in Florence were Giovanni da Milano and Nardo and Jacopo di Cione. Lack of any record of Giovanni da Milano in Florence between 1346 and 1363 probably means that he was absent from the city.[13] During this period he may have been in Siena, for his work shows some Sienese influence. Perhaps he eventually brought these punches back to Florence. They continued to be used in Florence by other painters, principally Giovanni del Biondo and Cenni di Francesco. Erling Skaug wondered whether the occurrence of these punch marks could mean something more unusual than a simple sharing of tools by younger artists within a common shop.[14] He proposed that a Florentine cooperative might have been formed to which the adherents brought their panels to be gilded and provided with punched decoration by a specialist.

This question of possible practical sharing of resources and distribution of tasks

among specialized artists brings me to the core of my remarks—a commission illuminated by a contractual arrangement. A contract concluded in 1384 in Lucca enables us to identify the dispersed parts of the Monte Oliveto altarpiece.[15] The left lateral in Budapest bears an inscription: *Magister Cini de Florentia intalavit* (fig. 14) and the right one, in the Fogg Art Museum, is inscribed: *Gabriellus Saracini de Senis doravit*. The contract names these two as well as another painter, Spinello Aretino, who was to be the painter of the figures. The two painters, Spinello and Gabriello, were to be paid equally. The arrangement whereby two painters were specified by contract to collaborate on a commission, each contributing a specific aspect of the work was, I believe, exceptional. Far more often the painter entrusted with the work also executed the decoration with his own punches. The Lucca contract stipulated that Gabriello was to use the same type of decoration as he had on the altarpiece for

San Ponziano, just completed. The remarkable feature of the San Ponziano altar was the inscriptions in the halos, executed in gilded *pastiglia*. Spinello's signed triptych painted in Lucca in 1391 for the local church of Sant'Andrea features the same distinctive *pastiglia* inscriptions, Gabriello's speciality (fig. 15).

The four punches present on the panels of the Monte Oliveto altarpiece must have belonged to Gabriello Saracini, an obscure painter, about whom we know only that he was listed in the 1357 Sienese rolls (fig. 16).[16] My comprehensive recording of all accessible instances of punch work over the years has enabled me to identify other works of Gabriello which, however, were fully executed by him. Several were grouped by Bernard Berenson under the name of the Master of Panzano.[17] This man, whom I identify as Gabriello, was a mediocre painter; the pressure of competition probably induced him to concentrate on his special skills by collaborating, in a decorator's capacity,

14. Spinello Aretino, Monte Oliveto altarpiece, 1385, part of the predella
Museum of Fine Arts, Budapest

15. Spinello Aretino, Enthroned Madonna, 1391, triptych from Sant'Andrea, Lucca
Accademia, Florence
Photograph: Alinari/Art Resource, New York

16. Details of halos in the lateral with Saints Nemesius and John the Baptist and of its predella portion, Monte Oliveto altarpiece
Museum of Fine Arts, Budapest (56)

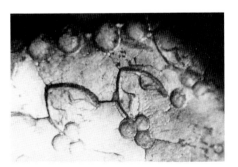

with other painters of higher artistic standing.

I proposed elsewhere that another painter with whom Gabriello collaborated was Giuliano di Simone, a painter in Lucca. For example, Gabriello's punches appear in Giuliano's Madonna Enthroned in Sarasota (fig. 17) and in two standing saints in Atlanta. It is quite possible that it was in the shop of this Lucchese painter that the two foreign painters, Spinello and Gabriello, executed their commissions. In exchange for a place to work, Gabriello decorated Giuliano's paintings, as can be seen by the appearance of his punches in some of Giuliano's works. Judging from the mixed style and the punch work, an Enthroned Madonna in the Civic Collections in Bologna seems to be a collaboration between Gabriello and Giuliano.[18]

Furthermore, Gabriello's punches and his apparent speciality—the gilded *pastiglia* inscriptions—appear in several paintings Taddeo di Bartolo executed both during his sojourn in Pisa in the nineties

As to Gabriello's companion in Lucca, Spinello Aretino, he in turn also formed a production team during his sojourns in other towns. After his stay in Lucca, Spinello went to Florence and associated himself with Niccolò di Pietro Gerini and Lorenzo di Niccolò. Their punches were used in the altarpiece that was signed by all three and dated 1401. On the basis of the Gerini punches, I would argue that Spinello's Madonnas in the museums in Saint Louis, Belgrade, and Cleveland belong to this same period (fig. 18). Primarily an itinerant expert fresco painter, Spinello probably did not own any motif punches of his own. Because a fresco painter has to work quickly, concern with intricate decorative procedures generally lies outside the scope of his interests and habits. Typically halos of frescoed figures were adorned by mere radiating scratched lines. (Of course Simone Martini's frescoed halos are notable exceptions.)[19]

The history of the making of the Enthroned Madonna pentaptych in the church of San Giovanni Fuorcivitas in Pistoia is also instructive. There are records of payments in 1345 to two woodworkers, Bartolomeo di Vanni and maestro Francesco da Siena, for the construction of the panels composing the altarpiece. The first reference to the contract with the painter is dated almost three years later. Painter Lesso (Alesso) di Andrea was paid in several installments for the work he carried out on the church premises. Also, local painter Filippo Lazaro was paid small sums for gilding ("per metere l'oro").[20] The painting apparently was not completed in 1348, and the desire to find a competent painter to finish the work is reflected in the *Entrata* and *Uscita* ledger, which lists the six best painters in Florence, two in Siena, and one in Lucca. The painter listed as first in the Florentine group, Taddeo Gaddi, eventually got the job after a prolonged disruption, perhaps caused by the aftermath of the Black Death. Taddeo received payments during 1353, at which time some additional gilding was done by the above-mentioned Filippo Lazaro. He must also have been a painter since he painted a curtain for the altarpiece. The small amount paid to Filippo for the gilding shows that he was not in charge of the

17. Giuliano di Simone, Madonna Enthroned with the Child Holding a Bird, c. 1384–1385
John and Mable Ringling Museum of Art, Sarasota, Florida (state 8)

and during a short period following his return to Siena. An example is the huge polyptych of 1402 in the Cathedral of Montepulciano. As Gabriello grew older and either ceased to work or died, Taddeo acquired some of Gabriello's punches.

Finally, there is also a possibility that Gabriello had previously collaborated as a specialist-decorator on another huge polyptych in 1375, this time with Florentine painters, in the Collegiata in Impruneta. Gabriello's arch appears in the predella and so does the typical gilded *pastiglia* that adorns the halos of the saints in the main zone.

18. Spinello Aretino, detail of an Enthroned Madonna, c. 1401
Cleveland Museum of Art, Leonard C. Hanna, Jr. Fund (77.145)

19a, 19b. Details of the halos in Taddeo Gaddi, Enthroned Madonna, 1353, pentaptych (begun 1348 by Alesso di Andrea)
San Giovanni Fuorcivitas, Pistoia

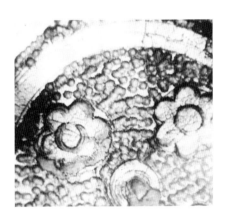

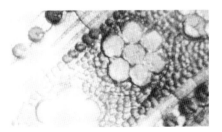

whole decoration, which differs from the equal disbursement made to the two painters of the Monte Oliveto altarpiece, Spinello and Gabriello. Thus, the three punches appearing on the present halos most likely belonged to the first painter, Alesso di Andrea, because the gilding and tooling always was done before the painting. In 1347 he painted the frescoes with four Virtues in the Pistoia Cathedral, but we do not know of any panel paintings by him.[21] The three punches in the Pistoia altarpiece, unfortunately, are of a more general type (figs. 19a, 19b); consequently, the task of their identification in specific panel paintings is more problematic than it was in the case of Gabriello Saracini, whose punches have very specific shapes.

The hexa-rosette present in the Pistoia altarpiece appears to be identical to that in a small Enthroned Madonna with Saints and Angels which bears a date of 1345 (figs. 19a, 20). This picture in the Budapest Museum of Fine Arts is there attributed, not very convincingly, to Jacopo del Casentino.[22] The gentleness of the facial types, however, is atypical of Jacopo and resembles the distinctive countenances depicted in Alesso's frescoes in the Pistoia Duomo. Likewise, we are obliquely provided with a lead toward a group of paintings assigned to the Master of San Lucchese, named after the altarpiece from San Lucchese (outside of Poggibonsi), which was destroyed during World War II. These gentle creations and the frescoes of Alesso are close in spirit both to the paintings of Nardo di Cione and to works tentatively attributed to Maso di Banco, and they represent the production of several kindred artists, though I have a feeling that some attributional readjustments will undoubtedly continue to be made concerning this group.[23]

In a similar way, the problem of separating the artistic personality of Niccolò di Tommaso and Bonaccorso di Cino has to be confronted. It seems to me that there is good reason to introduce a third personality working in a common style: philological examination of the document of 1372 concerning the execution of a Coronation panel for the Florentine mint (*Zecca*) suggests an alternative interpretation. Two painters are named as commissioned to execute it, Nicholao and Simone. For reasons that are still unclear, the first had been identified with Niccolò di Pietro Gerini.[24] Stylistically more justifiable is Miklós Boskovits' proposal, taken up by Andrew Ladis, that this painter was Niccolò di Tommaso, while Simone remains an unknown entity.[25] A document of 31 October 1373 names Jacobus Cini as having received 138 lire for completing the painting (a more substantial part because Nicholao and Simone received only 134 lire). Generally, this last is assumed to be Jacopo di Cione. It seems to me, however, that it is taking an easy way out to explain the discrepancy as a scribe's error. The patronym Cini (di Cino) instead refers to a well-known Pistoiese family of painters. I propose a hypothesis that this Jacopo was a brother of Bonaccorso di Cino whose personal style must have been close to that of Niccolò di Tommaso, as witnessed in the disagreement about the authorship of three frescoes in the Convento del Tau in Pistoia. To cite one illustration, a stylistically similar painting with a Last Judgment, of unknown whereabouts, was tentatively attributed by Millard Meiss (1971, fig. 28) to Niccolò di Tommaso or to Bonaccorso di Cino. Perhaps it is

another building block in the oeuvre of Jacopo di Cino, an addition to our ongoing struggle to gain a truer picture of the intermingling richness of trecento art production as new personalities emerge.

I submit that the general image of workshop structure and its functioning should be slightly modified in view of the examples investigated here: at times a workshop might have become an entity more elastic and diversified than previous definitions have suggested. For example, guest collaborators and specialized workers might have swelled the usual crew of the

20. Here attributed tentatively to Alesso di Andrea, Enthroned Madonna with Saints and Angels, 1345
Museum of Fine Arts, Budapest (6006)

workshop, or two masters (even three) would have joined their skills to cope with large commissions, perhaps more often than the rare double signatures on altarpieces and in the records would lead us to believe. We need additional objective criteria in our quest to enlarge the number of specific productions that can be related to recorded names of painters who otherwise remain unknown. Scrutiny of the distribution and appearances of distinctive punch shapes, combined to be sure with stylistic analysis, produces basic cognate groups that become cores of rationally justified entities. These entities represent independent workshops. The next step will be to try to connect these anonymous productions to the names of the "bodyless" painters. The tendency to rely on just the few names of known major artists as candidates for authorship necessarily skews perception of the historical situation. Too many painters passed unnoticed through the sieve into which is fed the entire extant corpus of trecento painting. The scrutiny of punch work potentially can identify previously unknown production units by introducing new names such as Mino Parcis, Gabriello Saracini, Simone di Gheri, Meo di Pero, and Jacopo Cini, whom I am presently engaged in researching; granted, some of these oeuvres are more tentative than others, depending on the availability of stylistic comparisons. Just to sketch the possibilities of the comparative punch-work method, let me mention that detection of forgeries is possible by punch analysis as well.[26]

Another of my concerns is proper evaluation of the master carpenter's contribution to the process of executing the structure of an altarpiece (which I like to call, with some exaggeration, the "apotheosis of the maestro legname"). In 1977 Creighton Gilbert published a pioneering article on this subject and discussed a number of cases, including the two altarpieces I have dealt with here.[27] Crucial was Gilbert's correction of the widely held view that the master painter was responsible for the design of the altarpiece. Indeed, in a number of instances we know the name of the master woodworker who was commissioned to execute the structure, and, in some cases, a number of years

passed before a painter was found. Should the client have been inclined to deal only with the painter for the sake of expediency, the painter would then have subcontracted the execution of the panel with a master carpenter. The relative artistic strengths of these two participants would probably have determined whether painter or carpenter would impose his concepts on the very shape of the altarpiece.

I shall briefly mention the complicated story of the making of the altarpiece for the Franciscans in Borgo San Sepolcro; in this case four years elapsed between the carpentry work of 1426 and the making of a contract with a painter. The largely incomplete altarpiece stood in the church for seven more years, until 1437 when Sassetta signed another contract to paint the altarpiece on an exact replica of the original structure; it was installed in San Francesco in 1444.[28]

It is important to our argument that the contracts both for the Rucellai *Maestà* and for the Siena Cathedral *Maestà* specified that Duccio would be given the panel to execute the painting ("accepit a dicto operario ad pingendam unam tabulam"): this makes it quite unlikely that he was responsible for the panels' designs.[29] These data rectify the current misconception that probably stems from the romantic nineteenth-century view of the painter as supreme artist-creator, one to whom all other participants in an enterprise were subjugated.[30] Whereas there were craftsmen-carpenters of average ambitions or less, there surely were others who possessed the intellectual capacity, experience, and authority to design projects without the painter's direction. The division of responsibilities and authorization for working in various media and materials were in fact essential arrangements and subject to guild jurisdiction. The accomplished master carpenters had considerable knowledge about designing complex structures and gave careful thought to matters of proportions. Surely some expertise was gained from their contacts with the architects for whom they provided large ceiling structures and partitions. Choir stall commissions, for example, certainly called for a precise knowledge of proportions, which the professional integ-

rity of the master's craft would have discouraged the carpenter from ceding to some other artist.

We need to know more about this aspect of artistic production. Once we learn how to discern individual characteristics in carpentry, such as specific methods of joining, extending, fastening, and reinforcing, we will be able to constitute the productions of specific carpenters' workshops.[31]

As an example of possible future research, let us return finally to the San Giovanni Fuorcivitas altarpiece. We note there a distinct trefoil depression in the spandrels which is specific enough to be worthy of attention from among the customary trilobe, quadrilobe, polylobe, or just common circular articulation of the spandrels or gables. This particular carved-out trefoil can be seen in several examples: the gable of a Madonna lunette by Taddeo Gaddi, in the Accademia, Florence; slightly modified, in the Enthroned Madonna by Giovanni di Bartolomeo Cristiani in Sant'Ambrogio, Florence; in an Enthroned Madonna with Four Saints triptych, also ascribed to Cristiani, once in Settignano, in the collection of Cavaliere

Alfredo Geri; in a Madonna triptych in Hampton Court, Her Majesty's Collection, attributed to Jacopo di Cione (fig. 21); and in an Assumption of the Virgin by Luca di Tommè in the Yale University Art Gallery. The gable of the Accademia lunette painting appears to have been added in the latter part of the century, when small figures were painted there supposedly by the shop of the Gerini. Even taking into account that portions of the framing in the Hampton Court triptych seem to belong to a restoration and that if there is no consensus on several related issues, we can propose affinities with the Pistoia altarpiece. If other characteristics of the execution and particulars of the craftsmanship on the panels and their decoration likewise accord in the five examples cited, we would conclude that the carpentry came from the shop of master Francesco da Siena and/or of Bartolomeo di Vanni, authors of the structure in San Giovanni Fuorcivitas in 1345 (discussed above), and that the activity of this shop continued over several decades. Established in Pistoia, it was a supplier to the Pistoiese painter Giovanni di Bartolomeo Cristiani who was also active in Florence.

A word of caution is in order when using the methodology employed here. For example, we should not reach premature conclusions by proposing a chronology of a painter's production on the basis of a change in the design of the framing portion of a panel from a circular shape at the top, supposedly the painter's earlier production, to a pointed arch. Rather than chronological evolution, the real cause might be that the painter dealt, at times, with two carpenters' shops: one conservative and the other more up-to-date.

I wish also to conclude with a plea for art historians to pay more significant attention to the discoveries made by art-technological methods. These still are not fully utilized and are often omitted from bibliographical sources.[32]

21. Detail of gable in School of the Cioni, Coronation of the Virgin, triptych
Hampton Court, Her Majesty's Collection (116)

NOTES

1. I first introduced this subject as a research project in 1965 ("An Investigation of the Punched Decoration of Mediaeval Italian and Non-Italian Panel Paintings," *Art Bulletin* 47 [June 1965], 261–265). It was followed by further publications. A catalogue raisonné of all punch shapes and the first half of the monograph *Punched Decoration on Medieval Panel Painting* are ready for publication (Obelisk Publishers, Prague), and the second volume is nearing completion.

2. Cennino d'Andrea Cennini, *Il Libro dell'arte*, ed. Daniel V. Thompson, Jr. (New Haven, 1932), 85–86: ". . . tapping in a few ornaments; stamping them with tiny punches, so that they sparkle like millet grains; embellish with other punches; and do stamping if there are any foliage ornaments. . . . This stamping which I am telling you about is one of our most delightful branches."

3. Jagged impressions of circular punches on some inferior paintings may possibly be interpreted as produced by tools fashioned from hollow bones or reed stalks. Nicholas Lochoff, who was charged by Tsar Nicholas to copy many Italian masterpieces, believed (falsely, it seems to me) that the original punches of Simone Martini were made of ivory and had his own imitations carved of ivory.

4. Frinta 1965, fig. 7; Luisa Marcucci, *Dipinti Toscani del secolo 14* (Rome, 1965), 44–45; Accademia, Florence, inv. 3449. It is interesting to ponder from the standpoint of our method the various opinions about the *Coronation*'s authorship. Osvald Sirén started on the right track when, in 1905, he first proposed Bernardo Daddi and, in 1917, refined his perception by claiming it for workshop production with a proposal of Bernardo's son Daddo di Bernardo as a possible painter. Although we lack any certain work by this painter, he surely can be a candidate because the *Coronation* features several of Bernardo's punches from his late period. Also the suggestion of Raymond Van Marle about a collaboration of Puccio di Simone on Bernardo's commission is plausible because Puccio used several of Bernardo's punches in his autograph altarpiece. On the other hand, Maso di Banco's participation (also suggested) is less tenable vis-à-vis our punch-work evidence, because he seems to have had a limited punch repertory of his own and it was not mixed with Bernardo's punches. The only plausible way Maso can be considered to have authored this panel is if we would enlarge our view of Maso's production, as did Miklós Boskovits, who attributed to Maso an Enthroned Madonna with Two Saints in San Giorgio a Ruballa. This latter painting features Daddi's punches exclusively.

5. From the immediate following of Bernardo Daddi comes a fragmentary *Madonna della Cintola* in the Metropolitan Museum of Art (Lehman Collection). The painter of the Accademia Coronation painted another Coronation, today split between the Kisters Collection, Kreuzlingen, and the Christ Church Gallery, Oxford (Music-making Angels). To one of these Coronations probably belonged two standing Saints in an English private collection; all these feature the rare monster punch impressions.

6. Enzo Carli, "Su alcuni smalti senesi," *Antichità Viva* 7 (1968), fig. 18.

7. Frinta 1965, figs. 20, 21, 24, 25. Hans Belting, "The 'Byzantine' Madonnas," *Studies in the History of Art* 2 (1982), 7–22, fig. 14.

8. Mojmír S. Frinta, "Unsettling Evidence in Some Panel Paintings of Simone Martini," in *La pittura nel 14 e 15 secolo. Il contributo dell'analisi tecnica alla storia dell'arte*, vol. 3 of *Atti del 24 Congresso Internazionale di Storia dell'Arte (Bologna, 1979)* (Bologna, 1983), 211–223. The chart of the punches was regrettably redrawn by the editors and their shapes wrongly defined or in some instances completely omitted, making it useless.

9. Alessandro Conti, "Oro e tempera: aspetti della tecnica di Simone Martini," in *Simone Martini: atti del convegno, Siena, 1985* (Florence, 1988), 122, figs. 6, 7. Henk Van Os ("Reply" to Gaudenz Freuler and Valerie Wainwright, "On Some Altarpieces of Bartolo di Fredi," *Art Bulletin* 68 [1986], 328) remarked: ". . . in the second half of the trecento huge commissions often necessitated incidental collaboration of otherwise independent masters with a stylistic idiom of their own," but was not aware of it in the early trecento.

10. Mojmír S. Frinta, "Evidence of the Italian Influence on Catalan Panel Painting of the Fourteenth Century," in *España entre el Mediterraneo y el Atlantico, Actas del 23 Congreso Internacional de Historia del Arte* (Granada, 1976), 1:361–371.

11. *Catalogue of Italian Paintings, John G. Johnson Collection* (Philadelphia, 1966), 48, no. 5: "close to Maso di Banco." Bernard Berenson ascribed it earlier to Giottino. Millard Meiss thought that the altarpiece originated in the "ambiente di Alesso di Andrea" ("Alesso di Andrea," in *Giotto e il suo tempo* [Rome, 1971], 401–418, fig. 59).

12. The arch punch continued to be used in Pisa in the works of Cecco di Pietro and others. Mojmír S. Frinta, "A Seemingly Florentine Yet Not Really Florentine Altar-piece," *Burlington Magazine* (August 1975), figs. 45–47, and the comparative chart on page 528.

13. Ugo Procacci, "Il primo ricordo di Giovanni da Milano a Firenze," *Arte Antica e Moderna* 13–16 (1961), 49–65.

14. Erling Skaug, "Punch Marks—What Are They Worth? Problems of Tuscan Workshop Interrelationships in the Mid-fourteenth Century: The Ovile Master and Giovanni da Milano," in Bologna, 1983, 257.

15. Sherwood A. Fehm, Jr., "Notes on Spinello Aretino's So-called Monte Oliveto Altarpiece," *Mitteilungen des Kunsthistorischen Institutes in Florenz* 17 (1973), 85–89. Mojmír S. Frinta, "Le peintre siénnois itinérant Gabriello Saracini," in Acts of the Colloquium: *Le Rayonnement de l'art siénnois du*

Trecento en Europe, Avignon 1983 (forthcoming).

16. Sherwood A. Fehm, Jr., "Notes on the Statutes of the Sienese Painters Guild," *Art Bulletin* 54 (1972), 199.

17. Bernard Berenson, *Homeless Paintings of the Renaissance* (Bloomington, 1970; repr. from *The International Studio*, 1929–1931), 43–46.

18. Frinta, "Le peintre siénnois" (forthcoming), fig. 10.

19. Mojmír S. Frinta, "Stamped Halos in the 'Maestà' of Simone Martini," in Florence, 1988, 39–45.

20. Ugo Procacci, "Appendice," in Rome, 1971, 360–361. Andrew Ladis, *Taddeo Gaddi* (Columbia, Missouri, 1982), 159–160.

21. Meiss 1971, 401–415, figs. 1–4.

22. Yet Miklós Boskovits (*Early Italian Panel Paintings in Hungarian Museums* [Budapest, 1966], no. 10) saw more affinity with the works ascribed to Stefano Fiorentino.

23. Procacci's change of attribution of the frescoes in the Convento del Tau in Pistoia from Niccolò di Tommaso to Bonaccorso di Cino, a former collaborator of Alesso di Andrea on the Pistoia Duomo frescoes ("Bonaccorso di Cino e gli affreschi della chiesa del Tau a Pistoia," in Rome, 1971, 349–359) leads me to a reevaluation of a Coronation panel in the Florence Accademia, no. 456.

24. Marcucci 1965, 99–100.

25. Andrew Ladis, "A High Altarpiece for San Giovanni Fuorcivitas in Pistoia and a Hypothesis about Niccolò di Tommaso," *Mitteilungen des Kunsthistorischen Institutes in Florenz* 33 (1989), 6, fig. 2.

26. Mojmír S. Frinta, "The Quest for a Restorer's Shop of Beguiling Invention: Restorations and Forgeries in Italian Panel Paintings," *Art Bulletin* 60 (March 1978), 7–23; Frinta, "Drawing the Net Closer: The Case of Illicito Federico Joni, Painter of Antique Pictures," *Pantheon* 40 (182), 217–224; Joseph Romano, "Connoisseurship and Photography: The Methodology of Mojmír Frinta," *Visual Resources* 7 (1990), 163–183.

27. Creighton Gilbert, "Peintres et menuisiers au début de la Renaissance en Italie," *Revue de l'Art* 37 (1977), 9–28.

28. Gilbert 1977, 12: "En 1426 . . . Bartholomeus carpentarius de dicto Burgo. . . . quatre ans après que les moines signèrent avec le peintre Antonio da Anghiari un contrat." Also Keith Christiansen in *Painting in Renaissance Siena, 1420–1500* (New York, 1988), 84.

29. James H. Stubblebine, *Duccio di Buoninsegna and His School*, 2 vols. (Princeton, 1979), 1:192–193. John White, *Duccio: Tuscan Art and the Medieval Workshop* (London, 1979), 186–187.

30. John White, "Carpentry and Design in Duccio's Workshop," *Journal of the Warburg and Courtauld Institutes* 36 (1973), 92–105; White, "Measurement, Design and Carpentry in Duccio's Maestà," *Art Bulletin* 55 (1973), 334–366; and 55 (1973), 547–569. I believe that the impetus toward the creation of several similar colossal ancona structures with representations of the *Maestà* would be unthinkable without the creative collaboration of the *maestro di legname* with the painter.

31. Monika Cämmerer-George, *Die Rahmung der Toskanischen Altarbilder im Trecento* (Strasbourg, 1966); Julian Gardner, "Fronts and Backs: Setting and Structure," in Bologna, 1983, 297–308.

I understand that Norman Muller, conservator of the Art Museum, Princeton University, is engaged in investigating the structures of the altarpieces.

32. This neglect might be partially the result of the art historians' training and interests, which generally lie in literary-, iconologically-, and nowadays sociologically-oriented studies. It is natural to underestimate and therefore to push aside other information if one is not familiar with the frame of mind or the reasoning of technologically-oriented researchers. These methods may provide innovative groupings and linking of artistic phenomena that may lead us toward understanding not only of questions of authorship but also of inspiration and influences. They move on separate tracks which, nevertheless, run parallel toward truer understanding of art. The troubling disagreement between scholars in the field might even reach to the level of language in that some of the technological studies cast as scientific reports lack the cherished art-historical "je ne sais quoi."

PETER M. LUKEHART
Trout Gallery, Dickinson College

Delineating the Genoese Studio: Giovani accartati *or* sotto padre?

In his essay "The Death of the Artist as Hero," the historian and philosopher Bernard Smith defines the artist-type of the specialized manufacturer (sixteenth to nineteenth century), an artist to be distinguished from the medieval and Renaissance model of one skilled in all aspects of his profession (fig. 1).

The ideal of the artist as craftsman-aristocrat was not . . . an heroic role but an accommodating one. In order to maintain their social success, such artists had to maintain large, complex workshops, and a division of labour typical of the Age of Manufacture. The master academician stood at the apex of a pyramid of manual work, supported by framers, guilders [sic], drapery painters, engravers, and many apprentices; an aristocrat of manual work in "that all-engrossing system of specialising and sorting men, that development in man of one single faculty at the expense of all other faculties." [1]

Whereas Smith's Marxist reading of the division of labor within the large studios during the late sixteenth through the seventeenth centuries might apply to those of Rubens, Van Dyck, or Bernini, it does not account for the majority of artists who lacked the princely patronage to finance such an elaborate system; nor does it account for the general shift in the role of the artist in society during that period. In fact, Smith's vocabulary suggests a crucial misunderstanding of the hard-won pedagogical and social reforms concerning the status of artists in the Renaissance. First, the true academic painter rarely worked in a space separate from his residence; he more often directed his students within his home or an attached studio.[2] Second, there were fewer traditional apprentices in the sixteenth century. A good number of *giovani*, or youths, of independent means—whose fathers were of the same, if not greater, social standing than the master artists—now entered the profession of painting, and their privileged status opposes the accepted paradigm of indentured service to a master, or what I shall define as the role of the *garzone*. A related point is that the jobs formerly undertaken by apprentices still needed to be performed, but a new exploitable mass had to be called in to do so. It is this revision of labor within the Italian studio during the late sixteenth and early seventeenth centuries that I wish to address.

Renaissance theoreticians, as is well known, pointed to antique precedents for the inclusion of painting within the liberal arts. Reciting a firmly held contemporary notion regarding the status of artists in antiquity,[3] Giovanni Battista Paggi, a Genoese nobleman's son who refused to follow his father's mercantile career, justified his decision to become a painter with the following: "First [painting] is a noble art because in ancient times it was such, in fact, it was counted among the liberal arts. . . ."[4]

After a brief career in Genoa, Paggi was banished for murdering one of his compatriots and spent nearly twenty years in Florence. During his exile Paggi campaigned for repatriation but was blocked by jealous artists who feared he might steal their commissions. The attempts by Genoese painters and gilders to exclude Paggi from practicing his art for remuneration led to legal hearings before the city fathers. In defense of his own awkward position as a nobleman who painted professionally, the exiled Paggi wrote that during the golden age painting "was practiced by noblemen in a manner consistent with their station and [it was] prohibited that any slave could learn it. . . ."[5] The source for Paggi's opinion was undoubtedly the *Natural History* in which Pliny writes that Pamphilos

was the first painter who was thoroughly trained in every branch of learning, more particularly in arithmetic and geometry. . . . It was owing to his influence that first at Sikyon, and afterwards throughout Greece drawing, or rather painting, on tablets of boxwood, was the earliest subject taught to freeborn boys, and that this art was accepted as the preliminary step towards liberal education. It was at any rate had [sic] in such honour that at all times the freeborn, and later persons of distinction practised it, while by standing prohibition no slaves might ever acquire it. . . .[6]

This comparison of gloss to source demonstrates the alternate agenda that Paggi intended in calling for the reform of the medieval guild statutes that were about to be enforced in Genoa in 1590–1591.[7] In the letters that he wrote to his brother Girolamo during the guild litigation, Paggi indicated that he wanted not only to prevent the application of moribund statutes to his practice, but also to argue that painting should be the exclusive province of the nobility: ". . . I would very much like to organize [painting] so that not every mean commoner could be admitted, and I would attempt to restrict it little by little into the hands of the nobility. . . ."[8]

In another letter Paggi added that

one should only accept as students sons of citizens in good standing, well off, and noble if possible. These [youths] are, for the most part,

on account of their good birth and education, more malleable than the others, and possess a more speculative genius, whence one should expect only good results; they are motivated by honor and not by money. They should have the ornament of letters and other fine studies so important to the painter.[9]

The emphasis on education and speculative genius—themes sounded by Cennino Cennini, Leon Battista Alberti, and Leonardo da Vinci—became linchpins around which countless sixteenth-century treatises turned.[10] Renaissance writers were

1. Cornelis Cort after Johannes Stradanus, *The Academy*, 1578, engraving Metropolitan Museum of Art, New York, Elisha Whittelsey Fund, 1953 (53.600.509)

well aware that if painting were to be accepted as a liberal art it would have to be demonstrated that the foundations of the profession were theoretical rather than manual, and its practitioners, according to Paggi, noble.

It is not my intention to rehearse the arguments for the nobility and liberality of painting, but to examine the ramifications of Paggi's model for the noble painter. What happened to the organization of the workshop when the sons of financially secure, and sometimes noble, parents were introduced to the painter's profession? And if, as Charles Dempsey has shown[11] (I would extend his model to include not only Bologna and Florence but also Genoa), educated young men with inquisitive and active minds were taught the principles of design, who was carrying out the manual labor that was also essential to the creation of a work of art? That is, who was now grinding pigments, mixing colors, preparing and priming the canvas or panel? Whose hands were responsible for the foundation on which the more highly valued, both economically and aesthetically, layers of paint were applied? The answers remain ambiguous. At this time I can only respond with any degree of certainty to the situation in Genoa; however, I will begin by drawing comparisons between Ligurian painters and their Lombard, Tuscan, Venetian, and Roman contemporaries.

Michelangelo Merisi da Caravaggio was born in 1571 to Fermo di Bernardino, *majordomo* and perhaps architect to Francesco Sforza, marchese of Caravaggio. Howard Hibbard hypothesized that Fermo belonged to a rising dignified class that approached the status of gentry in England, below the nobility but above peasants and workers.[12] Indeed, Fermo is known to have owned land in and around Caravaggio. After Caravaggio's family was decimated by the plague during the 1570s, his mother raised the surviving children. While they were living in Milan, Caravaggio is known to have been apprenticed to Simone Peterzano for four years beginning in 1584.[13] Thus Caravaggio, the son of a Lombard *mastro di casa*, followed a traditional path of apprenticeship: he studied with one master from the age of twelve and a half until

he was approximately sixteen and a half, if he honored the terms of the document. We do not know what Caravaggio was required to do in Peterzano's shop: specifically, there is no mention, in the documents or the biographies, of his training as a draftsman, of his responsibilities to the master, or of his education in the theoretical principles of painting. Although Giovanni Pietro Bellori erred on some points in his published account of Caravaggio's training, he makes an interesting comment in his *postille* to Giovanni Baglione's *Lives* (1642) concerning Caravaggio's early career: Caravaggio, he tells us, "ground pigments in Milan and learned how to manipulate color."[14] This phrase should not necessarily be taken literally, but rather as an acceptable seicento metaphor for an apprenticeship. If a *garzone* were contracted to serve a master, "grinding colors" and other manual tasks were to be assumed. Bellori, in other words, found nothing particularly disdainful in manual practices, which suggests that even a century later (1672) it was still perfectly appropriate for Lombard painters to come up through the ranks of the workshop in much the way that medieval and early Renaissance painters had.[15]

At approximately the same time in Bologna, Guido Reni, the son of a successful musician, was apprenticed to his father's colleague at the palace of the Bolognini family, Denys Calvaert, for some ten years between 1584 and 1594/ 1595. Achieving his independence only after his father's death, Guido transferred to the Carracci Academy at the age of twenty.[16] Malvasia, in the lives of Guido and Domenichino, paints a harsh picture of Calvaert's studio. According to the Bolognese biographer, Calvaert's *garzoni* were among the most oppressed of the later sixteenth century, suffering his outbursts of physical and verbal abuse.[17] In any case, Calvaert's apprentices, as Stephen Pepper indicates, were subject to a "kind of feudal relationship."[18] From this we can extrapolate that these *giovani*, or more appropriately *garzoni*, were required to execute all of the manual labors associated with the preparation of the pigments and canvases or panels. Additionally, Malvasia suggests that Guido might have been

motivated to depart from Calvaert's studio not only by his master's irascibility, but also because the Carracci pupils were allowed to keep any independent commissions they received.[19]

Artists in Venice seem to have been the most constrained by medieval guild laws, which controlled every aspect of artistic education and production

from apprenticeship as a garzone *to inscription as a* maestro dell'arte, *with the right to open a shop, employ assistants, and make and sell objects. . . . At the same time [the guild] protected the interests of its members, assuring a broad distribution of available work by limiting the number of apprentices and assistants permitted the head of each shop. The number of novices entering the trade was also limited, varying with circumstances.*[20]

Only those inscribed in the guild were allowed to make or sell paintings. This closed system was tested, unsuccessfully, by Pietro Malombra and Giovanni Contarini, both unusually "well born and educated for Venetian painters," and both of whom as dilettante painters decided, in 1596, to pursue painting as a profession. The Arte dei Depintori intervened and demanded that they be matriculated and inscribed into the guild.[21] Evidently, then, there were no exceptions to the apprenticeship system in Venice, and one imagines that there was little flexibility in the pedagogical program. The anomalous cases of liberally educated citizens like Malombra and Contarini—perhaps self-taught in the art of painting—point up the *retardataire* situation that prevailed in Venice.[22] It was this same traditional, juridical guild

model that the Genoese painters and gilders would have liked to enforce had Giovanni Battista and Girolamo Paggi not interceded.

The situation in Florence could not have been more different from those in Genoa and Venice. By 1563 Vasari, with the express directive of Cosimo I, established the Accademia del Disegno, an institution that radically limited the powers of the already moribund guilds—the Arte de' Medici e Speziali and the Arte dei Fabbricanti.[23] The Accademia reorganized painters, sculptors, and architects under the banner of the shared discipline: *disegno*. The new statutes of the Accademia provide only general details concerning who could join and the education that *giovani* would receive there: the Accademia was open to both dilettantes and professionals (statutes 2 and 3); the title of academician was open to all who excelled in their art (as an inspiration to the *giovani*); and poor *giovani* were supported by the academy.[24] This last statute may have been intended to protect *giovani* from becoming mere servants to a master rather than proper students. In Florence, then, the practice of the arts of design was open to all strata of society. We lack, however, detailed accounts of the experiences of *giovani* in the studios of established artists and we are forced to make generalizations based on earlier studies.

Nikolaus Pevsner, for example, described the training of artists before the institution of academies as follows:

. . . up to Michelangelo's time medieval methods had still been unchallenged. At about

2. Federico Zuccaro, *Taddeo Employed in Menial Tasks in the House of Calabrese*, c. 1580/1590s, pen and brown wash, traces of black chalk
Sotheby's, London

twelve a boy could enter a painter's shop as an apprentice and would in two to six years' time learn everything necessary from colour-grinding and preparing grounds to drawing and painting. At the same time he was expected to do all kinds of service in his master's house. After the end of his apprenticeship he could go out as a journeyman and then, when some years had passed, obtain his mastership certificate from the local company of painters or the company to which the painters happened to belong, and could settle down as an independent painter.[25]

Pevsner's study notwithstanding, we have little information concerning the actual studios, workshops, and pedagogical methods of Renaissance artists.

In one idiosyncratic instance, however, there is surviving evidence of a Florentine studio that has special significance here if only because of the famous tenants who occupied it in the seventeenth century. Recently some suggestions have been made about the role and decoration of Federico Zuccaro's studio in Florence which illuminate his pedagogical practices while a member of the Florentine Academy.[26] I introduce Zuccaro for several reasons: first, he was the most eminent painter in Florence after Vasari's death (from about 1576 to 1579), when he took over the decorative project for the cupola of the Florentine Duomo;[27] second, he was both an

artist and a theoretician, one who was extremely self-conscious about the role of the painter in society;[28] and third, Paggi rented Zuccaro's Florentine house and studio some years after the latter's departure in 1579.[29] While the renovation and decoration of the house, which formerly belonged to Andrea del Sarto, are interesting topics in and of themselves, I am here concerned only with the studio that Zuccaro had built as a place to teach and work and as a sort of dormitory for his *giovani* and assistants (especially those who worked on the cupola decoration).[30] The exterior of the studio was articulated in the rustic order to which were added sculpted reliefs showing the instruments of the three arts of design, as well as the Zuccaro coat of arms.[31]

On entering the studio in the late sixteenth century, one passed through a vestibule beneath a small vault whose fresco has since been covered. The studio proper also appears to have been decorated with frescoes on the ceiling and sculpture in niches along the walls.[32] Zygmunt Waźbiński has proposed that the program of the decoration was the life of Taddeo Zuccaro, the artist's brother and teacher. Although the frescoes are now covered with a layer of *intonaco*, the narratives can be reconstructed through a series of drawings (some are in the Uffizi, others were recently sold at auction): four groups of four drawings concerning the education and the accomplishments of Taddeo, allegorical figures of virtue, four portraits of artists, and the apotheosis of the Zuccaro family. The six of interest here concern the early career of Taddeo, from 1543, when Taddeo left his parents' home to pursue his career in Rome, until 1548, when after many hardships Taddeo triumphed with the decoration of the façade of the Palazzo Mattei.[33] The first image relates to Taddeo's apprenticeship with Calabrese, a rather unsuccessful Roman painter (fig 2). Calabrese did not teach Taddeo the rudiments of drawing and painting but forced him to perform the household chores of a servant: making beds, carrying wood, and starting fires.[34] In addition Taddeo was starved by Calabrese's wife (fig. 3), who feared that the earnest young painter would surpass his

3. Federico Zuccaro, *Taddeo in the House of Giovanni Piero Calabrese,* c. 1580/1590s, pen and brown wash, traces of red chalk
Sotheby's, London

4. Federico Zuccaro, *Taddeo Sent on an Errand by the Wife of Calabrese, and Admiring a Façade by Polidoro da Caravaggio*, c. 1580/1590s, pen and brown wash, traces of black chalk
Sotheby's, London

5. Federico Zuccaro, *Taddeo Drawing by Moonlight in the House of Calabrese*, c. 1580/1590s, pen and brown wash, traces of black chalk
Sotheby's, London

master. For this reason Calabrese and his wife also kept hidden their collection of Raphael's drawings. Thus, Taddeo was forced to draw and learn from the great masters of the past and present either by stopping to sketch during his errands (fig. 4) or to draw by moonlight in his chambers (fig. 5). He also made drawings on the mortar (fig. 4) while he was grinding pigments for Calabrese. Exasperated with the treatment of his master, Taddeo left Calabrese and took odd jobs in the workshops of other Roman painters, earning enough to subsist and leaving time to draw after

6. Federico Zuccaro, *Taddeo in the Vatican Belvedere, Drawing the Laocoön*, c. 1580/1590s, pen and brown ink, traces of red chalk
Sotheby's, London

7. Federico Zuccaro, *Mons Virtutis* (Garden of Liberal Arts), pen and brown ink, brown wash, white heightening
Pierpont Morgan Library, New York, Janos Scholz Collection (1983.67)

antiquity, as well as after the paintings of Polidoro da Caravaggio, Raphael, and Michelangelo (fig. 6).[35]

This program of study is not uncommon among artists of the sixteenth century. What is unique about Taddeo's circumstances is that he persevered through isolation, physical indignities, and poverty. Federico chose to emphasize neither Taddeo's grammar school education nor the artistic training he received under his father, but the arduous path that leads to fame and virtue (fig. 7). Waźbiński interprets this iconography as an ethical *exemplum* for the *giovani* in Federico's studio.[36] The theme of the decoration concerns equally the centrality of drawing to the artist's education; in nearly two-thirds of the scenes Taddeo is shown in the act of drawing, the skill shared by architects, sculptors, and painters.[37] Whereas Taddeo is also shown engaged in the menial tasks that comprised his service to Calabrese, they are here represented as injurious to the intellectual, social, and moral well-being of the artist.

Unfortunately, Federico probably left Florence before the cycle was completed, and it has been suggested that he left the drawings behind or sent them from Rome to be executed by the next resident in the studio. Who inhabited the house and studio between 1579 and 1588 has not been discovered, but we do know that Giovanni Battista Paggi rented the property from 1588 until 1599, at which time he was repatriated to Genoa.[38] This studio, as Detlef Heikamp has shown, later passed to Jacopo Vignali, Baldassare Franceschini, and Carlo Dolci.[39] If Waźbiński is correct in his identification of the decorative program and in his dating to the late sixteenth century, then the frescoes of the studio vault would have served as an inspiration to the *giovani* and as an admonition to a tyrannical teacher.

This leads us, finally, to two important junctures with Genoese artists: first, Paggi was probably the initial tenant in Zuccaro's Florentine house and its attached atelier, "the first structure of the period to be created (specifically) as a studio, to be distinguished . . . from the typical *bottega*";[40] second, two of the most influential teachers of the Genoese cinquecento, Ottavio and Andrea Semino, were studying the works of the ancients and moderns in Rome at exactly the time that Taddeo Zuccaro completed the Palazzo Mattei façade. I will address the two brothers first, as important models of an earlier generation, and conclude with Paggi.

Ottavio and Andrea were born in the mid- to late 1520s. Their father, Antonio Semino, provided their earliest education in his own shop in Genoa.[41] Sometime during their late teens or early twenties the Semino brothers traveled to Rome where they, like Taddeo Zuccaro and so many of their contemporaries, went to study and make drawings after the ancient and modern masters.[42] When they returned to Genoa around 1550/1551, they assumed control of their father's shop and matriculated through the guild, the Arte de' Pittori et Scuttari.[43] The Semino were in competition with the preeminent decorators of the second half of the cinquecento, especially Giovanni Battista Castello, better known as Bergamasco, and Luca Cambiaso. Yet they both received important commissions to paint mythological and dynastic cycles for the palaces and villas of the "nobili vecchi." Throughout the middle decades of the sixteenth century the Semino workshop seems to have divided work evenly between the two brothers: Ottavio undertook most of the poetic decorative programs and the façade decorations, and Andrea executed most of the historical and dynastic subjects, as well as the majority of easel paintings.[44]

Although both of the Semino had assistants and *garzoni*, Ottavio's personality proved insufferable if not hazardous to his students. In fact, Soprani reports that Ottavio was exiled in the 1560s for killing one of his *garzoni*.[45] After he made peace with (or rather a payoff to) the family of the deceased, he was allowed to return to Genoa. In a second scandalous incident, Ottavio was reputed to have seduced a young woman whom he forced to accompany him to Savona (probably in the early 1560s). In order to protect her identity and honor, Ottavio disguised her as a young boy, lying even to the Podestà and the

bargello about her gender. Adding insult to injury, Ottavio carried this deception further when he demanded that she engage in the tasks of a *garzone*; Soprani reports that Ottavio insisted that she "grind colors."[46] Thus we learn that not only was Ottavio a misogynist, but also an opportunist: he required his mistress to perform the menial labor reserved, as we shall see, for servants.

At the same time that Ottavio abused his authority as a teacher, he remained a highly acclaimed draftsman and fresco painter. His interior and exterior frescoes drew the praise of his contemporaries, as, for example, in the *Banquet of the Gods* for the Palazzo of Agostino Pallavicino on the Strada Nuova (later Palazzo Cambiaso; now the Banca di Napoli) or on the façade of the Palazzo Squarciafichi-Doria Invrea.[47] Together with Luca Cambiaso, Ottavio helped to establish the first recorded life-drawing academy in Genoa (probably in the 1530s–1540s) when they were still *giovani*. After their morning sessions, the two of them would often go to the stalls along the "Ripa" of the port in order to buy prints after the best masters.[48] That Ottavio was a serious artist Soprani did not question; it was his character, both as a teacher and as a citizen, that the biographer impugned.[49]

The best known of the pupils to study with the Semino was Bernardo Castello, born in 1557 to Antonio and Geronima Macchiavello, probably members of the *popolari*, in the parish of the Maddalena.[50] The traditional view of Castello's early career begins with his presumed studies in grammar school, after which he was apprenticed to Andrea Semino; Soprani reports that Bernardo also studied from time to time with Cambiaso.[51] Castello is known to have married quite young, in 1575, approximately the same time that he became an independent master. In the late 1570s or early 1580s, Castello traveled throughout Italy.[52] Don Angelo Grillo served as intermediary between Castello and Torquato Tasso, delivering the artist's illustrations for *Gerusalemme liberata* (fig. 8) to Ferrara in 1586.[53] In 1588, Castello was asked by the Accademia Fiorentina to make a portrait of Sofonisba Anguissola, the most famous woman painter of her

8. Bernardo Castello,
Presumed Death of Rinaldo,
c. 1617, red chalk
Palazzo Rosso, Genoa (no. 1994)

age, and, incidentally, the godmother of one of Castello's sixteen children. That same year Castello was elected *accademico* in the Florentine Accademia del Disegno on the basis of a single drawing. Meanwhile he was invited by a Genoese academy, probably the Addormentati, to read Aristotle's *Ethics* and *Poetics* at the Villa Lomellini in Pegli.[54] Throughout the 1590s Castello received numerous commissions for decorative cycles, portraits, devotional paintings, and altarpieces, often soliciting advice from his lifelong friend and correspondent, the poet Gabriello Chiabrera.[55] In 1590–1591, it is generally assumed that Castello, selfishly desiring to keep the most important Genoese com-

missions to himself, opposed Paggi—who never matriculated through the guild—and his efforts to dissolve the Arte de' Pittori et Scuttari, despite the fact that the guild statutes limited painters to a single apprentice (which would severely have limited his ability to undertake large-scale fresco commissions).[56]

Castello's career continued to flourish throughout the seventeenth century, and his reputation as the most eminent (or best connected) of Genoese painters led to a commission for one of the altarpieces in Saint Peter's. Despite these honors, when, in 1617, Castello's son, appropriately named Torquato, applied for admission into the Collegio de' Dottori, the exclusive college of doctors of law denied him on account of the manner in which his father practiced his profession.[57] The offenses, as we shall see, related to Castello's compromising of his *casa aperta*: he painted frescoes in palaces and churches; he made portraits for clients in their, rather than in his, home; and he established prices for his work (that is, he worked on commission). The depositions of Bernardo Castello's witnesses who testified before the Collegio provide a rare glimpse into the education and artistic practices of sixteenth-century painters, and the information provided therein allows us to emend the biographical accounts that have served as the basis of all previous studies of the artist.

One of the most fascinating revelations in the witnesses' testimonies was that distinctions were made between the students in an artist's shop or studio: some were obligated by contract (*accartato*) to serve the master for a specified period of time (as outlined in the guild statutes);[58] others remained under the jurisdiction of their fathers and appear to have been exempt from many of the manual labors associated with apprenticeships.[59] Previously, studies of sixteenth-century pedagogical practices assumed that either a guild system or an academic system (on the Florentine model) prevailed at one moment in a city's history; here we shall see that Genoese artists experienced a dichotomy. Since these unpublished testimonies contradict commonly held assumptions about the relationship between student and teacher during the late Renaissance, I would like to examine them carefully, quoting excerpts from the transcript.

The first witness called to testify was Andrea Merchano,[60] a colleague who had known Castello since 1573 when they were both in Semino's studio. Merchano told the lawyers that he himself had not been *accartato*, and he did not think that Bernardo had been either. Asked about the tasks that they had performed as *giovani*, Merchano stated, "M. Andrea summoned a man when he wanted to mix the colors and this same man prepared (or ground) the colors. We others cleaned the jars . . . where they were stored . . . and the servants carried the water, although the young boys did not carry the water. The

garzoni nailed the canvases on the stretchers (*quadri*) and also prepared (that is, applied gesso to, or primed) them. These same *garzoni* served the master in everything that he needed while he painted."[61] Merchano explained that Bernardo remained in Semino's studio for six years while he himself spent five years there; both of these terms would have fallen short of the seven years stipulated in the guild statutes.[62] Merchano also swore that Castello did not maintain a *bottega* (which exempted him from obeying the guild statutes), and later defined mechanical arts as those performed by *butegari* (those who worked in *botteghe*). "Painting," he insisted, ". . . is not mechanical."[63]

Throughout this testimony, the inquisitors and the witnesses emphasize the tasks appropriate, on the one hand, to liberal artists and, on the other, to manual laborers. In order to place this division within the framework of contemporary perceptions, it is instructive to examine Paggi's definitions of noble and non-noble practices in another letter to Girolamo.

Horsemanship is extremely noble and worthy of any lord, but the control of horses . . . washing them and brushing them, caring for them, bridling them, saddling them and getting them ready so that the cavaliere *can use them, is completely servile handwork and undignified for the* cavaliere*. . . . Horsemanship . . . jousting, making war and other similar affairs are one thing, and being a stable boy and preparing the horse are another. Similarly, painting and painting to express various conceits belonging to the Idea, making a pleasing deception for the eyes of others with imitated things, representing events that have already occurred as though they can be seen before your eyes, and innumerable other noble effects, which are the painter's province are one thing; and preparing canvases and panels, gessoing them, laying on the glue, grinding colors, making brushes . . . are the painter's "horse."*[64]

Paggi qualifies this division, saying that even if one accidentally touches inks, paint, sweat, mud, or any other intrinsically vilifying material in the act of a noble pursuit, it is still not ignoble (that is, in Aristotelian terms, the end is still noble).

Paggi himself had attended grammar school and then taught himself the rudiments of design. His association with Luca Cambiaso was an occasional one and probably took place after hours.[65] But Paggi's case is different from the others presented here: he was a nobleman extremely conscious of his status, which he did not wish to demean by serving another man or by compromising his *casa aperta*.[66] When Paggi returned to Genoa around 1600, he opened a studio in which all the participants were free (that is, *sotto padre*). I have not found any documents concerning an apprenticeship or periods of service for any of his students.[67] The only mention of a *giovane* performing manual tasks can be traced to Soprani, who discusses the circumstances in which Paggi accepted Giulio Bruno as a servant. Bruno had studied briefly with Lazzaro Tavarone before pursuing an independent career. According to Soprani, Bruno fell on hard times and asked Paggi to provide for him in exchange for his labors. Paggi later liberated Bruno from domestic responsibilities so he could devote himself entirely to painting. As I have argued elsewhere, Paggi accepted only liberal artists in his studio; thus when Bruno could again support himself, Paggi absolved him of menial tasks.[68]

Paggi, like Andrea Semino and other of their contemporaries, must have summoned servants and "hired men" to execute the manual labor for his free *giovani*, though Paggi's studio operated more homogeneously than other Genoese studios. I want to conclude by examining the mixed system of *giovani sotto padre* and *garzoni accartati* within a single studio because I feel certain that this was the system that prevailed, especially at the end of the sixteenth century. For this we can look at the example of Bernardo Castello, who, although not a nobleman, was a liberal artist trained in a studio where a more typical, mixed system was in place.

Information concerning Castello's studio derives from the testimony of a silk merchant summoned by the Collegio de' Dottori. Bernardo d'Amico, who frequented Castello's studio since about the mid-1590s, had not witnessed Castello's education, but he reasoned that his friend had not been *accartato* since the latter's

father had been able to provide for him. Castello, he argued, probably did not perform manual labor, but attended Semino's studio in order to learn how to draw and paint.[69]

The last witness that I would like to introduce, Battista Brignole, had studied with Castello in Semino's studio, although he himself was *accartato* for seven years.[70] Like Merchano, Brignole was rather certain that Castello was not *accartato*. Brignole's testimony illuminates the mixed system of training in Semino's studio: "He [Castello] did not perform the services that are accomplished by *garzoni*; that is . . . grinding colors and preparing canvases, for which task he [Semino] summoned other men."[71] Asked to describe who did the menial work for the master, Brignole answered: "These [menial] tasks[72] . . . are performed by people salaried by the master, that is these same *garzoni* who are *accartati* and governed by the master. However, these same things are not done by *figli di padri* who are governed by their fathers; they are obligated to do nothing except draw."[73] We also learn that although Semino always worked in his home, he continued to maintain a *bottega aperta*, by which Brignole may have meant that Semino either kept a separate shop for his large-scale commissions, or that even within his own home, Semino accepted commissions by the piece.[74] The actual disparity between the social and educational situations of Castello and Brignole are made the more poignant by the latter's admission at the end of his testimony: "I believe that all the things that I have done, I have done with my hands. For me they are mechanical because I prepare canvases with gesso. . . ."[75] Thus the division between the painters who were privilegd by circumstances and those who were forced by economic need to serve the master was most painfully obvious to the *giovani* and *garzoni* who worked side by side in the same master's shop or studio. The stigma of one's position within the social hierarchy of the studio was borne throughout one's career, as Brignole's testimony, or rather confession, illustrates.

This brief survey of the individual practices of painters throughout Italy points tentatively to a growing self-consciousness about which shop tasks (fig. 1) were considered appropriate to the education of different classes of artists at the end of the sixteenth century. Indeed, the pedagogical and apprenticeship systems seem to be more idiosyncratic at this stage than previously supposed. Whereas in Rome, Lombardy, Emilia, and Venice (except in the case of dilettantes) the traditional roles of apprenticeship and service to a master continued to be observed, the reforms of the Accademia del Disegno in Florence and the sharply delineated social hierarchy of the Genoese demanded new educational models for the *giovani* (sons of financially independent fathers). As we have observed in the testimony of Castello's colleagues, such as Brignole's comment that young boys who were *figli di padri* were expected only to draw, the education of artists in Genoa was already approaching the ideal set forth in Paggi's letters to his brother Girolamo some two decades prior to the litigation that sundered the guild in 1590/1591. Yet the earliest liberal practitioners of the art of painting in Genoa were not, as Paggi would have hoped, noblemen, but sons of *popolari*. Like their counterparts in the Accademia del Disegno in Florence, and in the Carracci Academy, and like the Sikyonian freeborn boys, these *giovani sotto padre* learned the principles of design; it remains to be investigated whether free students in Florence, Bologna, or even Sikyon were also absolved from any obligation to perform servile tasks.

APPENDIX

Below are excerpts from the testimony of the witnesses who were called on to speak on behalf of Torquato Angelo Castello at an inquiry preceding his election into the Collegio dei Dottori in Genoa. I have included the numbers of the questions (for example, "ad 25"), which are summarized in brackets, followed by transcriptions of the witnesses' responses. The testimonies are arranged chronologically, according to the dates and times of the depositions. Each response will be preceded by the initials of the witness: Andrea Merchano=AM; Battista Brignole=BB; Benedictus Gallus (Bénédicte, or Benedetto, Galle)= BG; Bernardo d'Amico=BA; and Ottavio Corrigiani=OC.

The document is found in the Archivio di Stato, Genoa, Notari Ignoti, no. 223, fascicle dated 2 December 1617. (Only the testimony of Ottavio Corrigiani was taken later, on 7 July 1618.)

For the convenience of the reader, I have tried to minimize the use of brackets. When I am certain of the missing letters in abbreviations and lacunae, I have italicized them. Ellipses indicate missing or illegible words; ellipses with brackets indicate that there is a break (my intervention) in the order of the testimony; and dashes indicate original cancellations of words. The quotation marks that precede each of the witnesses' testimonies are my additions to clarify the fact that they were given verbally.

OC: "[. . .] [Corrigiani answers a series of questions in one long statement that is unnumbered, from which I have excerpted the following] Et questo tocca al padre dico che sono diciotto o venti anni che io lo conosco et ho visto et inteso et sono anco stato in casa sua molte volte dove faceva piture diverse molto belle per questo parevanno [?] a me et di continuato in sua casa far l'esercitio della pitura facendola honorevolmente come fa il M.co Paggi il quale intendo che faccia il medesimo questo questo [sic] e publico e materia e secondo qualche ho detto qualche e a notitia mia ne il padre ne il figlio [Torquato Angelo] hanno fatto professione mecanica hoc est etc."

[. . .]

ad 14 [When, for how long, and under what circumstances did you meet Bernardo Castello?]

AM: "L'anno 1573: — con occasione che io andai @ Roma con M. Andrea Semino."

BB: "Sarano da 40 @ 45 anni che continuo col detto B.nardo per conto della pitura perche io l'esercitavo se bene hora ho aperta butega."

BA: "L'ho continuato @ conoscere da quarant'anni in qua con ocasion di esserli vicini."

BG: "L'ho detto sopra [in question 2: "Io lo conosciuto il padre di detto M. B.nardo che havea la sua — butega in le vigne di Sartore et so che è statto per il spatio di venticinque anni a Genova essendo stato in casa sua molte volte e farli fare delli — ancone e quadri."] et l'o. . . fa e ponno essere da 50 anni."

OC: "Son da 18 o 20 anni con ocasione di vederle sue piture condic. . . da qualche dono."

[. . .]

ad 16 [What professions did Bernardo Castello practice from his childhood to the present?]

AM: "Non posso prima di haverlo conosciuto, tengo bene — per certo che non habbi fatto altro esercitio — e poi di haverlo conosciuto non ha — fatto altro esercitio che la pittura e questo lo posso dire per certissimo."

BB: "Tutti li esercitij che ha fato li ha fatti nella casa della pittura, et non ho inteso altri esercitij."

BA: "Io non so quando egli sij nato ma parlo [?] solamente di quello quando l'ho conosciuto che ha — sempre fato la pitura in casa sua."

BG: "Non l'ho mai conosciuto ne visto fare altro esercitio che dipintore."

OC: "Io non posso m. . . solo del [tem]po detto."

[. . .]

ad 19 [Was Bernardo Castello ever a consul of the painters' guild?]

AM: "Io non mi racordo che egli sia statto console ne l'arte fa [fra?] consoli."

BB: "Hora mi ricordo di queste cose che sij mai stato console et io — sono statto console — e prima di 13 o 14 anni si facevano i consoli, ma hora non si fa per qualche differenze [a?] che entri li pitori di casa e quelli che tengono di butega."

BA: "Non so che egli e stato console."

BG: "Io non so che sij mai stato console."

OC: "Ne scire."

[. . .]

ad 24 [In order to learn his profession, did Bernardo Castello serve as a *garzone* with one master, or with others?]

AM: "Non lo so solito col sud*etto* [Andrea Semino]."

BB: "Non ho mai saputo solo che ha impreso l'arte di d*etto* Semino."

BA: "Io credo che non sij stato p*er* garzone con carta altrimente mache sij andato p*er* imparare senzaltro."

OC: "Non lo so."

ad 25 [How long was Bernardo Castello a *garzone*?]

AM: "Da haverà servito da sei anni et io li son stato solo per — — — cinque anni p*er* garzone."

BB: "Se c. . . servire p*er* garzone p*er* sette anni, ma io non so quale lui vi [?] sij stato."

BA: "Non so che habbi servito p*er* garzone."

BG: "No lo so, e non so se ne anche se servisse p*er* garzone."

OC: "Ne scire."

ad 26 [Was Bernardo Castello 'accartato'?]

AM: "Non ne so niente, se fusse accartato so bene che io non l'ho havuto carta, e perciò credo che ne anco lui non ne habbi havuto ne . . . — — habbiano notato alcuno."

BB: "Io non so se fusse acartato o no, ma più presto credo di no — perch'era — — — ne anco col'era."

BA: "Mi credo che non fusse acartato p*er*che il padre havea comodità di governarla."

BG: "No — so se fusse acartato ma io ho un figlio che ha servito il M.co Gio B.ta Paggi senza carta."

OC: "Ne scire."

ad 27 [Did Bernardo Castello perform the chores that other *garzoni* did?]

AM: "Faceva li esercitij che sogliono fare li altri garzoni de — pitori per conto dell'arte."

BB: "Lui non facia li servitorj che soliano fare li altri garzoni delli pitori perche li altri servitorj sono macinare colori et apparechiar telle p*er* il q*ua*le offitio suppliava altri huomini."

BA: "Io non ero in casa del maestro che potessi [?] vedere se facia li servitorj che fanno li altri garzoni."

BG: "Non lo so."

OC: "Non lo so."

ad 28 [Who prepared the paintings? What exactly did the *garzoni* do: mix colors; prepare and clean the paint dishes; carry the water and the tools needed for painting; stretch canvases and prepare them; and serve the master in whatever way necessary?]

AM: "M. Andrea [Semino] chiamava un huomo quando volea distemperare de colori et tal istesso huomo che chiamava apparechiava li colori et noi altri netopavanno li vasi . . . e arcelle dove si tengono et le cuchete e vasi dove si tengono i colori et le — aque li portarano li fanteschi [?], et li garzoni di parvi non portano aqua e le telle sopra li quadri li piantavano li garzoni et anco li aparechiavano et li istessi anco servirvano il maestro in tutto quello che ha bisogno mentre depinge."

BB: "Questi esercitij son tenuti nele Interroga*tione* son fatti da persone — salariate dal maestro ch*e* medemi garzoni che sono acartat[i] e governati dal maestro facii ma queste cose p*er*li — figli de padri i qualli si governano dal padre non son solia far altri salvo dessignare."

BA: "Io m . . . do che sia chiaro quello che si contiene nell'Interroga*tione*."

BG: "Io non lo so."

OC: "Chi vuole [?] imparare un arte credo che faccia delle cose per minute p*er* introdursi alle altre maggiori, pero non so quello — et p . . . in questa arte particulare."

ad 29 [Did Bernardo Castello also have to serve the master in many manual labors around the house or outside it?]

AM: "S*ignore* no. E non [?] si fa niente."

BB: "Quelli che sono governati delli padri non ne fano nessune di queste cose."

BA: "Io credo che questo non lo facessi — et vi sono di [?] a quelli garzoni che fano le cose contenute nell'Interro*gatione* ad quelli no."

BG: "Si puo ne [?] servire ma io non li sono quando li comandano."

OC: "Ne scire."

ad 30 [Did Andrea Semino have a *bottega aperta*?]

AM: "— Non tenea boteghà aperta, ma stava nel chiostro di S. Siro."

BB: "M. And.ea Semino ha sempre laverato [sic] nelle stanze ma havea butega aperta."

BA: "Ho sempre inteso dire che il pitore Semino hanno [sic] lavorato in casa e non in butega aperta."

BG: "Il Semino lavorava in casa."

OC: "Non lo so."

ad 31 [Did Bernardo Castello ever have a *bottega aperta*, even for a brief time?]

AM: "Signor no. Che non la mai teneva botega."

BB: "Signor no. Ne vogli ne ho mai visto."

BA: "Non mi ricordo ne ho inteso che detto B.nardo habbi mai aperta butega."

BG: "Questo no."

OC: "Come sopra [question 30: "Non lo so."]."

ad 32 [Did or does Bernardo Castello receive payment for his work (*manifatura*)?]

AM: "Ha esercitato et esercita l'arte con farsi pagare."

BB: "— Esercita la pitura e quando fa dell'opere si fa pagare."

BA: "D'ogn'uno che fa lavori si fa pagare."

BG: "Dipinge per esser pagato."

OC: "Io credo che detto B.nardo riceva mercede delle sue fatiche come sogliono fare tutti i pitori eccetto intendo che faceva il Mag.co Paggi."

[...]

ad 56 [What, in your opinion, are vile or mechanical arts?]

AM: "Li butegari."

BB: "Li fromaggiani li . . . casi e simili sono arti vili."

BA: "— Io intenderei — per vile arte li fromaggiai et altre arte [sic] simile [sic]."

BG: "Non lo so qua . . . i decernare ne le sto qua . . . i su; essendo francese."

OC: "La legge de [15]76, quella dest . . . secondo luso di questa Serenissima Repubblica con quella mir. . . ."

ad 57 [Do you know which arts, requiring manual labor for remuneration—money or goods—are considered mechanical?]

AM: "Non so quale e tengo che la pitura non sij mecanica."

BB: "Io posso judicare che tutte le cose facevo che le facevo con le mani et che mi sono mecaniche p— et [?] io apparecchio delle telle con del gesso e stimo che queste cose siano mecaniche."

BA: "Io non so judicare quelli che si contiene nell'Interrogatione."

BG: "Io mi credo de si per quanto — dicono[?]"

OC: "Me lasso il giudicare la decisione alla [legge]."

ad 68 [What is your profession? How old are you? What is your financial situation?]

AM: "Son pitore, son di etta d'anni cinquanta sette, vale scudi [?] 100 e piu."

BB: "Son pitore son di etti [sic] d'anni 65 e possedo in beni sc. 100 e piu."

BA: "Son di etta danni 50 de professione seatero."

BG: "Ho 65 anni o circa la professione l'ho detto [I have not found any statement in his testimony] possedo in beni scudi 100 e piu."

OC: "Io ho anni 54 sono notaro di Collegio possedo in beni sc. 100 e piu."

NOTES

I would like to thank Tracy Cooper, Ellen Todd, and Alessandra Galizzi for their helpful comments and criticisms. I must also single out Rodolfo Savelli and Carlo Bitossi in Genoa for their expert assistance with the documentary material and Piero Boccardo and Elizabeth Llewellyn, who provided photographs of important images. Last, Timothy Wardell checked the notes for this and all the essays in this volume.

1. Bernard Smith, "The Death of the Artist as Hero," in *The Death of the Artist as Hero: Essays in History and Culture* (Melbourne/Oxford, 1988), 17. The internal quotation is a passage from Marx's *Das Kapital.*

2. As I argue elsewhere, Genoese painters, at a ratio of about two to three, had studios in their own homes. Those who maintained *botteghe* were forced to obey the guild statutes, while those who confined their teaching and working to their *case aperte* were exempt. See Peter Lukehart, "Contending Ideals: The Nobility of Painting and the Nobility of G.B. Paggi" (Ph.D. diss., Johns Hopkins University, 1987), 245–246, 287–289, 291–292, 296–298.

3. Leon Battista Alberti, *De pictura*, trans. and ed. John R. Spencer (New Haven, 1966), 64–65; Leonardo da Vinci, *The Notebooks of Leonardo da Vinci*, trans. and ed. Edward MacCurdy, 2 vols. (New York, 1938), 2:227–229, 257; Benedetto Varchi, "Della maggioranza delle arti," in Paola Barocchi, ed., *Scritti d'arte del cinquecento*, 3 vols. (Milan/Naples, 1971), 1:137–140; Romano Alberti, *Trattato della nobiltà della pittura*, in Paola Barocchi, ed., *Trattati d'arte del cinquecento fra manierismo e controriforma*, 3 vols. (Bari, 1962), 3:197–235.

Paggi's library contained all of these texts except (possibly) L. B. Alberti's. See Lukehart 1987, app. 5.

4. Giovanni Battista Paggi in "Arte della pittura nella città di Genova," ed. Giovanna Rosso del Brenna, *La Berio* 16, no. 3 (1976), 8; "Giovanni Battista Paggi: lettere al fratello Girolamo," in Barocchi 1971, 1:196. I will be citing the letters transcribed from the *La Berio* manuscript throughout; the references to Barocchi are generally easier to locate because of the small circulation of *La Berio.*

5. Paggi, in *La Berio* 16, no. 3 (1976), 7: ". . . che ne tempi antichi essa arte era da persone nobili et da tali nobilmente esercitata, con proibizione che serva alcuno la potesse imparare. . . ." See also Barocchi 1971, 1:194.

6. Pliny, *Natural History*, trans. and ed. K. Jex-Blake and E. Sellers (London, 1896; repr. Chicago, 1968), Book 35:76–77, 119. See also the passage by Romano Alberti (Barocchi 1962, 3:204), in which he discusses the origin of the term *graphikos.*

7. For a more detailed discussion of guild reform in Genoa, see Lukehart 1987, chap. 4: "About the Nobility of Painting and the Arte de' Pittori et Doratori: Guild Reform in Late Sixteenth-Century Genoa"; and Franco Renzo Pesenti, "La disputa a Genova del 1590 sull'Arte della Pittura e Giovan Battista Paggi," in *La pittura in Liguria: artisti del primo seicento* (Genoa, 1986), 9–22.

8. Paggi, in *La Berio* 16, no. 3 (1976), 15: "ma vorrei ben ordinarla in modo che non vi s'immetesse [sic] ogni poveraccio plebeo, et tentarei con bon modo di ridurla a poco a poco nelle mani della nobiltà. . . ." See also Barocchi 1971, 1:204.

9. Paggi, in *La Berio* 17, nos. 1–2 (1977), 12: ". . . bisogna che non si accettino per discepoli se non figliuoli di Cittadini di honesta fortuna et benestanti, et nobili se è possibile. Questi per lo più, per la buona creanza et educazione, sono più docili de gl' altri, et di più speculativo igegno, onde non se potrebbe aspettare se non buona riuscita, si moveriano per stimolo d'onore, et non per guadagno haverebbero l'ornamento delle lettere et altre buone discipline che troppo importano al Pittore, et finalmente sarebbero stromenti tante più atti a fare questa professione, ch'ella in poco tempo ne salirebbe nella sua prima grandezza." See also Barocchi 1971, 1:211–212.

10. Cennino Cennini, *Il libro dell'arte*, trans. and ed. Daniel V. Thompson (New York, 1960), 1–2; L.B. Alberti 1966, 90–91; Leonardo 1938, 2:256–257.

11. Charles Dempsey, "Some Observations on the Early Education of Artists in Florence and Bologna," *Art Bulletin* 62 (1980), 552–569.

12. Howard Hibbard, *Caravaggio* (New York, 1983), 1. Hibbard's source is probably Giulio Mancini's *Considerazioni sulla pittura*, ed. A. Marucchi and Luigi Salerno, 2 vols. (Rome, 1956–1957), 1:5, 7–10, which is published in his own appendix 2, 346–351. For the land holdings, property sales, dowries, and other evidence of personal wealth, see Mia Cinotti, *Michelangelo Merisi detto il Caravaggio*, vol. 1, I Pittori Bergamaschi. Il Seicento (Bergamo, 1983), 233–238.

13. Hibbard 1983, 1–2. For the documents concerning Caravaggio's apprenticeship, see Cinotti 1983, 236: [6 April 1584] ". . . il Caravaggio poco più di tredicenne, abitante a Milano nella parrocchia di S. Giorgio al Pozzo Bianco, stringe un contratto col pittore Simone Peterzano, abitante nella stessa parrocchia, per quattro anni di apprendistato, durante i quali vivrà ininterrottamente presso il maestro, che s'impegna a fare di lui un pittore capace di lavorare in proprio (probabilmente il rapporto è già in atto ed egli abita già presso il Peterzano, come sembra indicare la communanza di indirizzo)." (Archivio di Stato di Milano, Registri 1574–1576.) My own research suggests that the fact that the apprentices lived with the master indicates a relationship of *garzone*, or almost servant to master. Caravaggio did not go to Peterzano's home merely to learn to draw and paint, but to do chores, especially in the early years.

14. Giovanni Pietro Bellori, *Le vite de' pittori, scultori et architetti*, ed. Evelina Borea (Turin, 1976), 212; reprinted in Hibbard 1983, 361. For the *postille* to Baglione's *Vite de' pittori, scultori, et architetti* (Rome, 1642), see Hibbard 1983, 356 n. 1: "Macinava li colori in Milano, et apprese a colorire et per haver occiso un suo compagno fuggì dal paese in bottega di Mess. Lorenzo Siciliano ricovero in Roma. . . ."

15. The tradition of having apprentices grind colors dates at least to the Middle Ages. We know this was a major part of an artist's craft both from Cennini and from the surviving documents of commissions requesting that the master himself oversee, or even take personal responsibility for, the colors. This practice continued into the fifteenth century as we learn that Luca Signorelli was requested to paint all the figures in the vault of the Orvieto Cathedral (especially faces and hands); similarly, he was to oversee all the work and was personally responsible for mixing the colors. Michael Baxandall, *Painting and Experience in Fifteenth-Century Italy* (Oxford/New York, 1972), 23.

16. D. Stephen Pepper, *Guido Reni: A Complete Catalogue of His Works with an Introductory Text* (Oxford, 1984), 19. Carlo Cesare Malvasia (*Felsina Pittrice. Vite de' Pittori bolognesi* [Bologna, 1678], ed. Giampietro Zanotti, 2 vols. [Bologna, 1841], 2:6–7) says that Guido was about nine years old when he came to Calvaert's attention, but we do not know whether he was immediately relieved of his obligation to follow his father's career as a musician. In any case, Guido excelled in Calvaert's studio and was selected "dal maestro (appena compiva anni tredici) a dar l'esemplare agli altri condiscepoli. . . ."

Pepper, following Malvasia's notes for the *Felsina Pittrice*, suggests that Guido was free to leave Calvaert's shop after his father's death, either because of the end of his father's influence or the end of his ten-year apprenticeship. Malvasia's published account indicates, falsely, that Daniele Reni was still alive at that time.

17. Malvasia 1678, 2:6–7 (Guido), 222 (Domenichino). Calvaert is supposed to have attacked Guido both for using a special jar of lake reserved for the master and for his emulation of the Carracci manner. Similarly, Domenichino was beaten and, on another occasion, physically abused for trying to copy an engraving by Agostino Carracci. See the discussion in Pepper 1984, 19 and 54 nn. 3–4.

18. Pepper (1984, 19) states that Calvaert's bursts of corporal and verbal punishment show "that in Calvaert's studio a kind of feudal relationship of master and pupil still survived, while within the Carracci Academy a special kind of collective purpose limited the older and younger members, Reni's subordinate relation to Calvaert was reinforced by paternal authority. Upon the death of his father he felt released from his obligations, and Calvaert's pretensions became insupportable."

19. Malvasia 1678, 2:7: ". . . anzi di qualche operetta, che a lui direttivamente veniva commessa, [Calvaert] riscuoteva con molta confidenza lo stabilito prezzo, con farne a lui pocchissima parte: che fu il principio della alienazione del primiero affetto di Guido. . . ." And later he marks the contrast to the Carracci, ". . . convenendo essi di procurare, e lasciargli le fatture di minor conto, e' l prezzo intero di quelle, che a lui direttamente venissero ordinate." Pepper (1984, 54 n. 6) publishes a document from 1595 in which Guido is paid for a God the Father in the church of Santa Sabina, Bologna. What Pepper does not explicitly state is that this very commis-

sion may have precipitated Reni's leaving Calvaert's shop. Is it possible that he wished to sign a contract for an independent commission and was challenged by Calvaert?

Gail Feigenbaum presents her interpretation of the enlightened practices of the Carracci Academy elsewhere in this volume. In fact, her theories and observations regarding the situation in Bologna would corroborate my interpretation of the free enterprise system that was in place in studios (or academies) that trained liberal artists in Genoa and probably in Florence as well.

20. David Rosand, "The Crisis of the Venetian Tradition," *L'Arte* 3, nos. 11–12 (1970), 26. According to Rosand (26–27), Venice upheld the "modo et ordine antiquo" until 1679. Prior to the establishment of the Collegio dei Pittori (1682) only Giovanni Bellini, while painter of the State in 1483, was ever exempted from the guild statutes.

21. Rosand 1970, 38; see also the quotations from the archival documents, 52, nn. 157–160. Contarini was studying to become a notary and Malombra was to follow in his father's career as a state official (and poet). When they took up painting independently as an avocation the guild was disinterested; however, when they devoted themselves professionally to painting "the *Arte* brought suit against them, accusing them of practising the art of painting without having been properly inscribed in the guild, and demanded that they be forced to matriculate." The guild no longer accepted the argument that they were dilettantes and accused them of self-delusion and contravention.

22. On the guild statutes and the statutes of painters prior to the founding on the Collegio dei Pittori, see, in addition to Rosand 1970, 4–53, Alice Binion, "The 'Collegio dei Pittori' in Venice," *L'Arte* 3, nos. 11–12 (1970), 92–101; Daniela Puppulin, "Lotto e l'arte dei dipintori," in *Interpretazioni veneziane: studi di storia dell'arte in onore di Michelangelo Muraro*, ed. David Rosand (Venice, 1984), 351–357. I would like to thank Tracy Cooper for her generous bibliographic suggestions and for invaluable discussions concerning the social condition of Venetian painters.

23. On the history of the Accademia del Disegno, see Nikolaus Pevsner, *Academies of Art, Past and Present* (Cambridge, 1940), 42–55; Dempsey 1980, 552–559; Karen-edis Barzman, "The Università, Compagnia, ed Accademia del Disegno" (Ph.D. diss., Johns Hopkins University, 1986); Zygmunt Waźbiński, *L'Accademia Medicea del Disegno a Firenze nel Cinquecento. Idea e istituzione* (Florence, 1987); see also the review of Waźbiński's book by Barzman, *Burlington Magazine* 130 (1988), 856–857.

24. The statutes of 1563 are published by Pevsner 1940, 296–304: Statute II (297–298), Statute III (298). See also Barzman 1986, 114–154. The language of the Florentine statutes is generally more positive concerning the role and status of *giovani* within the academy than any other contemporary city, most of which were still under the guild system.

For a discussion of the diversity of the membership of the academy, see especially Dempsey 1980, 554–557 and Barzman 1986, 219–307. In Paggi's letters to his brother Girolamo (*La Berio* 16, no. 3 [1976], 9) we learn that even princes, dukes, and kings of the sixteenth century learned to paint.

25. Pevsner (1940, 34) cites J. Meder, *Die Handzeichnung* (Vienna, 1919), and H. Huth, *Künstler und Werkstatt der Spätgothik* (Augsburg, 1923).

26. See Detlef Heikamp, "Federico Zuccari a Firenze (1575–1579), II," *Paragone* 18 (May 1967b), 3–34; and, more recently, Zygmunt Waźbiński, "Lo studiola scuola fiorentina di Federico Zuccari," *Mitteilungen des Kunsthistorischen Institutes in Florenz* 29 (1985), 275–346. When the ex-Rosenbach drawings were recently auctioned, J. A. Gere ("The Life of Taddeo Zuccaro by Federico Zuccaro," auction cat., Sotheby's, New York [11 January 1990], n.p.) reproposed the hypothesis that Federico Zuccaro's drawings were probably made in the 1590s and intended for his Roman palazzo and studio. Gere does not believe that the formats of all the drawings would conform to the specifications of the cross-vault in Federico's Florentine studio.

27. In addition to the sources cited above in note 26, see also Heikamp, "Federico Zuccari a Firenze (1575–1579), I," *Paragone* 18 (March 1967a), 44–68, in which the author discusses at length Zuccaro's role in the decoration of the cupola of the Florentine Duomo.

28. Concerning Federico Zuccaro's theoretical interests, see his own *Lettera a Prencipi, et Signori Amatori del Dissegno, Pittura, Scultura et Architettura . . . con un Lamento della Pittura. . . .* (Mantua, 1605) and *L'Idea de' Pittori, scultori et architetti* (Turin, 1607) (both of these are reprinted in *Scritti d'arte di Federico Zuccaro*, ed. Detlef Heikamp [Florence, 1961]), as well as his joint work with Romano Alberti, *Origine, et progresso dell'Accademia del Dissegno, de' Pittori, Scultori, et Architetti di Roma* (Pavia, 1604; repr. Ann Arbor, 1975). For scholarly discussions of his theories, see, in particular, Erwin Panofsky, *Idea: A Concept of Art History* (New York, 1968); Ludwig Frommel, "Der Palazzo Zuccari. Vom Künstlerhaus zum Max-Planck-Institut," in *Max-Planck Gesellschaft Jahrbuch* (1982), 37–57; and Elizabeth Cropper, *The Ideal of Painting: Pietro Testa's Düsseldorf Notebook* (Princeton, 1984), 49–52, 155–156, 163–164.

29. Heikamp 1967b, 8 and 31 nn. 14–15.

30. For twentieth-century photographs, plans, and reconstructions, as well as earlier prints, see Heikamp 1967b, figs. 1–5 and pls. 2–3; Waźbiński 1985, figs. 1–3.

31. Waźbiński (1985, figs. 1–2) reprints Ferdinando Ruggeri's 1724 engraving and a detail of the surviving relief.

32. See the reconstructed plans of Federico Zuccari's studio by Mario di Giampaolo in Heikamp 1967b, figs. 1, 3; and Waźbiński's enlarged detail (1985, fig. 3). Waźbiński (278–279) suggests that Zuccaro had two studios: one private, the other public.

33. For the entire program and a tentative reconstruction, see Waźbiński 1985, 277–296, fig. 12, and app. 1–3, 342–345. The first description of the cycle of extant drawings for the frescoes was made by P.J. Mariette, *Abecedario*. Archives de l'art français (Paris, 1859–1860), 162–164.

34. Waźbiński 1985, 293–294; see also the appendices referred to in note 33 above.

35. Waźbiński 1985, 294–295; see also the appendices referred to in note 33 above.

36. Waźbiński 1985, 295–296. The placement of these scenes on the ceiling of the studio would have indicated a "specchio morale." The author diverges from earlier readings of the ceiling in suggesting that the central area was not blank, but may have contained Federico Zuccaro's *Mons virtutis* (fig. 7 in this study). See also Werner Körte, *Der Palazzo Zuccari in Rom. Sein Freskenschmuck und seine Geschichte* (Leipzig, 1935), 68–70.

37. This is a point about which Waźbiński does not remark. One of the drawings from the cycle, in fact, shows Taddeo—now cured of his malady and leaving his parents' home once again—en route to Rome, accompanied by allegorical figures of *Disegno* and *Spirito*, when he meets the Three Graces (Uffizi 11018 F, reproduced by Waźbiński 1985, fig. 29).

38. It is Waźbiński (1985, 281) who suggests that Paggi may have executed the frescoes on Federico's designs. See note 26 for Gere's alternative hypothesis. If this is true, it would mark the only other known frescoes that Paggi ever executed; the first was *Saint Catherine Converting Two Criminals* for the *chiostro grande* in Santa Maria Novella, Florence (c. 1582). Because the former frescoes would have been accomplished within Paggi's own home and studio, they would not have constituted a compromise of his *casa aperta*. For a discussion of the delicate question of leaving one's house in order to work, see Lukehart 1987, 147–160; and note 66 below.

39. Heikamp 1967b, 8.

40. Heikamp 1967b, 12–13: "Di abitazione di artisti che alludono con la decorazione in maniera specifica alla professione dell'artista ne esistono altre più antiche in Italia. Lo studio dello Zuccari [in Florence] è però la più lontana nel tempo che può averla pretesa di essere nata veramente come *studio* allo scopo di distinguersi in modo chiaro e pretenzioso dalla fino allora usuale *bottega*. Per la storia di come l'artista si valuta nell'epoca del Manierismo è un momento di prim'ordine."

41. On the lives of Andrea and Ottavio Semino, see Raffaele Soprani, *Le vite de' pittori, scultori et architetti genovesi* (Genoa, 1674), 57–66; Soprani and Giovanni Carlo Ratti, *Le vite de' pittori, scultori et architetti genovesi*, 2 vols. (Genoa, 1768–1797), 1: 60–71; Licia Ragghianti Collobi, "Andrea Semino disegnatore," *Critica d'Arte* (March 1954), 133–143; Fiorella Caraceni Poleggi, "La committenza borghese e il manierismo a Genova," in *La pittura a Genova e in Liguria dagli inizi al cinquecento*, ed. Ennio Poleggi, 2 vols. (Genoa, 1970–1971), 1:264–281, 308–310; Ezia Gavazza, *La grande decorazione a*

Genova, 2 vols. (Genoa, 1974–1989), 1:17–35; and F. Poleggi, "La committenza borghese e il manierismo a Genova," in *La pittura a Genova e in Liguria dagli inizi al cinquecento*, ed. E. Poleggi, 2 vols. (Genoa, 1987), 1:244–258, 286–289.

42. Soprani 1674, 57–58.

43. F. Poleggi 1987, 1:286. Andrea Semino was matriculated in the guild before Luca Cambiaso or G.B. Castello, il Bergamasco. See also the list of guild members published by Rosso del Brenna, in *La Berio* 16, no. 1 (1976), 26–28, where Andrea and Ottavio are listed in the matriculations immediately above Cambiaso and Bergamasco.

44. F. Poleggi 1987, 1:251–254: "Si opera ormai nella bottega dei Semino una netta distribuzione delle opere in commissione dettata dalla diversa inclinazione dei due fratelli, ma anche dall'esigenza di 'autoriformazione' che grava anche sull'ambiente pittorico genovese: Ottavio attende alle ultime trasposizioni mitiligiche ormai spoglie di intellectualismo e grondanti eros domestico e simbologie familiari nelle sale dei palazzi privati, mentre Andrea dipinge pale d'altare e assolva ai riti delle celebrazioni dinastiche che, pur nel chiuso delle dimore, alludono al severo ruolo pubblico del padrone di casa." See also the discussion, 287–288.

45. Soprani 1674, 62: "Et invero per quanto si possa dire, ch'egli fosse nell'arte sua senza difetto; gran pregiudicio ad ogni modo gli apportò l'esser fregolatissimo nel vivere: dedito a suoi capricci, e così facile all'ira, che (per quanto ne riporta la fama) per causa molto leggiera uccidesse a sproposito un suo garzone; e perciò fosse sbandito da Genova: mà che aiutato poi da suoi amici, e sborzata alli parenti del defonto certa somma di denari, fù assai tosto richiamato dal bando. . . ." Fiorella Poleggi (1987, 1:288) suggests a date in the 1560s for this event.

46. Soprani 1674, 64: "Era egli [Ottavio] oltre di ciò molto dedito a piaceri non leciti; si che invaghitosi un giorno d'una bella Giovanetta, così ben la persuase, che da suoi parenti alontandola, alla Città di Savona seco di nascosta la condusse: dove presa in affitto una casa stimò di assicurarsi dal disturbo della giustitia tenendo seco la sua cara in habito di maschio, et occupandola ben spesso in macinare i colori. Mà non potendo i parenti della giovane soffrire un torto così grande . . . fu perciò ordinato al Podestà di Savona che procurasse di assicurarsi se veramente in casa d'Ottavio v'era la sudetta giovanetta. In esecuzione del qual ordine mandò egli con ogni prestezza il suo Bargello alla casa di Ottavio; il quale sentendosi gli sbirri alla Porta, nascose prestmaente [*sic*] la treccie della donzella in una succidissima berretta, et havendole anche lordata la faccia gli ordinò che senza ponto alterarsi attendesse a macinare i colori. Quindi aprendo la Porta iutrodusse [*sic*] di buona voglia il Bargello, che seguitato da suoi famigli con la diligenza, in somiglianti casi dovuta, cercò per ogni cantone la Donna, e non havendola trovata, riferrì al Podestà, che altri non erano in quella casa che Ottavio col suo garzone, e restarono in tal modo beffati i parenti della giovane dell'astutia del Pittore. . . ."

47. The frescoes are illustrated in F. Poleggi 1987, 1: figs. 244–248 (Palazzo Cambiaso/Banco di Napoli), 251 (façade of Palazzo Squarciafichi-Doria Invrea); see also the discussion, 246–251.

48. Soprani 1674, 62: "Hebbe Ottavio gran familiarità col Cambiaso, e mentre erano giovani solevano spesse volte fra la settimana ritirarsi nelle loro case, dove . . . disegnavano a gara dal naturale e continuarono per qualche tempo, non senza frutto; così lodevol fatica.

"Havendo donque una mattina i due giovani studiosi finita la loro accademia, uscirono di casa, et avidi di veder qualche cosa di nuovo intorno al dissegno, si condussero sotto la Ripa, dove ne' i giorni di festa si solevano vendere le carte stampate in rame, et in legno. . . ."

49. Soprani 1674, 63–64: "Et a dir il vero trapassò egli in questa parte termini della convenienza, e del dovere; poiche per quanto sembri propria de'Pittori la bizzaria, questo però s'intende sempre ne'termini della modestia. Mà egli uscendo fuori de'limiti si rese esoso, et abbominevole. . . ."

50. For Bernardo Castello's life, see Soprani 1674, 115–125; Soprani and Ratti 1768, 1: 105–111; Luigi Alfonso, "Bernardo e Valerio Castello," *La Berio* 8, nos. 1–2 (1968) and "Gian Battista Castello," *La Berio* 9, no. 2 (1969), 27–36; F. Poleggi 1970, 1:288–293, 315–317; Gavazza 1974, 1:37–49; Mary Newcome, "Drawings by Bernardo Castello in German Collections," *Jahrbuch der Berliner Museen* (1979), 137–151; Dante Bernini, *Luca Cambiaso e la sua cerchia. Disegni inediti da un album palermitano del '700* [exh. cat., Galleria Nazionale di Palazzo Spinola] (Genoa, 1985), 11–12, 56–57; F. Poleggi 1987, 1:258–261, 269–280, 292–295, and Regina Erbentraut, *Der Genueser Maler Bernardo Castello 1557–1629* (Freren, 1989).

51. Soprani 1674, 115. If Castello did study with Cambiaso it was almost certainly on an irregular "after-hours" basis. There is no mention of a second teacher in any of the testimony made on Castello's behalf, for which see Archivio di Stato, Genoa (= ASG), Notari Ignoti, no. 223, Collegio de' Dottori (1602–1623), fascicle dated 2 December 1617, parts of which are transcribed here in the appendix.

52. Soprani 1674, 115–116; F. Poleggi 1987, 1:258–260, 292–293.

53. Soprani 1674, 116, 118; F. Poleggi 1987, 1:292. For illustrations of Castello's preliminary drawings for the series, see Bernini 1985, figs. 51a–51t and color plates 22–24. See also Newcome 1979, 137–151.

54. Soprani 1674, 116, 121; F. Poleggi 1987, 1:292. In 1589 Castello was commissioned to paint *Coriolanus and Vetruria* for the same Villa Lomellini Rostan in Pegli.

55. For Castello's commissions, see the bibliography in n.50 above. Much of the correspondence between Chiabrera and Castello has been preserved and published in *Lettere di Gabriello Chiabrera a Bernardo Castello* (Genoa, 1838). A recent study of Chiabrera's liaisons with artists, literati, and patrons was

produced for the 350th anniversary of the poet's death: Giulia Fusconi, Graziano Ruffini, and Silvia Bottaro, eds., *Gabriello Chiabrera: Iconografia e documenti* (Genoa, 1988); see especially the chapter by Giulia Fusconi, "Gabriello Chiabrera e la cultura figurativa del suo tempo," 7–38. I owe this reference to Timothy Standring. See also Erbentraut 1989, who cites many letters from Chiabrera to Castello in her text, esp. 30–46, 221–231.

56. Giovanni Bottari, ed., *Raccolta di lettere sulla pittura, scultura, ed architettura* (Rome, 1767), with additions by Stefano Ticozzi, 8 vols. (Rome, 1822), 6:57 n.1, 79 n.1. Barocchi (1971, 1:191–192 n.5) accepts Bottari's judgment without comment. For a discussion of the evidence for this tension and possible animosity between Bernardo Castello and Paggi, see Lukehart 1987, 233–235, 239–240 (where I argue against this interpretation).

57. ASG, Notari Ignoti, no. 223, Collegio de' Dottori (1602–1623), fascicle dated 2 December 1617. I have transcribed the relevant passages from the document here in the appendix.

In another, later letter (ASG, Notari Ignoti, no. 225, fascicle 83 dated 20 November 1627) to the Collegio de' Dottori, Torquato Castello begs them to reconsider his plight after he had been absent from Genoa for ten years. The case was still not resolved, and the Collegio once again refused to act in Torquato's favor.

58. This is *capitolo* 21 of the undated statutes of the "Arte della Scutaria et Pittoria." Since there are amendments and additions to these statutes on 18 December 1481, I would use this as a *terminus ante quem.*

Statute 21 reads: "Et primo quod nullus magister artis predicte non possit accipere pro famulo vel discipulo aliquem ad minus, et pro minori tempore annorum septem et hoc per publicum instrumentum manu pubblici notarij." A bit further, they added, ". . . et steterit annis septem continuis cum aliquo ex magistris dicte artis . . . sub poena florentinorum decem usque in viginti quinque. . . ." Rosso del Brenna, *La Berio* 16, no.1 (1976), 18–19.

When the statutes were redrafted, in Italian, by the consuls Giovanni Battista Castello and Battista Brignole in 1590, the first *capitolo* read: "Che niuno maestro dell'arte del Pittore possa accettare alcuno garzone, o discepolo per manco tempo di sette anni, et ciò per publico istromento per mano dell' nottaro di detta arte et non altri. . . ." (*La Berio* 16, no. 2 [1976], 7–8). During his apprenticeship the *garzone* could not sell or exhibit any work of his own in public (statute 5, *La Berio* 16, no. 2 [1976], 9). Compare this system to the practices of Calvaert in the text.

59. The "Arte de' Maestri Muratori Lombardi" included stone workers, masons, mortar mixers, and architects. To date the most thorough discussion of this guild is Armando di Raimondo's, with Luciana Müller Profumo, *Bartolomeo Bianco e Genova. La controversa paternità dell'opera architettonica tra '500 e '600* (Genoa, 1982), 143–151. What is fascinating about Genoa is that the architects, unlike contemporary painters, did not seek independence from

the guild even well into the seventeenth century. For example, Bartolomeo Bianco, who is perhaps best known for his designs for villas throughout Liguria, as well as for the new walls of Genoa (1630), remained a member throughout his entire career.

According to the new statutes of their guild (approved by the Senate on 20 September 1600), apprentices were *accartati* for at least five years before becoming eligible to be approved as masters (see Luigi Alfonso, *Tomaso Orsolino ed altri artisti di 'Natione Lombarda' a Genova e in Liguria del secolo XIV al XIX* [Genoa, 1985]). I would like to thank Donna Salzer for bringing this valuable comparative material to my attention.

60. The name may also be spelled Merilano. To date the only other reference that I have found is in the matriculation of the guild members: "Andreas Merilanus" appears below (that is, later than) the names of Bernardo Castello, Cesare Corte, and Battista Brignole. Unfortunately, there are no specific dates for the matriculation.

61. ASG, Notari Ignoti, no. 223, Collegio de' Dottori (1602–1623), fascicle dated 2 December 1617. See the passages transcribed here in the appendix for the original text of this testimony.

62. See the references above in note 58.

63. This passage is transcribed *in toto* in the appendix.

64. Rosso del Brenna in *La Berio* 16, no. 3 (1976), 11: "Hora si come della Pittura è avvenuto, così avenisse del cavalcare, che per qualche abuso alcuni cavaglieri, o per povertà o per poco accorgimento usassino far di sua mano tutte le predette cose intorno a cavalli loro, non per questo sarebbe retto giudizio il dire che l'arte o la professione del cavagliere fose vile et abietta, imbrattandosi le mani in si fatta maniera. Altra cosa è il cavalcare et cavalcando armegiare, giostra, combattere et far cose tali nobilissime, et altro è il governare et apparechiare il cavallo, si come altra cosa è il dipignere et dipignendo esprimere varij concetti dell'[I]dea, combatere con la Natura istessa come già ha detto, far grazioso inganno a gli occhi altrui con le contrafatte cose, rapresentar le storie già seguite et quasi farcele vedere di presenza, et inifiniti altri nobilissimi effetti, che son proprij del Pittore et altro l'apparecchiar tele, e tavole, ingessarle, mesticarle, macinar colori, far pennelli, et mettere in punto queste cose tali che sono il cavallo del Pittore, et se egli avviene che qualche Pittore nobile metta tal'volta le mani in alcuna di queste cose, per zelo che egli ha dall'eternità d'altro simile rispetto, si assimiglia in tal caso al Cavagliero che apparecchiandosi a qualche giostra, o pur battaglia, non si fidano di servidori suoi vuole di sua mano assicurarsi che le cingie, le staffe, la briglia, et ogn'altra cosa sia accomodata bene et se non sono le rassetta [*sic*] a modo suo." Compare to the same passage in Barocchi 1971, 1:200.

65. Soprani (1674, 91–94) never mentions that Paggi was a student or *garzone* of Cambiaso; rather he makes note of several important moments at which the latter, along with the sculptor Gaspare Forzano,

provided guidance, encouragement, or suggestions. For a longer discussion of Paggi's early education, see Lukehart 1987, 21–25.

66. This is a very important issue among many of the nobility who had to work in order to maintain their standard of living. Briefly, a *casa aperta* means that the professional (be it a notary, physician, or silk merchant) had to conduct all his business activities within his own home, and not in a separate *bottega*. For a detailed discussion of the careers and practices suitable to the nobility in Genoa, see Giorgio Doria and Rodolfo Savelli, "'Cittadini di governo' a Genova: richezza e potere fra Cinque e Seicento," in *Materiali per una storia della cultura giuridica* 10, no. 2 (December 1980), 277–354.

When the Genoese Senate liberated painters from the guild statutes on 10 October 1590, they made a distinction between those who maintained a *casa aperta* (liberal artists) and those who maintained *botteghe* (manual artists) (Soprani and Ratti 1768, 1: 136–138; trans. into Italian by Barocchi, 1971, 1:216–219). Those with *botteghe* had still to obey the guild statutes. I presented my ideas concerning these issues in a paper entitled "About the Nobility of Painting, Paggi, and Artistic Practices in Genoa," College Art Association, Boston, February 1987.

67. I have read through the documents of Paggi's notaries between 1600 and his death in 1627: ASG, Notari, Filippo Camere (Paggi's notary from c. 1600 to c. 1618) and Bartolomeo Borsotto (Paggi's notary from c. 1618 to 1627).

Interestingly, one of Paggi's students, Castellino Castello, accepted an apprentice, Giovanni Tommaso de Barberi, age twelve, in 1614 (ASG, Notari, Bartolomeo Borsotto, filza 5, scansia 765 [1614–1615], fascicle 382 dated 19 November 1614; first published by Venanzio Belloni, *La pittura genovese del seicento*, 2 vols. [Genoa, 1969–1974], 2:56–57]. Thus Paggi's practices were not universally adopted, even by his own students.

68. Soprani and Ratti 1768, 1:460. Information concerning Bruno's service to Paggi comes to light in the codicil to Paggi's will (ASG, Notari, Bartolomeo Borsotto, filza 91, scansia 776, fascicle dated 3 March 1627, appended to the will dated 9 February 1627; published in part by Venanzio Belloni, *Penne, pennelli e quadrerie* [Genoa, 1973], 48–51): "Item lascia sian pagate a Giulio Bruno pittore, o, vero a suoi heredi scudi sette d'argento per suo salario della servitù che fece in casa di esso M.co codicillante."

69. ASG, Notari Ignoti, no. 223, Collegio de' Dottori (1602–1623), fascicle dated 2 December 1617. See the appropriate passages transcribed here in the appendix. Henceforth all testimony will be assumed to derive from this document, transcribed in the appendix.

On Castello's education, see Soprani (1674, 115–116), who tells us that Bernardo already possessed "le vere regole dell'arte [della pittura]" at age 15. It is equally remarkable that Castello, the esteemed friend of poets, should not have had a formal education in letters. In this sense his pedagogical experience is the inversion of Paggi's, who

attended grammar school and taught himself the rudiments of painting. See also Erbentraut 1989, 27–30, 61–84.

70. Brignole—a consul of the Arte della Pittura in 1590, the year of the litigation to free painters from the guild statutes—is mentioned only in passing by Soprani (1674, 76). None of his works survives, and the testimony he provides for Bernardo Castello (as in note 69 above) is the richest resource we have for the artist. Because he was both a painter and a gilder, Brignole was not allowed to leave the guild after 1591. See my discussion of the guild reform in Genoa (Lukehart 1987, 223–224, 288–289) in which it becomes apparent that Brignole and G.B. Castello (Bernardo's brother) both originally endorsed the new statutes. By the end of the trial, however, they abandoned their positions and threw their support behind Girolamo and G.B. Paggi.

71. ASG, Notari Ignoti, no. 223.

72. The statements in the document are responses to an Interrogation, a numbered list of questions that is asked in identical order of all the witnesses. In this instance the list comprises forty-five questions in numerical order, plus three out of sequence—numbered 60, 68, and 69—for a total of forty-eight. Some of the questions focused on Torquato Castello's legitimate birth, his residency in Genoa, proper schooling in law and liberal professional practices; the remainder are directed toward Bernardo Castello's birth, citizenship, residency, profession and professional practices. Manfredo Ravascher and Ottavio Contardo, syndics of the Collegio, compiled the Interrogation for Torquato's admission.

For the history of the Collegio de' Dottori, see Maria Grazia Merello Altea, "La professione legale in Genova nel secolo XVII," *Annali della facoltà di Giurisprudenza di Genova* (Milan, 1962), 297–344; Giovanni Montagna, "Il Collegio dei Dottori a Genova: la documentazione dal 1541 al 1603," *Annali della Facoltà di Giurisprudenza di Genova*, 18 (1980–1981), fasc. 1–2, 77–115; and the forthcoming study of Rodolfo Savelli, "Le mani della Repubblica. La Cancelleria genovese dalla fine del trecento agli inizi del seicento."

73. ASG, Notari Ignoti, no. 223.

74. See the discussion and bibliography in note 66 above.

75. ASG, Notari Ignoti, no. 223.

GAIL FEIGENBAUM
National Gallery of Art

Practice in the Carracci Academy

In Bologna, probably in 1582, the brothers Agostino and Annibale Carracci, together with their cousin Lodovico, founded an academy of art.[1] It was their invention of the academy as an institution whose mission was to teach students what they needed to learn in order to become artists that may be the Carraccis' most enduring legacy. Their creation of this new institution fundamentally changed the concept of the artist and the standards of artistic education for future generations, and the academy was the crucible in which the Carracci forged the reform of painting, charting the future course of the Italian baroque.

The earliest reference to this academy is found in the account books of the father of the Carraccis' first pupil, Giovampaolo Bonconti. It records contributions toward the academy's start-up expenses as follows: for the making of a big beautiful Madonna; for an *impresa* (an emblematic image combined with a Latin motto); and for work benches.[2] Of the Madonna and the benches we know nothing. But we do know that the academy's *impresa* combined the Carracci family insignia of the constellation Ursa Major, the Great Bear, commonly called *il Carro*, with the motto *contentione perfectus*. The bear is a leitmotif on a sheet of sketches by Agostino— a collage of thoughts confided to the page—in which stars of the constellation are indicated by rays (fig. 1).[3] Names of various members of the Carracci family appear in the sketch, and several times the word *"inmortali"*; at the upper left Agostino practiced drawing eyes like the ones later engraved in a manual designed to teach his step-by-step method of drawing—the *Scuola perfetta per imparare a disegnare tutto il corpo humano*. Of the several emblematic meanings of the bear I will mention only two. First, Titian is said to have chosen it for his *impresa* because the she-bear's offspring was thought to have been born without form, and then licked into shape by the mother, just as the artist improved on nature by giving form to nature's raw material. Second, as Charles Dempsey has noted, the collective aims of the Carracci Academy are best expressed in Ursa Major, the constellation that never sets, forever pointing to the polestar, the traveler's beacon.[4] The bear was a fitting guide for the academicians, teachers and pupils who called themselves the *incamminati*—travelers on the path to the unattainable end of perfection.

I introduce these images here for a purpose: how one is disposed to conceptualize the academy seems to determine how one interprets all the evidence that pertains to it. Although this is not the place to address the extensive art-historical literature, it must be admitted that essentially the same facts were available to this writer as were available to earlier scholars who constructed interpretations of the academy very much at odds with the one proposed in this paper. First is the view that the Carracci Academy was no different from a traditional workshop, but affected a pretentious title.[5] Equally far off the mark is the widespread, and usually tacit, assumption that the Carracci Academy was like a nineteenth-century academy—as if it could somehow have predicted and assimilated centuries of subsequent academic evolution in its self-invention. It can be argued that the latter anachronistic fallacy was itself behind the rejection of the Carracci Academy's existence by many modern scholars. If it was the nineteenth-century academic model that one had in mind, it was, of course, absurd to conceive of a similar institution coming into being in late sixteenth-century Italy. Both notions died hard, however, and they continue to haunt us even after being laid to rest most convincingly in studies of the Carracci Academy in its intellectual, theoretical, and historical contexts in which the academy's purpose emerges with greater clarity than ever before. These latter provide the foundation on which rests the interpretation outlined here.[6]

Agostino's sketch makes perceptible something of the self-consciousness that was midwife to the birth of the Carracci Academy, and that set it apart from traditional workshops in Bologna, despite the fact that they fulfilled many of the same functions. The sketch also conjures the ambivalence and overlappings of family identity and institutional identity that pervaded the academy. And, conveniently, it alludes to the meanings of the word "practice" considered in this paper: first, as in the practice of art, or how artistic skill is ensconced in, and carried out as, a professional endeavor—and for which the Carracci invented the new vehicle of the academy; second, as in "practice makes perfect," or performing exercises in order to acquire or improve skills; and third, as in practice as an embodiment and index of theory. These aspects of practice constituted the quotidian substance of the Carracci Academy that is the central issue of this paper.

The organization of roles and functions in the academy is far from being sorted

out, and the questions raised here outnumber the answers. One might begin by calling attention to some facts about the first fifteen or so years of the academy, the "prima Accademia."[7] When it opened Lodovico was twenty-seven years old, Agostino twenty-five, and Annibale twenty-two. All three were at a stage in their lives when they might otherwise have been working as what we for want of a precise term would call journeymen or fully trained artists working for other masters. Lodovico had become a master five years before, and Agostino had for several years been building a successful career as an engraver. The Carracci enterprise was unusual in Bologna in being a family workshop formed not by fathers and sons, but

1. Agostino Carracci, *Heads, Eyes, and a Bear*, pen and brown ink
Royal Library, Windsor Castle

by three men very close in age and all endowed with conspicuous talent. It may have been this unique situation that prompted the Carracci to create an alternative to the traditional hierarchical structure of the *bottega*.[8] As the eldest, Lodovico was *caposcuola*, but he abdicated part of the authority that customarily devolved on this position; and as a result the direction of the academy appears to have been determined by the three Carracci collectively.[9] The relations between the family and the other members of the academy are not yet well understood. Nor is much known about how the practical and intellectual instruction was integrated with the work of carrying out commissions in this new institution that was, in some sense, a cross between the traditional family workshop and the relatively new model of the Florentine Accademia del Disegno, which was officially incorporated in 1563.

Presumably the traditional work of apprentices—from grinding pigments to assisting in the execution of commissions—was accomplished in the academy, but the means by which the customary apportionment of responsibilities and privileges of the *bottega* system translated to the new, and possibly more fluid structures of the academy is unknown. One perhaps surprising feature of the academy is that so many of its members came not as young boys, but as adults, and many had already been trained under other artists. Lucio Massari, for example, joined at age twenty-four, after training under Bartolomeo Passerotti. Pietro Faccini entered at twenty-six, although as a novice. When Alessandro Tiarini tried unsuccessfully to gain admission, he was already twenty, and had trained under Lodovico's teacher, Prospero Fontana. Guido Reni was turning twenty and Francesco Albani was in his late teens when they transferred to the academy after breaking off their training under Denys Calvaert, a ranking member of the Bolognese artistic establishment.[10] These artists remained for several years. Bonconti, the Carraccis' first recorded pupil, was a member of the academy for two decades until his death in 1603.[11] Thus artists in their twenties and older, who

otherwise might have been working independently or as paid assistants for other masters, comprised a sizable segment of the academy.

Were any of them working as paid assistants for the Carracci? Did the Carracci employ journeymen painters as assistants as Rubens was to employ Van Dyck? According to Malvasia, Guido Reni's duties included sketching out and assisting in the execution of works the Carracci assigned him, for which he received no compensation. Could it have been this policy that prompted one of the Carraccis' most mature pupils, the gifted but disgruntled Faccini, to strike off and establish his own rival academy? On the other end of the spectrum might one—perhaps the young noblemen who were the Carracci pupils—have taken advantage of instruction but avoided the customary duties of apprenticeship? Presumably special arrangements were made for children of the aristocracy like Camillo Bolognetti, who attended drawing lessons in the academy and must have been excused from the kind of manual labor expected of apprentices in workshops.[12] How and where was a distinction made between pupil and dilettante? The answers to these questions are elusive. It seems that the *bottega* system embodied the belief that art was a skill first to be learned and then practiced. By contrast, the academy viewed learning as the artist's lifelong pursuit, his path to perfection; education was neither limited to the years when one was a pupil in training nor limited to the knowledge strictly necessary for a young artist to become a master.

There is evidence that some pupils in the academy were permitted to accept and execute outside commissions, as well as to keep the money from their sale.[13] Several of the advanced *incamminati*, including Reni and Albani, collaborated on a major fresco cycle in the Oratory of San Colombano, an all-Carracci Academy project that apparently employed no member of the Carracci family. Malvasia also reports that as *caposcuola*, Lodovico passed along the low-paying jobs to the pupils and often helped them by finishing their designs.[14] As *caposcuola*, Lodovico was also called on to mediate fees for his pupils' works: according to Malvasia, Reni asked thirty *scudi* for an Adoration of the Magi he painted for the Bolognetti, but Lodovico set the price at ten *scudi* based on Reni's status as a *scolare* rather than on the merit of the picture.[15] Reni was deeply insulted by this, and the episode points to a source of tension within an institution that was improvising new structures intended not only to enhance the dignity of the painter as a liberal artist, but also to conduct the practical business of training artists, and making and marketing art.

The nature of the dialogue of the Carracci with earlier art has been the subject of much scholarship—from the pejorative labeling of eclecticism to Elizabeth Cropper's perceptive analysis of how, through this dialogue, the Carracci responded to the new educational conditions of the artist, whose sources had now been organized by Vasari into a history of art.[16] The Carraccis' relations with their contemporaries have not been similarly examined; rather, most scholars have been content with the set piece that the Carracci, in a few decisive skirmishes, broke with, conquered, and supplanted an exhausted local tradition of late mannerism. Yet their actions suggest that from the beginning their relations with the Bolognese artistic establishment were more complicated and less inimical: that the Carracci in fact sought to embrace their colleagues and bring them into the academy and they also joined in their activities outside the academy. There is stylistic evidence for this which could make the subject of another paper, but the historical facts are themselves surprising. While enrolled in the Carracci Academy, for example, pupils could study with masters other than the Carracci. Although it is not clear precisely how this worked, the case of Bonconti is suggestive. Three years after coming to them, in 1585 and again as late as 1591, during which time Bonconti was a member of the academy, his father's accounts record gifts and money to Passerotti who was called "suo precettore del disegnari."[17] Whether Bonconti went to Passerotti's studio, or whether Passerotti taught in the Carracci Academy is not stated in this document. But in 1583, Bonconti's father

also gave a lavish gift to two of Bologna's most prominent painters, Ercole and Camillo Procaccini, for their efforts in teaching his son—and here it *is* specified "nell' Accademia," presumably that of the Carracci.[18] The document indicates that artists beside the Carracci served as teachers in the academy, and that the members contributed toward what might be called their honoraria. This pedagogical program may have amounted to a system of preceptors analogous to the guest lecturers in fields outside of painting, such as Lanzoni, who performed anatomical dissections in the academy. Other artists were brought in to judge bimonthly competitions to which pupils submitted drawings on an assigned topic. Conversely, the Carracci and some of their pupils, including Albani, are said to have been regular attendants at life-drawing sessions held in the evenings at the academy of Bernardino Baldi. This was an institution sometimes called the Accademia degli Indifferenti, or Accademia del nudo, about which little more is known but that it preexisted the Carracci Academy and offered life-drawing sessions as well as drawing from casts.[19]

What emerges from these as well as other fragments of information gleaned from Malvasia's biographies of the Bolognese painters and from the oration by Lucio Faberio at Agostino Carracci's funeral in 1603 is an atmosphere that fostered permeability to the outside—"dato libero adito" in Malvasia's words.[20] The Carracci Academy, experimenting with new structures in order to realize new goals, invented itself with not only its windows but its doors open to the city. Having more than one teacher in the form of examples from the past—like Correggio and Titian—and from the present—in the form of living masters—was part of the Carraccis' program of giving their pupils the freedom and the means to invent the art of the future: as Malvasia portrayed Lodovico advising his nephew Annibale, ". . . l'imitare un solo è un farsi di lui seguace, e l'secondo, che il tor da tutti e sceglier dagli altri, è farsi di esse il giudice e l'caporione."[21] Just as the authority of the unsurpassable masters—like the ancients, or Michelangelo—could not be allowed to "foreclose the future,"[22] neither

2. Agostino Carracci, Sheet of Caricatures with an Antique Altar, pen
British Museum, London

3. Lodovico Carracci, *Antique Ruins with a Colossal Vase*, pen
Uffizi, Florence, Gabinetto Disegni e Stampe

could the single authority of one's teacher—as representative of the authoritarian and hierarchical *bottega*-apprenticeship system—be allowed to set the course for the *incamminati*. To realize this theoretical position the Carracci had to create new institutional structures for teaching art.

The desecration of the altar of antiquity in a pair of sketches by Agostino and Lodovico suggests the Carraccis' attitude toward the enshrinement of at least one of the cinquecento's most revered authorities (figs. 2, 3). If the "reform of painting" entailed releasing artists from the obligation to forever imitate a prescribed and limited slate of authorities, the writer suspects that the freedom to decide which examples to heed—the very prospect of not being oppressed by authority—must have made the new academy more attractive to students, especially since most subjects taught there were in some form or another available in the *botteghe* of other leading Bolognese artists. Training in Passerotti's studio, for instance, included drawing from the nude and after casts, and studying anatomy. Neither was the presence of literati and intellectuals

from the university a novelty of the Carracci Academy: the great naturalist Ulisse Aldrovandi frequented the studio of Prospero Fontana as did the writer Achille Bocchi. Denys Calvaert ran what Malvasia called a "school for learning to paint," offering instruction in architecture, perspective, anatomy, and decorum.[23] But Malvasia's description makes Calvaert's teaching methods sound, probably intentionally, authoritarian and old-fashioned: reading the rules of perspective to his students; showing them the anatomy, reciting the parts, naming every bone and nerve; declaiming the orders of architecture and the rules of their use. This was learning by rote, with no guest lecturers, no anatomical dissections, no analyses, and no lively debates as in the Carracci Academy—just Calvaert, an old pedant, reciting the rules. Elsewhere Malvasia tells of pupils growing bored and restive during long lessons on perspective in Bernardino Baldi's academy.[24] Both Baldi and Calvaert lost many students to the Carracci. The exhilarating atmosphere said to have characterized learning in the Carracci Academy—that is, learning there

was fun—must have been at least partly the result of new, less authoritarian approaches to teaching.

The Carracci, especially Lodovico, had a reputation for being solicitous of their pupils' sense of pride and dignity. In a letter to Federigo Borromeo about the academy, Lodovico remarked that nothing was more discouraging to the young academicians than having their errors pointed out before their cohorts by the people whose good opinion they most ardently desired. He described how in the academy in order to temper the effects of criticism and still correct the errors, the pupils would make their drawings of an assigned subject and submit them to judges who were carefully chosen for their long experience and impartiality. The judges would write on the drawings "first, second, or third" and so on according to their excellence. Then the drawings would be passed around in turn so that each pupil could learn, without exposure to public criticism, how his own work was judged, but also understand the qualities of what was judged to be best.[25] What a contrast to Denys Calvaert who was reputed to be quick-tempered, and who at the slightest annoyance would holler at his pupils, kick them, and beat them. Calvaert also exploited his pupils by selling as his own, and for high prices, their copies of his works, and keeping the money. Also, according to Malvasia, he secretly took for himself the larger part of fees for works commissioned directly from his pupils.[26] Such practices, while common perhaps throughout Italy, seem somehow alien to the character of the Carracci Academy, and it would be interesting to know if they went on there. It would also be helpful to know something about the financial arrangements of the academy, and how they compared to the *bottega* system in the rest of the city, but this is uncharted territory.

It is useful to turn now to a neglected body of evidence that provides direct testimony to the activities of the academy: the masses of drawings that are misattributed to the Carracci or classified as Carracci school.[27] They are what remains in the boxes of the world's collections of Carracci drawings after the autograph Car-

4. Annibale Carracci, *Figure Study* (verso), detail, red chalk
Uffizi, Florence, Gabinetto Disegni e Stampe

racci have been plucked out. Attention to this category is normally limited to whether this or that sheet is strong enough to be by one of the Carracci or one of the more famous pupils like Reni or Faccini, whose distinctive drawing styles are coming to be recognized. It is a difficult category to sort out, wildly disparate, much of it consisting of later copies and drawings that have nothing to do with the Carracci. It taxes the connoisseur's skills to the utmost, yet in coming to know the patterns of this material, one begins to discern a body of works that are truly by the Carracci school, that is, drawings by the *incamminati*. As such they constitute an archive of practice in the academy. If most sheets will never be connected with specific names, those that can be linked with some assurance to the academy shed much light on practice.[28]

One such sheet is a chalk study from the nude in the Uffizi. It is attributed to Annibale, but not with much confidence (fig. 4). Nor is it likely to be by Lodovico or Agostino. It is, however, very much a Carracci Academy product: the model reclines in a casual sprawl; the draftsman revels in the challenge of a steep and awkward foreshortening and is concerned with the disruptive disposition of light and shade on the body. Whereas these are the kinds of problems the Carracci were exploring even in the 1580s, the figure's abrupt cropping, largeness, and bold occupation of space suggest a date in the nineties. (It is, however, worth asking whether the Carraccis' and their pupils' patterns of development coincided to the extent that one can think of dating an academy drawing by the same criteria.) In Lodovico's *Flagellation of Christ* (fig. 5) a similar figure is sprawled in the right corner. Although the model with his misshapen ear is the same as the one in the study and whose pose corresponds almost exactly to it, he is seen in the drawing from a steeper angle. The painting shows more of the chest and stomach, less of the back, and the hand is modified to suit the action of the figure who cradles a flail and braces himself to watch the scene. But the drawing is not a preparatory study. As the disparity between the two views of the same model in the same pose discloses,

5. Lodovico Carracci, *Flagellation of Christ*, oil on canvas
Pinacoteca Nazionale, Bologna

the drawing preserves a moment in one life-drawing session, which by its nature as a group activity implies other views of this same pose drawn from different parts of the room by other artists. It can then be inferred that the drawing eventually used for the painting was made by whichever artist—not necessarily Lodovico—was sitting just to the left of the one who made this study in the Uffizi. If indeed a drawing made in life-drawing class did double duty as a preparatory study for this painting, then this dual function represents the conflation of a process that has been assumed—mainly on the basis of later academic practice—to be Carracci practice as well. There are many other instances of life-drawing-class poses employed in the Carraccis' paintings.[29] We tend to separate the Carraccis' figure drawings done as a preparation for a painting from those made from the model in life-drawing sessions, but is this a real boundary? Should we assume that any drawing used as a modello for a painting was necessarily by one of the Carracci, or could a competent study by a pupil have served if it worked out the needed pose? Was the model asked to assume the pose in the life class because the Carracci needed such a figure for the painting they were working on? Or might such a drawing have been saved and consulted later when it was of use? It has been supposed that academic studies were made purely for the sake of learning; the evidence that the author has examined suggests that so firm a distinction was not made in the early Carracci Academy between the preparatory study, in which the model was asked to assume a pose intended for a painting, and the exercise of drawing from life—between practice, as it were, and theory.

In reintegrating the Carracci and the *incamminati* material, one begins to recognize in clusters of drawings how certain problems were attacked in the academy at a particular moment. From this kind of evidence begins to emerge a context for the paintings. Judging from the flurry of early drawings that experiment with every manner of difficult foreshortening, Annibale's *Dead Christ* of around 1584 is but one manifestation of an intensive exploration of this problem in the academy.[30]

6. Carracci school, *Figure Study*, chalk
Wallraf-Richartz Museum, Cologne

Sometimes the same model appears in different drawings. It seems that the slim youth with his pug nose, broad face, and low protruding ears in a Carracci school drawing in Cologne (fig. 6) also posed for a study in the Uffizi (fig. 7), which is an autograph Annibale associated with his altarpiece of the *Pietà* (fig. 8) painted in 1585. I raise this point about the reuse of models in part to dispute an interpretation of Annibale's study that seems out of keeping with what the drawings in general suggest about Carracci practice. In his recent book on the Carracci Academy,

7. Annibale Carracci, *Study of a Seated Man*, red chalk
Uffizi, Florence, Gabinetto Disegni e Stampe

8. Annibale Carracci, *Pietà*, 1585, oil on canvas
Galleria Nazionale, Parma

9. Annibale Carracci, *Study of a Seated Man*, red chalk
Uffizi, Florence, Gabinetto Disegni e Stampe

10. Agostino Carracci, *Pietà*, engraving
Albertina, Vienna

11. Agostino Carracci, *Seated Figure*, detail, red chalk
Uffizi, Florence, Gabinetto Disegni e Stampe

Carl Goldstein argued that in this drawing for the *Pietà* Annibale grafted a leg from a life study attributed to him in the Uffizi (fig. 9), onto an upper body based on the *Pietà* by Michelangelo, which had previously been recognized as the source for the pose, by means of Agostino's engraving (fig. 10).[31] But the languid, flaccid torso in Annibale's drawing exhibits none of the taut structure of the Michelangelo. The soft surfaces of what, to this writer, looks like a real, somewhat underdeveloped young body whose hip bone and ribs press out to deform the silhouette, are palpably different from both Michelangelo's marble and the engraving that records it. The arms and pitch of the torso also depart from Agostino's print. It is difficult to escape the conclusion that Annibale drew this figure from a living model, and that the model was directed to pose like Michelangelo's *Pietà*.

Furthermore this relationship discloses the Carraccis' habitual method of mastering a whole repertoire of poses from the canon of Michelangelo. When they wanted to use Michelangelo in their own art they got a model into position—as in the Carracci school study of one closely posed after Jonah in the Sistine ceiling (fig. 11)—

and they studied the pose from the model.[32] Like many other Michelangelo poses, the Jonah reappears in several Carracci variations as in Lodovico's chalk study, at Oslo, for an angel in his altarpiece of *Saint Hyacinth* (fig. 12).[33] The Carracci thus tended to demonumentalize Michelangelo and somehow domesticate his manner. It is striking how often one sees this, as in the *Butcher Shop*, which transposes Michelangelo (the *Sacrifice of Noah* from the Sistine ceiling) from a heroic key to a humble one, or the transposition from the sublime to the sensual, as in Lodovico's painting of *Susanna* (fig. 13).[34] His red chalk study for the painting (fig. 14) was made from a model posed after Eve in the Sistine ceiling.[35]

12. Lodovico Carracci, *Study for an Angel*, 1594, black chalk
National Gallery, Oslo

13. Lodovico Carracci, *Susanna and the Elders*, oil on canvas
Banco Popolare dell'Emilia, Modena

14. Annibale Carracci (here attributed to Lodovico), *Figure Study of a Woman*, red chalk
Uffizi, Florence, Gabinetto Disegni e Stampe

15. Lodovico Carracci,
Deposition, pen and wash
with red chalk
Musée du Louvre, Paris

16. Lodovico Carracci,
Deposition, pen and wash
over red chalk
Christ Church, Oxford

17. Annibale Carracci,
Figure Studies, detail,
red chalk
Uffizi, Florence, Gabinetto Disegni
e Stampe

That the Carracci occasionally quoted Michelangelo has long been recognized. The great frequency with which they did has not been appreciated, and has important implications. What should be emphasized in the cases noted here is that the Carracci referred to Michelangelo's art not directly, but via the living model—a critical distinction. By re-posing the model the Carracci and their pupils regrounded Michelangelo's art in nature, rather than submitting to Michelangelo's absolute authority. In so doing they confirmed nature—that is, the actual model—and not art as the higher authority, a conviction crucial to their reform of painting.

Returning to Annibale's *Pietà* offers the opportunity to make some observations about collaboration in the academy. On stylistic grounds a pair of sketches of the *Deposition* by Lodovico (figs. 15, 16; in the Louvre and at Christ Church, Oxford) can be dated to the early 1580s; yet there is no evidence that Lodovico painted this subject until much later. The Christ Church drawing, at first glance, has little in com-

mon with Annibale's painting, except that the Magdalen in the right corner of each assumes a similar pose. This should be compared, however, to another of Anni-

bale's drawings for a *Deposition*, also in the Uffizi, that seems to record an earlier stage of the composition (fig. 17). Here Christ is carried in much the same way as in Lodovico's drawing in Christ Church. Similarly, Lodovico's sketch in the Louvre, again a quick *invenzione*, should be compared to Annibale's altarpiece. There are marked similarities in the fainting Virgin, the details of the landscape background, and the diagonal orientation of the composition itself. How should these relationships be interpreted?

Malvasia reports that the *Pietà* was one of the low-paying commissions Lodovico passed along to his younger cousin, promising the patron to provide every assistance and retouching.[36] Malvasia observes also that Lodovico was a fount of invention, which is certainly attested in his drawings, and in the inspiration he could provide to his colleagues, with twenty variations on any theme.[37] The evidence suggests that in working out his own concept for the *Pietà*, Annibale was nourished and inspired by Lodovico's inventions. The existence of Lodovico's bright, free sketches of several subjects he did not paint, but which were painted by his cousins, raises the likelihood that the exchange of inventions in this form— collaboration at the deepest level of invention as well as in the phase of execution— was academy practice.

That the Carraccis' collaborative attitude pervaded their early practice is abundantly attested, from sharing the directing of the academy to the thirteen commissions on which the three worked together between the birth of the academy and the departure of Annibale and Agostino for Rome.[38] When the Carracci were asked which artist had been responsible for which parts of one of these projects, the frescoes in the Palazzo Magnani, Malvasia reports that they answered: "It is by the Carracci, we did it together."[39] Most scholars have dismissed this as a pose, as if to say, "Yes, but who really did it?" I think this is a mistake. Whatever praise or blame their work was to receive, it was important to the Carracci that their art be understood not as an accident of personal style, but as a manifestation of a new, suprapersonal, reformed style of painting.

In a joking way, Malvasia suggests that they exercised a kind of intellectual quality control in their criticism of each other's work. When one of them finished a picture, the other two would pretend to visit as strangers and challenge the painter to justify what he had done. If he failed to satisfy his critics, the painter would have to revise his work, else the other two would pick up the brush and do it for him.[40] Who can say if this charade truly was the custom of the Carracci, or if it accounts for their remarkably numerous pentimenti? But it is a story of the authority of the group outweighing the authority of the individual. Another check by the collective on the individual was the Carraccis' apparent decision to fix prices, although the evidence for this cannot be explored here.[41]

In subordinating their diverging individual stylistic propensities to a strong and specific unity of purpose, the Carraccis ensured, in practical terms, that the collective would dominate the personal. Elsewhere this writer has argued that the near-total lack of agreement on attributions within the collaborative projects results partly from the Carraccis' working procedures, in which there is no reason to assume that the same artist who sketched the compositional invention also studied the poses from life, prepared the *modello*, drew the cartoons, and wielded the brush on the scaffold.[42] It therefore may have been the exception rather than the rule that one artist carried out a scene from conception through execution. What could not have been any but a conscious strategy is the effort of the individual painters to subordinate their personal manners to the unity of the group style. While this is the attitude expected from a traditional workshop team in which the assistant's job is to imitate his leader, here the artists deferred to a style generated by their own interaction. Although the collaboration of the Carracci is sometimes shrugged off as a pragmatic response to the exigencies of the fresco technique, it extended to easel paintings as well. For instance, Malvasia noted that the three Carracci together painted a *Flight into Egypt* on copper as a gift for the nun of San Bernardino who bleached their shirt collars.[43] Until rather

18. Attributed to the
Carracci, *Ecce Homo*, oil
on canvas
Piero Corsini Gallery, New York

recently the view that the Carracci collaborated in easel paintings was not uncommon—Roberto Longhi proposed it regarding Lodovico's *Preaching of the Baptist* and Denis Mahon did not rule it out in *The Butcher Shop*.[44] Not long after the great Carracci exhibition in 1956, in which so much was learned, but so much set in stone, the notion of such collaboration somehow became discredited as the refuge of the inadequate connoisseur afraid to take a stand. In the intervening decades, no one had the temerity to propose that any given easel painting was executed by more than one of the Carracci, although some of the persistent arguments over attributions might be resolved by such an explanation.

Rather than risk being embroiled in one of these old controversies, the writer would prefer to start anew with an unpublished *Ecce Homo* that fits comfortably into the Carracci style of the mid-1580s (fig. 18).[45] The figures are life-size, and it is probably an overdoor. Certain passages, like the plumed helmet, monster-faced epaulets, and broadly modeled forearm betray distinctive rhythmic brushwork typical of Lodovico. But in other areas, a stiffer movement of the brush and more conscientiously descriptive modeling stand out. Compare the head and turban of this fig-

ure with the softer, almost washlike transitions of the modeling of Christ. The differences in handling emerge with great force in the original, and the writer is inclined to interpret this work as having been executed by at least two artists, most likely Lodovico and Agostino, probably with the assistance of other members of the academy. If that is the case, then it is noteworthy that in this relatively early collaboration their personal manners were not more thoroughly meshed.

It has been easier for scholars to accept a greater depth of collaboration in the earlier projects, as in the Jason cycle, when it can be difficult to tell the young Carracci apart in their more independent paintings. The tacit assumption has been that, with time, as each of the Carracci came more into his own, it became harder for him to disguise his personal style and thus easier for us to distinguish the hands in the collaborations. As tempting as this conclusion is, the opposite may also be true: with time the Carracci became more, not less, skillful in combining their individual manners.

This leads to a last example. On the eve of Annibale's and Agostino's departure for Rome, the Carracci decorated a suite of three rooms in the Palazzo Sampieri. Each room contained an overdoor in oil on canvas, a frescoed chimney, and a ceiling medallion. It has been demonstrated that in a series of drawings Annibale revised Agostino's ideas for his overdoor, while the kernel of Annibale's overdoor composition has been recognized in a drawing, now called Lodovico (but in the writer's view probably by Agostino).[46] Regarding the authorship of these frescoes, Anton Boschloo's assertion that there is no evidence of close collaboration invites challenge.[47] Disagreement has persisted since the seventeenth century over the attributions of all but two of the frescoes.[48] One exception was the *Hercules and Jupiter* ceiling (fig. 19), always given to Lodovico. The *Hercules and Atlas* ceiling (fig. 20) has been tossed back and forth between Agostino and Annibale, with Lodovico's name never proposed. But a careful look discloses that in both ceilings the same cartoon was used for Hercules' arm, although in the reversed orientation. Whose cartoon? If not Lodovico's drawing, then it was by the hand that contributed to the very bones and flesh of Lodovico's painting. If Lodovico's, then the *Hercules and Atlas*, always thought to be by one of his cousins, is also partly his. One could go on. For example, the Enceladus chimney (fig. 21) displays the bulbous, exaggerated anatomical structure typical of Lodovico's contemporary work, but has none of his fluid execution: surely it is a collaboration. To search for purity even in these later projects is a vain exercise. In a sense one could say that at this point the Carracci no longer needed to dissemble. As they became more the masters of their own manners they could be themselves at full strength, confident that the strength of the others would serve as a balance and produce a unified Carracci work.

Those familiar with scholarship on the Carracci will recognize that the emphasis in this study on collaboration in Carracci practice, in the invention of the academy, and in accomplishing the reform of painting does not accommodate certain commonly held notions about the roles of the individuals; for example, that the dry, intellectual Agostino was responsible for the theoretical apparatus that distinguished the academy from a workshop. Or that Annibale was a painter's painter who talked with his brush and regarded Agostino's theoretical speculations as hot air. Or the attempts, beginning with Bellori and Malvasia and continuing to the present day, to single out the true teacher of the Carracci as either Annibale or Lodovico; or the attempts to determine which was the one Carracci truly responsible for the reform of painting. In fact no one can know how the art of each of the Carracci might have developed had they not been collaborators, and efforts to pull them apart have engendered much misunderstanding.

It has been gratifying to learn that scholars in other fields have recently taken up related issues. In very different ways, which both depend on a revised understanding of the workshop, Arthur Wheelock and Svetlana Alpers have used the scientific findings of the Rembrandt Research Project to challenge the assumption that Rembrandt is reducible to his

19. Lodovico Carracci, *Hercules and Jupiter*, fresco
Palazzo Sampieri, Bologna

20. Agostino or Annibale Carracci, *Hercules and Atlas*, fresco
Palazzo Sampieri, Bologna

21. Attributed to Lodovico Carracci, *Enceladus*, fresco Palazzo Sampieri, Bologna

dialectic between art and nature that was a prime mover in the reform, actually functioned. For Annibale to say, as Malvasia has him do, that painters talk with their hands, is not to deny that the Carracci held theoretical principles, but rather to explain that the best expression of these principles was not in words. For the Carracci, theory and practice were not only inseparable but synergistic. And the more intimately we come to know how they learned and taught and worked in the academy, the more we find that Annibale was speaking the truth—that the Carraccis' theory is embedded in, and can be read in, their practice.

My operating assumption has been that the Carracci would have invested the new structures they devised for the practice of art with their deepest convictions about art. I have proposed that they ran the academy as partners, ensuring that their collective aims and principles, and not the authority of one individual, would guide the institution. By introducing a wide array of viewpoints into the academy, they freed themselves and then their pupils from enslavement by authority. Pupils were given a broad education to train their intellects and judgment and to equip them for their new freedom. The Carracci Academy formulated the problem of practice in a historically conscious age. It offered a new paradigm for artistic creativity, and it was in this aspect, as much as in its working procedures, that the Carracci Academy became the foundation for all art academies that would follow; how ironic that in later centuries the academy would so often become the very instrument that enforced the authority of the history of art.

autograph works.[49] Alpers has also argued that "modern attempts to separate works by Rubens' hand from those by others in the studio, and the taste for his *eigenhändig* oil sketches, intrude a notion of value inappropriate to his mode of production and to the commodity he produced."[50] I have tried to raise similar questions about the academy and the notorious confusion over distinguishing the Carraccis' hands. For it must surely be argued that connoisseurship is not an abstract or absolute process applicable to all points and places in art history. To have validity, it must be related to a concept of the artist that is contingent on historical circumstance, different from moment to moment, and place to place.

Some writers in this century have doubted whether the Carracci could be said ever to have had a theory of art. Others have suggested that there was a cleavage between contemporary art theory and Carracci practice, as if the two were out of step. To reintegrate the paintings with their context and process of creation and with the Carraccis' teaching method is to discover how the theory, such as the

NOTES

For support of my research I would like to express my gratitude to: J. P. Getty Postdoctoral Fellowships; Charles S. Singleton Center for Italian Studies, Johns Hopkins University, Florence; Center for Advanced Study in the Visual Arts and National Gallery of Art, Washington. To Charles Dempsey and William Tronzo, who read a draft of this paper and offered excellent suggestions, and to Irving Lavin, who prompted me to consider the Carracci Academy in relation to the subsequent history of academies of art, my heartfelt thanks.

1. The date for the foundation of the academy is now generally accepted to be 1582. This is based on a document published by Malvasia recording that in 1582 the Carraccis' pupil Giovampaolo Bonconti contributed his "proporzionabil parte occorsa la prima volta, nel passare all'Accademia de' Carracci; e questo per fare una grande e bella Madonna, la Impresa, banchi, e altre cose necessarie in essa." Carlo Cesare Malvasia, *Felsina pittrice* (1678), ed. Giampietro Zanotti (Bologna, 1841), 1:404–405.

2. On the academy see particularly Heinrich Bodmer, "L'Accademia dei Carracci," *Il commune di Bologna* 13 (1935); Charles Dempsey, "Some Observations on the Education of Artists in Florence and Bologna During the Later Sixteenth Century," *Art Bulletin* 62 (1980), 552–569; and Dempsey, "The Carracci Academy," *Leids Kunsthistorisch Jaarboek* 5–6 (1989), 33–43, which Charles Dempsey very kindly allowed me to read in manuscript.

3. Windsor inv. 2002, *Heads, Eyes, and a Bear*, pen and brown ink, brown wash, 259 x 195 mm, catalogued by Rudolf Wittkower, *The Drawings of the Carracci at Windsor Castle* (London, 1952), no. 158, pl. 39. Wittkower observed that the inclusion of the name Francesco, Agostino's nephew born in 1595, provided the *terminus post quem* for this sheet. The points from which the rays emanate seem to suggest, rather than map precisely, the constellation Ursa Major, whose seven brightest stars form the characteristic dipper or plough shape, especially since in this drawing the bear is drawn in the reverse sense to the constellation.

4. Charles Dempsey chose this image with which to conclude his monograph, *Annibale Carracci and the Beginnings of Baroque Style* (Glückstadt, 1977), 74.

5. This view was most directly, and influentially, expressed in Hans Tietze's pioneering study, "Annibale Carraccis Galerie im Palazzo Farnese und seine römische Werkstätte," *Jahrbuch der kunsthistorischen Sammlungen des Allerhöchsten Kaiserhauses* 26 (1906–1907).

6. Dempsey 1977, 1980, and 1989. Elizabeth Cropper, "Tuscan History and Emilian Style," in *Emilian Painting of the Sixteenth and Seventeenth Centuries: A Symposium*, National Gallery of Art (Bologna, 1987), 49–62. For a valuable discussion of teaching in the Carracci Academy, see especially Dempsey 1977, and of course, Malvasia's biographies.

7. The academy was a rapidly evolving entity, and to consider it monolithically leads to misunderstanding. After Annibale and Agostino left Bologna in the mid-1590s, and especially after efforts were undertaken in the early years of the new century to transform the Carracci Academy from a family enterprise into a public organization for the artists of Bologna, the situation changed dramatically; see especially Dempsey 1980 for the history of the later phases. My study focuses on the first phases of the academy, during the period of the reform of painting.

8. My thanks to Linda Klinger for her observations on the importance of the family and kinship to the structure of the Carracci Academy.

9. Luigi Spezzaferro is the only writer to have perceived the importance of the new academy's eschewal of hierarchical organization. His brief observations on the Carraccis' collaboration prepare the ground for a new consideration of the subject. Luigi Spezzaferro, "I Carracci tra naturalismo e classicismo," in *Le Arti a Bologna e in Emilia dal 16 al 17 secolo*, Atti del 24 Congresso C. I. H.A., 1979 (Bologna, 1982), 4:203–228.

10. Malvasia 1841, 2:6–7, makes a drama of Guido's break with Calvaert, attributing it partly to Calvaert's ill treatment of his pupil, and partly to the irresistible pull of the innovative Carracci. Domenichino, only fourteen years old when he left Calvaert's studio to join the academy, may have been an unusually young *incamminato*. Malvasia tells the story of the bimonthly contests where the pupils anonymously submitted their drawings on an assigned topic: Domenichino won three times before he overcame his shyness in the midst of older competitors to admit that the winning drawings were his own. As Malvasia reported, Domenichino was ". . . acclamato per maggior d'ogni altro, ancorchè il più picciolo." Malvasia 1841, 2:221.

11. Malvasia 1841, 1:405.

12. For an important discussion of how similar situations were met in contemporary Genoa, see Peter Lukehart's essay elsewhere in this volume.

13. See for example Malvasia 1841, 2:7, the life of Guido Reni; and for an example of an independent work by a pupil, Reni's *Judgment of Solomon*, private collection, illustrated in *Guido Reni, 1575–1642* [exh. cat., Pinacoteca Nazionale] (Bologna, 1988), no. 7.

14. Malvasia 1841, 1:274, 330.

15. Malvasia 1841, 2:10.

16. The implications of Vasari's publications of the *Lives of the Artists* are explored by Cropper 1987.

17. Malvasia 1841, 1:404–405.

18. Malvasia 1841, 1:405, "Del medesimo anno [1583], una castellata d'uva squisita, mandata a donare ad Ercole Procaccini e Camillo suo figliuolo, per le fatiche ch'usano nell'insegnare a Gio. Paolo suo figlio, nell'Accademia. Dell'anno stesso un altro regalo à medesimi, per l'istessa cagione."

19. Malvasia 1841, 1:334.

20. Malvasia 1841, 2:7. This is not the occasion to discuss the arguments about Malvasia's reliability as

a source, although I should stress that I have taken them very much into account in my interpretation. My reading of Malvasia suggests that he fully recognized the exceptional nature of the Carraccis' enterprise and highlighted it in his biographies of the Carracci and others of the Bolognese school.

21. Malvasia 1841, 1:284.

22. Cropper 1987.

23. Malvasia 1841, 1:198.

24. Malvasia 1841, 1:385.

25. The letter of 1614 was published by Giorgio Nicodemi, "L'Accademia di pittura, scultura ed architettura (fondata dal card. Federigo Borromeo all'Ambrosiana)," in *Studi in onore di Carlo Castiglioni, prefetto dell'Ambrosiana* (Milan, 1957), 653–696. Having gone unremarked in the Carracci literature, this extraordinary document was reprinted in Gail Feigenbaum, "Lodovico Carracci: A Study of His Later Career and a Catalogue of His Paintings" (Ph.D. diss., Princeton, 1984). An English translation of key sections of the letter appears in Dempsey, "The Carracci Academy," 1989.

26. Malvasia 1841, 2:7.

27. This is evidence the writer first discussed in a paper given at the Institute for Advanced Study in 1987 and subsequently published as "Drawing and Collaboration in the Carracci Academy," in Marilyn Aronberg Lavin, ed., *IL 60: Essays Honoring Irving Lavin on His Sixtieth Birthday* (New York, 1990), 145–165.

28. It should be mentioned that these drawings are rarely illustrated, except by mistake, and therefore are difficult to discuss. And I am only now beginning to undertake the special study that this material deserves. It slowly dawned on me, after going through thousands of such sheets in the ordinary way of eliminating them as autograph Carraccis, that they might have their own stories to tell.

29. See Feigenbaum 1990 for further examples and discussion.

30. Annibale Carracci, *Dead Christ*, oil on canvas, 70.8 x 88.8 cm, Staatsgalerie, Stuttgart.

31. Carl Goldstein, *Visual Fact over Verbal Fiction: A Study of the Carracci and the Criticism, Theory, and Practice of Art in Renaissance and Baroque Italy* (Cambridge, 1988). Fundamental errors in this book are pointed out in reviews by Charles Dempsey, *Times Literary Supplement* (March 1989), and Diane De Grazia, *Renaissance Quarterly* 42 (Winter 1989), 866–868.

32. Uffizi 12374 F, verso, is a copy in black chalk after one of the gods in the Jason frieze, Palazzo Fava, Bologna; at the crotch of the figure was sketched a visual pun of a devil's profile in pen and ink.

33. First noted in Feigenbaum 1984, 303. The drawing bears an old attribution to Lodovico. It was acquired from the collection of J. C. Dahl, a Swedish painter who lived in Germany and was a friend of Otto Runge. Runge left Dahl his collection of paint-

ings and drawings, which may have included this study by Lodovico. I am indebted to Bodil Sørensen for the information on the provenance of this drawing. The Sistine Chapel Jonah is also the inspiration behind the pose of Polyphemus in the Aeneas cycle frescoed by the Carracci in the Palazzo Fava, Bologna.

34. The painting in the collection of the Banca Popolare dell'Emilia was recognized as Lodovico's by Carlo Volpe, who very kindly drew it to my attention. It was catalogued in Feigenbaum 1984, no. 90, and Volpe's entry appeared posthumously in *I dipinti antichi della Banca Popolare dell'Emilia* (Modena, 1987), 78–80. In this case there were iconographic reasons to evoke Michelangelo's prototype of the temptation of Eve, as discussed in Feigenbaum 1984.

35. Uffizi 1547 Orn., unpublished. The author recognized this small study among the unmounted drawings attributed to Annibale.

36. It should be pointed out that this report of Lodovico passing along and helping with these early commissions tends to be dismissed as Malvasia's way to minimize a phenomenon that many critics perceive: that Annibale quickly outstripped Lodovico in his series of extraordinary altarpieces dating 1583–1585.

37. Malvasia 1841, 1:267. This is discussed in Feigenbaum 1990.

38. For the collaborative commissions, see Feigenbaum 1984. These are treated more fully in my forthcoming monograph and catalogue on Lodovico.

39. Malvasia 1841, 1:287.

40. Malvasia 1841, 1:277.

41. See for example the letter published by Malvasia 1841, 1:175, written by Pompeo Vizani, acting as an agent for Dionigio Ratta, who wanted an altarpiece for the new church of San Pietro Martire that he was building in Bologna. Vizani reported to Ratta, "quanto alla pittura della tavola, io ho parlato con i Carracci, e li ho fatto parlare anco da altri per disponergli, e si sono risoluti, che serviranno; ma venuto a trattar del prezzo non mi è piaciuta la lora risoluzione, poichè hanno detto di voler dugento scudi, che mi pare un gran pagare, avendo essi fino ad ora fatto le loro tavole per sesanta e per settanta, ma vogliono cominciare a vendere per riputazione; ho poi inteso, che sono soliti a calar molto poco dalla prima domanda." It is worth noting that Vizani was negotiating with the Carracci as a collective entity. The rest of the letter makes clear that Vizani recommended the Ratta commission instead to Prospero Fontana, who was willing to provide the picture quickly and for half the price. Lodovico executed the commission and was paid the high price of 600 *lire*, for which see the document published in Feigenbaum 1984, cat. 77, 320.

42. Feigenbaum 1984; Feigenbaum 1990.

43. Malvasia 1841, 1:332.

44. Roberto Longhi, "Annibale, 1584?," *Paragone* 89 (1957), 35, ". . . punge più che il sospetto di una col-

laborazione, perchè alcune tra le teste di giovani a sinistra e persino la famosa figura del giovane barcaiolo, nonostante i disegni di Ludovico, si direbbero eseguiti dalla mano di Annibale." *The Butcher Shop* has been attributed at various times to all three Carracci, as well as to Passerotti. For a full discussion see Donald Posner, *Annibale Carracci* (London, 1971), 3–4. Denis Mahon in *Mostra dei Carracci, Disegni* [exh. cat., Palazzo Dell'Archiginnasio] (Bologna, 1956), no. 84, wrote that while he favored an attribution to the young Annibale, "Lo scrivente non si sente disposto ad escludere in modo assoluto un'eventuale limitata partecipazione di Agostino . . . ."

45. Piero Corsini Gallery, New York. A pen and wash drawing ascribed to the French artist Georges Lallemand (died 1635) copies the composition of this painting in the reverse sense, which suggests that a print was made after the painting; illustrated in *French Drawings from European Collections: The Former Armand Gobiet Collection* [exh. cat., Pennsylvania State University] (University Park, 1979), no. 6. My thanks to Mary Jane Harris for calling this drawing to my attention.

46. That the British Museum sketch, inv. 1858–11–13–34, was related to Annibale's overdoor was pointed out by Posner, who believed the drawing to be by Lodovico. Posner's insight was reported by Dwight Miller in his article analyzing the "process of critique and counter-critique" in the development of the composition for Agostino's overdoor: "A Drawing by Agostino Carracci for His *Christ and the Adulteress*," *Master Drawings* 7 (Winter 1969), 412.

47. A.W.A. Boschloo, *Annibale Carracci in Bologna* (The Hague, 1974), 2:195–196, no. 13, ". . . there is no evidence of such a close collaboration in the Palazzo Sampieri as there was in the palazzi Fava and Magnani, where often one member of the family drew the preliminary study, while another painted the fresco, so that a unique possibility presented itself of comparing the interpretations of the three Carracci. Nor did the commission in the Palazzo Sampieri give occasion for such an intensive collaboration. It was for six separate scenes divided over three rooms, not a continuous narrative combined into a frieze . . . ." Where Boschloo saw the possibility of comparing individual interpretations, the present writer sees rather the near impossibility of separating out the "Platonically true" individual styles.

48. The attribution to Lodovico of the *Hercules and Jupiter* ceiling in the first room has not been questioned. Usually the *Ceres Searching for Persephone* chimney in that room is assigned to Lodovico, although some writers have wondered if the execution was wholly by his hand. The *Punishment of Enceladus* chimney in the second room has been attributed to Agostino, Lodovico, Annibale, and various combinations of the three hands. The ceiling in the second room, *Hercules and Virtue*, is always given to Annibale. Writers are divided between Agostino and Annibale for the third room's ceiling of *Hercules and Atlas*, and the authorship of the chim-

ney, *Hercules and Cacus*, is also disputed between Annibale and Agostino. For the most recent discussion of the Sampieri frescoes see Giampiero Cammarota, "Gabriele Fiorini: Uno scultore all'Accademia degli Incamminati," *Atti e memorie della Accademia Clementina di Bologna* 19 (1986), 34–46. Cammarota's attractive thesis that each of the rooms was decorated by one of the Carracci is difficult to sustain. For attributions, see especially Posner 1971, 2:33; Michael Jaffé, "Carracci Frescoes in Palazzo Sampieri-Talon," *Paragone* 85 (1957), 108; and my forthcoming monograph on Lodovico.

49. Arthur Wheelock kindly let me read the introduction to his session on Rubens and Rembrandt at the 1989 College Art Association Annual Meeting in San Francisco. Svetlana Alpers, *Rembrandt's Enterprise* (Chicago, 1988), 11.

50. Alpers 1988, 101.

JOHN M. ROSENFIELD
Harvard University (emeritus)

Japanese Studio Practice: The Tosa Family and the Imperial Painting Office in the Seventeenth Century

In 1657 the Japanese imperial household appointed Tosa Mitsuoki (1617–1691) to serve as *edokoro azukari*, superintendent of its Painting Office in Kyoto. As chief painter in the imperial court, Mitsuoki was the leading exponent of a central element in the nation's artistic heritage: the abstract, brightly colored mode of narrative painting called *yamato-e*. His workshop, however, was the smallest of the half-dozen professional painting ateliers active in Kyoto, for the income and authority of the imperial household had been severely restricted by the military government in distant Edo (present-day Tokyo).

Mitsuoki, a learned and resourceful man, restored the Tosa family to prosperity and influence. It had once provided the hereditary heads of the Painting Office, but for nearly a century the family had lived in self-exile in Sakai, a port city south of Osaka. There, isolated from patrons and overshadowed by the other workshops, the Tosa workshop had struggled simply to survive.

Mitsuoki, in responding to great changes in social and cultural life taking place around him, ventured away from the family's traditional painting styles. He had been trained in a workshop organized according to the standards of the Japanese middle ages (1185–1568), an environment that encouraged self-effacement and conformity. He matured in one that promoted individualism and competition. Later generations would rank him as one of three historic masters of the Tosa tradition, but his achievements had little impact after his death.[1] His successors failed to adapt to the continual changes in Japanese cultural life, and the family enterprise gradually weakened and then ceased to exist by the end of the nineteenth century.

Many schools of painting and decorative arts flourished in seventeenth-century Japan.[2] Two of them—Tosa and Kanō—were intimately linked to the national government and to deep fissures and contradictions that divided the national polity. Tosa painters were employed chiefly by the imperial court in Kyoto. The court sheltered a sacrosanct emperor who, though wielding little direct power, embodied the mystical sources of state authority.[3]

The Kanō school worked primarily for the samurai class, whose military regime in Edo controlled land tenure, distribution of tax revenues, and even the income of the emperor and the funds available to him to build his palaces. If Mitsuoki was head of the imperial Painting Office in Kyoto and preeminent leader of the Tosa school, he had a Kanō equivalent, Tan'yū (1602–1674), head of the main Kanō family workshop in Edo. Tan'yū was the shogun's private painter (*oku no eshi*) and, without question, the most prestigious artist in the empire.

79

Tosa and Kanō schools, serving the Japanese ruling establishments, embodied the two dominant currents in the nation's high culture: native Japanese customs and imported Chinese learning. While these currents opposed each other, they had also mingled in a dialectical fashion for centuries. Tosa artists specialized in the so-called Japanese mode of painting (yamato-e). Kanō artists specialized in ink painting derived from southern Song China. The small Tosa workshop served the relatively impoverished monarch. The Kanō artists, as rich and aggressive as their samurai patrons, operated many workshops throughout the empire—fourteen in Edo alone.

The courts of emperor and shogun, antagonistic and yet mutually dependent, provided stable government for the nearly three centuries of the Early Modern Era (c. 1568–1868). The Tosa and Kanō schools of painting—at once rivals and allies, dif-fering in their ideals but freely copying from each other—provided authoritative norms for virtually every other school of Japanese pictorial art.

One of the last surviving Kanō workshops is shown (fig. 1) as it was remembered by Kawanabe Gyōsai (1831–1889), an eccentric artist who had apprenticed there forty years earlier.[4] The woodblock illustration, satirical in spirit, shows the studio in a high state of disorder as apprentices chase a large carp (lower right, right page). Gyōsai had caught the magnificent fish and brought it to the studio to sketch it, but his foolish colleagues wanted only to slice it up for lunch—proof in Gyōsai's eyes of the Kanō school's failure to respect nature.

Gyōsai depicted the senior artist sitting at the upper left (left page), holding a feather pointer and criticizing an unfinished painting done by the man to his left. Behind him is a large storage box marked

1. Kawanabe Gyōsai, *Atelier of Kanō Tōhaku at Surugadai*, woodblock print book illustration of *Gyōsai gadan*, 1 (Kyoto, 1877) (21.5 x 28.6 cm)
Harvard University Art Museums, Cambridge, Gift of Mrs. Henry Osborn Taylor

"Screen Picture Books" (byōbu ehon)—books with standardized compositions. An old assistant seated next to him is painting a screen panel on the floor. To the far right another senior figure interviews a customer, a samurai judging by his sword and jacket. Prominent in the picture are several sheaves of paper, which appear to be account books from paint and paper merchants.

Kanō painters have been abundantly studied.[5] Tosa artists, despite a foundation of careful research on individual works, have not yet been given the attention on which comprehensive scholarship is established: special exhibitions, detailed biographies, iconographic studies, and compilations of authentic signatures and seal impressions. I thus have attempted to bring together scattered sources of information to provide a preliminary review of the aesthetic and sociological character of the family workshops, and especially that of Mitsuoki.[6]

Working at great distance from most original paintings, I have been obliged to depend on others for judgments of connoisseurship. I have instead concentrated on issues germane to this volume: workshop practices and organization, artists' training, stylistic response to patronage and market forces, commercial rivalries (or collaboration), and material and non-material compensation to workshop artists.

The Japanese Court Painter

Court artists like Mitsuoki provided paintings required by the imperial establishment. Two products, for example, were accorded the utmost symbolic and ceremonial prestige. The first were the portraits of thirty-two Chinese sages, emblems of loyalty and responsible statecraft, which were painted on sliding screens in the Hall of State of the imperial palace immediately behind the thrones of the emperor and his consort. Owing to the frequency of fires at the palace, the portraits were often repainted.[7] The second were the emperor's folding fans. New ones were provided at the beginning of each month, with special emphasis given to the one painted for New Year ceremonials.

The painting workshop made ornate sliding and folding screens for ceremonial halls and apartments; picture albums to be given to important visitors and aristocratic bridal couples; and portraits of courtiers and Buddhist monks. The workshop provided narrative handscrolls depicting legendary histories of Buddhist temples or Shinto shrines. Commissioned by courtiers as an act of piety, these scrolls were usually donated to the sanctuaries. Other screens and handscrolls depicted great historical events (such as battles and coronations) and court ceremonies.

Court painters served as connoisseurs and curators, studying and attributing older paintings and overseeing their repairs. They seem to have been quasi-dealers as well, serving as middlemen when works of art changed hands. They frequently made copies to replace older paintings that had been damaged. Some even provided designs to handicraftsmen making robes, lacquerware, and iron tea kettles for use by courtiers.

Painters' ranks and titles
Ranking courtiers were often appointed provincial governors, and the Tosa family name, in fact, was derived from the designation of family heads as governors of remote Tosa Province on Shikoku island. Some painters were appointed to administrative posts such as assistant minister of justice; some were officers of the imperial bodyguard; and most were assigned to the fourth or fifth level of the eight-grade system of court ranks. The governorships were strictly honorary. Documentary evidence throws little light on how much authority or responsibility the other posts conveyed, but judging from similar appointments for calligraphers and poets, such persons, if gifted in administration, would be assigned substantial duties in the court bureaucracy.

The Painting Office and its organization
Though the existence of an imperial Painting Office can be verified in documents dating as early as the ninth century A.D., written accounts are few, disconnected, and unsubstantial. Tables of government organization show that the

Painting Office came under the general jurisdiction of the Central Affairs Ministry (*nakatsukasa-shō*) and specifically under the *kurodō*, the office of the emperor's private secretary (or chamberlain).[8]

The physical location of the Painting Office in Kyoto, however, has rarely been documented. An eleventh-century text states that the office was within the palace compound—inside the Kenshun Gate, the eastern entry to the precinct of the sovereign's private quarters (*Dairi*).[9] In later times the atelier could well have been outside the palace compound. Indeed, Mitsuoki is said to have received authorization to use his own house as the Painting Office, but no other information about this is available.[10]

The administration of the Painting Office changed over the centuries.[11] Documents from the Heian period (794–1185) state that the head was originally a *bettō*, a generic title often assigned to chiefs of administrative divisions. Beneath him was the *azukari* (literally, "in-charge"), either a bureaucrat or a scholar trained at the court's Confucian academy (*Daigaku*) or the *Kangaku-in*, private school of the leading family of aristocrats, the Fujiwara. Next in rank were the ink draftsmen (*sumigaki*), the painting specialists (*eshi*) who drew the main compositions.[12] Beneath them were assistants and apprentices (*jisshoku*), who ground the pigments, prepared painting surfaces, and did some of the underpainting. (Scholars today consider most workshop products as collaborative efforts.) In documents of the Kamakura period (1185–1333) the *bettō* are no longer mentioned; the head of workshop was the *azukari*, who by then was usually a painter.

Evidence about compensation is scanty. It has been surmised that when serving as superintendent of the Painting Office, the family head must have received an annual stipend, a share of the budget of the imperial household. He, in turn, would divide this sum among members of the workshop. In the sixteenth century the Tosa family annual allotment was one hundred *koku* of rice from estates in the Sakai district, a relatively generous amount.[13] In addition to annual salaries or stipends, documents indicate that the court would also compensate its painters at fixed rates—so many ounces of silver for so many panels of sliding screens.[14]

Honors to artists

The imperial household honored its favorite artists and other professionals by granting them Buddhist titles: Bridge of the Law (*hokkyō*), Eye of the Law (*hōgen*), and highest and rarest, Seal of the Law (*hōin*). The custom originated in the ninth century, when the emperor Saga authorized the three titles for distinguished Buddhist monks.[15] The award was a prerogative of the throne, issued in the form of a written proclamation signed by a minister. Monks were always the primary recipients, and the first artist known to have been so honored was the celebrated Buddhist sculptor Jōchō (died 1057) for projects sponsored by the Fujiwara family. Thereafter Buddhist sculptors and painters were increasingly honored, and the custom gradually spread to lay artists, Confucian scholars, and medical doctors. These titles were purely honorary and, apart from the prestige, conferred no other benefit. By the early nineteenth century, the number of honorees had become much inflated.

Yamato-e

The Tosa workshop specialized in *yamato-e*, literally "Japanese painting."[16] In simplest terms this may be defined as depictions of themes specific to Japan in a style that is strongly patterned and usually brightly colored. Album leaves attributed to Mitsuoki's grandfather (fig. 2), father (fig. 3), and father's workshop (fig. 4) clearly demonstrate this mode. All three works depict episodes from the eleventh-century romantic novel *Tale of Genji*, the most popular and enduring classic of Japanese court fiction.

Linear perspective and spatial conventions

In the three paintings, buildings and gardens are shown from a bird's-eye perspective that radically tilts up the ground plane. The human figures and trees, however, are represented as though seen at eye

2. Tosa Mitsuyoshi, *The Third Princess, Chasing a Kitten, Catches a Glimpse of Kashiwagi Playing Football*, c. 1613, album leaf illustrating chapter 34, *Tale of Genji*, by Murasaki Shikibu, ink, color, and gold leaf on paper (26.1 x 22.5 cm)
Kyoto National Museum
Photograph from *Kokka* 996 (March 1976)

Technique

Brush handling is called *tsukuri-e* (literally "manufactured painting"), a method so refined and meticulous that it obscures its own processes and presents the viewer with a smooth, unified surface. This technique is the direct opposite of that used in Chinese-style ink painting, in which each fluid stroke of the calligraphic brush is visible on the paper and the artist has little opportunity to make changes.

Yamato-e painters employ a straight-edge to draw architectural members—posts, beams, railings, and sliding doors. They use expensive mineral pigments, such as malachite green or cinnabar, and much gold paint and thin foil, thereby endowing their pictures with a luxurious opulence befitting their court patrons.

Historicism in style and subject matter

Much of seventeenth-century Tosa painting was strongly retrospective in character, inspired by the art and literature of the golden age of Japanese court culture of the eleventh and twelfth centuries. The devastation of recent civil wars and the ascent to power of uncultured samurai had prompted the Kyoto aristocracy to cherish Heian and early Kamakura period poetry and narrative painting as part of their cultural identity. By contrast, the samurai in eastern Japan embraced "Chinese learning," exemplified by their endorsement of Confucian social philosophy and their patronage of the Kanō school. The decorative arts of the late Ming court—lacquerware, cloisonné, and ceramics—afforded the ruling Tokugawa family models for the lavish ornament seen today at the family mortuary shrines at Nikkō.

The subject-matter repertory of the Tosa artists was of vital importance to their Kyoto patrons, who were steeped in the poignant romances of *Tales of Ise*, attributed to Ariwara no Narihira (825–880), and the *Tale of Genji* by Murasaki Shikibu (died c. 1014), and had revived the study of classical court poetry. But the Tosa repertory extended to portraits of courtiers, battle scenes (compositions based on careful study of thirteenth-century imagery), and narrative scrolls depicting shrine and temple legends. Tosa painting had strongly nationalist overtones. Mitsuoki, for exam-

level. Bands of clouds enter the compositions from all sides, obscuring incidental detail and directing the viewer's attention to the events taking place. The cloud bands, painted in gold or sprinkled with flakes of gold and silver leaf, minimize suggestions of pictorial depth. Like the gold grounds of Italian medieval votive paintings, they reinforce the decorative, two-dimensional qualities of the design.

Room interiors are shown without their ceilings. This arbitrary pictorial device, unique to Japan, sacrifices realistic architecture to narrative. The missing roof and steep angle of vision afford a clear view of what is happening within. The human figures are relatively large in scale. Heavy garments enclose the bodies. Faces are shown with minimal detail, a convention nicknamed *hikime-kagihana* (eye drawn with a straight line, nose with a hook). Altogether the traits of this stiff, impersonal figural style are closely attuned to the constrained atmosphere of court decorum.

ple, wrote in his theoretical treatise of 1690, *Great Tradition of Japanese Painting* (*Honchō gahō daiden*), that foreign painting was like prose, Japanese painting was like poetry, and that the Tosa patriarch Mitsunobu (died 1521/1522) surpassed all Chinese painters in his narrative techniques.[17]

Stylistic pluralism
Tosa painting modes were adopted by virtually every school of Japanese pictorial art of the sixteenth and seventeenth centuries; the Tosa artists borrowed widely as well. A simplified version of Tosa *yamato-e* was used by the so-called artisan painters (*machi eshi*; literally, "city picture masters").[18] These anonymous professional craftsmen, operating small family workshops, produced a vast number of books and scrolls illustrating religious tales and popular fiction. The more prestigious Kyoto ateliers—Kanō, Hasegawa, Kaihō, Unkoku—executed *yamato-e* screens and albums that are virtually in-

distinguishable from those made by Tosa artists. The famous Tawaraya Sōtatsu (died c. 1640) adapted the Tosa mode for his paintings of classical literary themes which he executed with much more spontaneity. Plebeian artists of the *ukiyo* ("Floating World") school (which rose during the seventeenth century in entertainment districts in Kyoto, Osaka, and Edo) depicted courtesans and entertainers with much of the abstraction and polished technique found in the Tosa figural style.

Mutual borrowing among schools of artists, though little noted in premodern texts, is a deeply rooted feature of Japanese art history. Artists in most media seem to have been free to work in a variety of styles provided they established clear identity as master of one of them. This last proviso was essential; most artists would locate themselves unmistakably in a well-defined stylistic tradition, but thereafter they experimented widely. None did so more than Mitsuoki, as we shall see.

3. Tosa Mitsunori, *Genji Eavesdropping*, c. 1635, album leaf illustrating chapter 7, *Tale of Genji*, ink, color, and gold leaf on paper (15.5 x 14.1 cm) Tokugawa Museum, Nagoya Photograph from Baba Ichirō, ed., *Genji Monogatari*, *Taiyō* special issue (Tokyo, 1976), 73

Westerners accustomed to greater consistency in style and ideology are disturbed by such pluralism and believe it to be unprincipled and expedient.[19] On the contrary, Japanese pluralism was in itself a cultural principle, one that enabled artists to adapt and survive in changing cultural environments; it also took the edge off their professional rivalries. Workshops competed with one another, at times heatedly; but the history of Japanese patronage also abounds in cases where commissions were spread among contending workshops whose members managed to collaborate harmoniously—this in a nation in which Confucian and Buddhist ethics promoted ideals of social harmony.

Hereditary workshops

Tosa painters are a prime example of another Japanese cultural trait: a single family maintaining its craft in a hereditary fashion over many generations (appendix 2). Hereditary lineages of this kind appear in every corner of Japanese society—among farmers, carpenters, potters, literary critics, metalsmiths, weavers, sumo wrestlers, and moneylenders. In a nation that proudly claims to have been ruled by a single family in an unbroken line since the dawn of history, the psychological need to belong to a long-established lineage seems to have been enormous. In fact many newly founded workshops, the Tosa among them, invented fictitious genealogies to strengthen their historical credentials.

Workshops were linked to a family structure quite different from its counterparts in the West.[20] A professional family, or *ie* (literally "house" or "household"), was a vocational and economic unit that transmitted skills and property from one generation to the next. Membership in the *ie* was not restricted to blood relations but extended to kin by marriage and even to employees. Workshop records often make no distinction between relatives, employees, or disciples. When designating a new family head (*iemoto*, literally "household foundation"), family elders preferred to choose the oldest son of the previous *iemoto*, but many a first son was bypassed in favor of a more gifted junior relative, in-law, or adopted outsider. The ability to produce outstanding work—and thereby to attract business—was a major criterion in selection.

Members of an atelier, regardless of blood affiliation, usually took both the same family name and a characteristic personal name (*na*). Workers in the Tosa atelier, for example, called themselves Tosa and used the characters *mitsu* ("bright") or *hiro* ("extensive") as the first element in their two-character personal names. (A by-product of this custom is the great similarity of names so confusing to Westerners.) If artists changed affiliation, they would change both their family and personal names. (See discussion in appendix 1.)

Workshops handed down documents, drawings, and sales records from generation to generation, but in only a few cases have the records been kept intact.[21] Those of the Tosa family, unfortunately, are scattered and incomplete.[22] The few surviving Tosa drawings consist of prelimi-

4. Tosa school, *Genji Watches Court Women Playing Gō*, c. 1640, album leaf illustrating chapter 3, *Tale of Genji*, ink, color, and gold leaf on paper (24 x 20.7 cm) Harvard University Art Museums, Cambridge, Gift of Charles Parker

nary sketches for important commissions (fig. 15), miniature copies of completed works (with notations about customers), and albums of sketches from nature. Among the Tosa written documents is Mitsuoki's theoretical treatise of 1690, which was intended as a guide to pupils and descendants.

Workshop lineages often produced offshoots, and the Tosa was no exception. In 1662 Emperor Gosai, to strengthen the revival of *yamato-e*, ordered a gifted senior member of the Tosa atelier in Kyoto to establish a new workshop. This man, who then was called Tosa Hiromichi (1598–1670), exchanged the Tosa family name for another one, Sumiyoshi, which was that of a semi-legendary artist of the mid-twelfth century, Sumiyoshi Kei'in.[23] In so doing he fashioned an entirely fictitious connection with a famous figure in court painting. Hiromichi had already received a religious name, Jokei, which he took as his new personal name and thus became Sumiyoshi Jokei. He soon began to work for the shogunate and was appointed artist in service (*goyō eshi*) to the military government. His son Gukei (1631–1705) moved the Sumiyoshi atelier to Edo in 1683, where it rapidly took on a stylistic identity different from that of the Tosa family.

The Tosa Workshop in Sakai and Kyoto

Modern scholars believe that the effective founder of the Tosa school was Mitsunobu (died 1521/1522), the most thoroughly studied of its artists.[24] I am not concerned here with accounts that trace the lineage farther back (see appendix 2) and show the strong connections between the school and the Ashikaga military regime.[25] My main purpose is to explore the background from which Mitsuoki emerged.

Tosa Mitsunobu became superintendent of the Painting Office in 1469—a most baleful time in Japanese history. Two years earlier the Ōnin War (1467–1477) had broken out; it was the first of a series of brutal conflicts among regional lords that raged for over a century and brought about the collapse of the Ashikaga shogunate.[26] During this era, Kyoto was burned several times, and the imperial

establishment was reduced to a parlous condition. Annual ceremonies of the court were abandoned; burials and coronations of the emperors were postponed owing to a lack of funds; and the imperial palace was described as overgrown with weeds, its dwellings no different from commoners' lodgings. Courtiers were reduced to selling their calligraphies. The last of the Ashikaga shoguns became virtual pawns of the contending samurai leaders. Equally imperiled were the fortunes of the Tosa artists, who were obliged to seek patronage outside of the courts of emperor and shogun.

As Japan's samurai clans struggled among themselves, the middle classes— merchants, moneylenders, craftsmen— managed not only to survive but to develop a strong consumer economy and assert themselves culturally. In the process a ready market developed for the prolific output of artisan painters in Kyoto, Nara, Sakai, and other urban centers. These self-trained professionals produced handscrolls and albums illustrating Buddhist legends, popular folktales, historical events, and Japanese literary classics. Their paintings, closely based on the Tosa style, usually offer vitality and gusto instead of technical refinement. In fact the artisan painters flourished so vigorously that they influenced the Kanō and Tosa schools. Narrative handscrolls of Tosa Mitsunobu and his son and successor Mitsushige (1496–after 1569), even when done for elite patrons, reveal much of the bravura of artisan painting.

The third head of the Tosa workshop, Mitsumoto (born c. 1530) was killed in 1569 in the bloody seige at Honkoku-ji, Kyoto, when Nobunaga rescued the puppet Ashikaga shogun Teruaki. The second head, Mitsushige—still alive and in his seventies—resumed his position as *iemoto*. His son having fallen in the lethal power struggles in Kyoto, Mitsushige arranged for the Tosa family to flee the capital for his birthplace, the port city of Sakai south of Osaka. There they were sustained by the annual stipend of one hundred *koku* of rice discussed earlier.[27]

Sakai was no remote backwater. With a population of nearly thirty thousand, it had prospered from trade with Ming

China and from its textile and ironworking industries. Moreover, Sakai merchants and bankers were well known for their cultivation.[28] They supported the eccentric Zen monk poet and painter Ikkyū Sōjun (1394–1481), who had lived there in the late 1420s; they also supported a number of gifted linked-verse poets. The tea ceremony flourished in Sakai, where the tea master Sen no Rikyū (1522–1591) was born; and a friend of Mitsushige, the well-known Sakai merchant and tea adept, Imai Sōkyū (1520–1593), seems to have helped the Tosa family settle there.

In 1572 the imperial Painting Office in Kyoto was turned over to an adopted son of the fallen Mitsumoto; otherwise little is known about him. Soon thereafter the Kanō family seems to have been given *de facto* control over the office. Kanō Takanobu (1571–1618), father of Tan'yū, began to provide the emperor's fans and, in the 1596 rebuilding of the imperial palace, he painted the thirty-two Chinese sages on screens in the Hall of State (Shishin-den). These paintings were later transferred to Ninna-ji in Kyoto, where—miraculously—they still survive.[29] In 1599 Takanobu was formally appointed *azukari*, and the Tosa family would not reclaim the post until Mitsuoki, over a half-century later.

During the six decades in which the Tosa school worked in Sakai, Japan experienced tumultuous social change: the Ashikaga military government fell; and three successive generals—Oda Nobunaga, Toyotomi Hideyoshi, and Tokugawa Ieyasu—gradually brought the nation under their control. They also began a fifty-year period of castle and palace building that required the services of artists and craftsmen and created a vast market for decorated screens.

Tosa Mitsuyoshi (1539–1613)
The precise date and circumstances of Mitsushige's death are unknown. His successor as *iemoto* was most likely a student who took the name Mitsuyoshi. Letters tell of the atelier in Sakai under Mitsuyoshi actively helping Kanō school painters on projects that required *yamato-e* style or subject matter.[30] Tosa painters assisted Kanō Eitoku (1543–1590) working for Toyotomi Hideyoshi; they helped Kanō

Sanraku (1559–1635) at Osaka Castle and Kanō Takanobu at the imperial palace.

Mitsuyoshi seems to have expanded the scope of Tosa painting in a number of ways. He placed much emphasis, for example, on Chinese-style bird painting. Previous generations of Tosa painters, emulating Chinese court customs, had begun working in the style of imported pictures of quail attributed to Emperor Hui Zong (1082–1135) and Li An-zhong (active in the court of the emperor and his successor).[31] Though quail painting possessed few traits of *yamato-e*, the imported Chinese examples had established it as an idiom of court painting, and it became a major stock in trade of the Tosa school from Mitsuyoshi's time on (fig. 13).

Mitsuyoshi's workshop responded to the increasing demand for large decorative screens.[32] At that time screens were usually unsigned, and present-day Japanese specialists generally attribute only two pairs to the workshop with any confidence; these nonetheless seem to demonstrate the impact of the expanding market. In the older of the two, Mitsuyoshi placed five Genji episodes over the surface of an eight-fold screen, enlarging in a hesitant fashion the type of compositions he used on album leaves.[33] In the later one, he reduced the number of scenes to three and dramatically changed the composition to a more scenic, panoramic view.[34] This clearly parallels developments in screen composition in the major Kyoto professional ateliers of the day.

An equally clear pattern of stylistic development is seen in two sets of album paintings, both illustrating the *Tale of Genji*, that are datable to Mitsuyoshi's last years. Both albums contain pages of poems inscribed by men whose court ranks testify to the fact that the Tosa school under Mitsuyoshi had begun to restore its standing among the Kyoto aristocracy. The school was also beginning to achieve the kind of elegance and fine craftsmanship demanded in a new era of growing prosperity and opulence.

The older of the two albums contains no less than eighty paintings by Mitsuyoshi and eighty calligraphy pages written by middle-ranking court officials.[35] Of those officials the best known today is Karasumaru Mitsuhiro (1579–1638), a flamboyant personality, accomplished calligrapher, amateur painter, adept of tea, student of Zen, and patron of Sōtatsu and Kōetsu.[36] Among the others were members of families that staffed the middle levels of the court bureaucracy, the Reizei, Asukai, Hino, and Ano families. Judging from their dates, the album must have been completed in 1612 or 1613.

The second set, finished in 1613, has smaller pages and contains fifty-four paintings (as, for example, fig. 2) and fifty-four calligraphy pages—one for each chapter of the novel.[37] Here the calligraphers were from the highest levels of the Kyoto aristocratic elite. The first three pages were inscribed by the retired emperor Go-Yōzei, who had abdicated in 1611 after reigning during the crucial years of the establishment of Tokugawa hegemony. The others were by the retired senior regent Konoe Nobutada (1565–1614), one of the most creative painters and calligraphers of the day;[38] his daughter—unnamed (a rare instance of a woman included in such projects); Prince Toshihito (1579–1629), builder of the Katsura Villa and one-time adoptive son of Hideyoshi;[39] Karasumaru Mitsuhiro, who inscribed the earlier album; the imperial prince Sonjun (1591–1653), abbot of the Shōren-in monastery and leading calligrapher. The rest of the collaborators were close relatives of the emperor or members of aristocratic families such as the Nakanoin, Saionji, Reizei, and Hino.

Scholars speculate that Mitsuyoshi died before this album was completed. The last six paintings bear seal impressions reading "Chōjirō," identified most likely as the youthful name of Mitsunori, Mitsuyoshi's successor as head of the Tosa family. The six paintings with the Chōjirō seal are notably more delicate and finely executed than the preceding forty-eight by Mitsuyoshi. Even those by Mitsuyoshi in this album, however, are more delicate and detailed than those in the album that he painted slightly earlier. Just as Mitsuyoshi learned to adapt his compositions to large-scale screen painting in response to demands for decorative imagery, he also refined his craft technique in response to the tastes of his aristocratic patrons.

Tosa Mitsunori (1583–1638)
Upon Mitsuyoshi's death in 1613, his son (or disciple) Mitsunori became *iemoto*. After spending most of his life in Sakai, Mitsunori moved the atelier to Kyoto in 1634, hoping to solidify the family's connections with the throne. He died, however, only four years later at age fifty-six without regaining the post of head of the Painting Office.

Mitsunori's devotion to refined, miniature techniques led him to revive the distinctive form of Chinese court painting called "white drawing" (J: *hakubyō*; C: *bai miao*). As first practiced by northern Song court painters such as Li Gong-lin (c. 1049–1106), the *bai miao* technique purged the palette of all color; the image was drawn on silk or paper in ink alone with delicate brushes, producing a thin and unmodulated line.[40] The earliest Japanese court paintings in this technique are datable to the thirteenth century and continue sporadically thereafter in *yamato-e* renditions of courtly themes.[41] Mitsunori, perhaps seeking a distinctive formal idiom to give his atelier competitive advantage, used this refined technique in tiny *Genji* albums whose images are so small, delicate, and pale that they defy the most sophisticated photographic reproduction.[42]

That Mitsunori himself received aristocratic patronage is revealed by the names of mostly middle-ranking courtiers who inscribed leaves in his album of Genji paintings in the Tokugawa Collection (fig. 3).[43] Considered his finest work from a technical standpoint, the paintings' jewellike opulence is all the more remarkable for its miniature scale (15.5 x 14.1 cm).

Despite this evidence of approval, Mitsunori's low standing relative to his main competitors, the Kanō school, is shown by the minor role he played in an ambitious three-scroll set of *Illustrated Legends of the Taima-dera (Taima-dera-engi-emaki)*, completed in 1633—one year before he moved his atelier back to Kyoto.[44] The courtier donors, headed by the imperial prince Yoshinori, assigned different painters to illustrate each of twenty-seven episodes. Although the scrolls were modeled on an older set painted by Tosa Mitsushige, the pictures

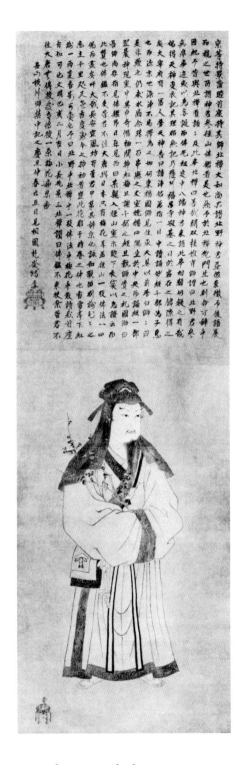

5. Tosa Mitsuoki, *Sugawara Michizane in Chinese Dress*, 1649, hanging scroll, ink and color on silk (113 x 35.4 cm) Iwasaki Collection, Tokyo (1922) Photograph from *Kokka* 390 (November 1922)

were done mostly by Kanō artists and in the Kanō style; Mitsunori was allotted only one scene to illustrate. The colophon states that Sanraku (1559–1635), head of the Kyoto Kanō atelier, executed the first painting. The other artists included Sansetsu (1589/1590–1651), who was Sanraku's disciple and adopted heir; Kōi (died 1636), the teacher of Tan'yū (1601–1674);

Naganobu (1607–1650), active mostly in Edo; Tan'yū himself—on his way to becoming the most prestigious painter in the empire—and Tan'yū's younger brother Yasunobu (1613–1695). Several more obscure Kanō painters were also listed, as were Buddhist painters working at the Kasuga atelier in Nara.

The Tosa workshop in Sakai employed many painters, but with the exception of Tosa Hiromichi, their biographies and works remain largely unknown today. (I list them separately in appendix 1.)

Tosa Mitsuoki (1617–1691)

Early years

Mitsuoki, son of Mitsunori, was born in 1617 in Sakai. Though very little data on his youth and education is available, he was surely trained as an apprentice to his father and other members of the workshop. In 1634, when still in his teens, Mitsuoki moved to Kyoto with his father. When Mitsunori died four years later, Mitsuoki continued his training, presumably under his father's assistants Hiromichi and Mitsuzumi. He must also have become fully conversant with the currents of Kyoto painting of the day.

Among the few works that may be assigned to the first phase of Mitsuoki's career is a painting, dated 1649, of the court poet Sugawara no Michizane (845–903; also called Kitano Tenjin) dressed in Chinese costume (fig. 5).[45] Done in the stiff, detailed manner of Tosa *yamato-e* portraiture, this work was inscribed by the monk Sesshin Bongin (died c. 1660), ninety-sixth abbot of the Kyoto Zen temple of Shōkoku-ji. Mitsuoki employed a distinctive Chinese-style seal in the shape of a table; his signature reads *Tosa*.

The same seal and signature appear on Mitsuoki's Chinese-style landscape painted on silk in a manner reminiscent of the well-known medieval Kyoto painter Sōami (died 1525) (fig. 6).[46] This work is not well realized; heavy brush handling, over-large boat in the middle ground, and inarticulate treatment of spatial depth reveal a lack of mastery of the pictorial idiom. A similar essay in ink painting may be dated later in Mitsuoki's career.[47]

Paintings like this in the Chinese manner lend credence to a remark in the mid-nineteenth century *Koga bikō* that Mitsuoki had studied the work of two masters of ink painting: Kanō Naonobu (1607–1650), the innovative younger brother of Tan'yū, and Shōkadō Shōjō (1582/1584–1639), tea master, calligrapher, and painter in the Zen amateur tradition.[48] Ink painting remained a primary pictorial mode for most Kyoto painters, and many Tosa artists felt obliged at least to familiarize themselves with it if not to master it.

Middle years: 1654–1685

In 1654 Mitsuoki was granted full court recognition with his appointments to the Junior Fifth Rank, as Lieutenant of the Left Bodyguard (*sakonoe shōgen*), and as *edokoro azukari*. For the next three decades—a period of great productivity—Mitsuoki proudly inserted his court titles into his signatory inscriptions and seals; he also used a seal reading *Fujiwara*, asserting that his family, like many others at court, had been awarded honorary association with that ancient aristocratic lineage.

Coinciding with Mitsuoki's appointment in 1654 was a project to rebuild the imperial palace compound, which had been completely destroyed by fire the previous year. Mitsuoki was employed to paint sliding screens for the Ordinary Palace (*Tsune-goten*); Hiromichi, leading assistant of Mitsunori and later the founder of the Sumiyoshi atelier, painted screens for the Small Palace (*Ko-gosho*). The military government, which financed the project, imported the majority of artists from the Kanō school in Edo and designated Tan'yū supervisor and chief painter for the project. Tan'yū's high standing is reflected by the fact that he was paid a third more than Hiromichi and almost twice as much as Mitsuoki for the same amount of work.[49]

The palace paintings were consumed by fire in 1661; in the reconstruction that followed, Mitsuoki was again employed, but that work, too, was lost in the fire of 1672. (Fires destroyed all or part of the palace five times during the seventeenth century alone.) Among the subjects assigned to Mitsuoki were topographic landscapes of famous Japanese beauty spots such as the coast at Wakanoura. Though these landscapes have been lost, his surviving middle-period oeuvre contains a fine pair of landscape screens depicting the famous Itsukushima Shrine and the pine-clad islands of Matsushima.[50]

A pair of screens depicting *New Year's Celebrations at the Imperial Court* reveal Mitsuoki as a conservative journeyman recording ceremonial events.[51] With stiff, formalized placement of figures and architecture, they give no evidence of his ability to devise novel variations on old

6. Tosa Mitsuoki, *Chinese-style Landscape*, c. 1650, hanging scroll, ink on paper (93 x 36 cm)
Collection unknown
Photograph from *Kokka* 911 (February 1968)

compositions. More artistically innovative is a pair of screens painted for Empress Tōfukumon-in (1607–1678), consort of Emperor Go-Mizunoo and daughter of the second Tokugawa shogun, Hidetada (fig. 7).[52] (The shogun's success, in 1621, in forcing his daughter on an unwilling emperor was a major episode in the domination of the court by the military regime.) In the right screen is a cherry tree in bloom; the left shows a maple with leaves of autumnal red. From the branches of both trees hang long slips of paper inscribed with *waka* poems.

None of the poems is signed, but a connoisseur's document of 1698 accompanying the screens identifies the writers as twenty-five courtiers and Buddhist priests who comprised the imperial cultural establishment of the 1670s and 1680s. They include members of such aristocratic families as Kūjō, Gojō, Aburanokoji, Saionji, and Karasumaru; also listed are imperial princes who served as abbots of Sambō-in and Shōren-in monasteries. The connoisseur's document, like many such traditional certificates, contains inconsistencies, but Japanese specialists provisionally accept the connection with Tōfukumon-in and the status of the

courtiers who inscribed it. This evidence indeed suggests that the Tosa atelier may once more have gained the support of the very highest strata of the imperial court.

In stylistic terms the screens are a radical departure from conventional Tosa painting. Mitsuoki's bold composition of a single tree extending over most of the picture surface overpowers the literary value of the poem slips. The composition reflects the large-scale decorative modes of the other Kyoto professional studios, especially that of the Hasegawa family, whose screen paintings of trees and rocks have a similar sense of swirling energy. Mitsuoki's brush handling in the rocks and tree trunks is indebted to other rival ateliers, mostly the Kanō school.

Mitsuoki's powers of synthesis reach their height in a pair of middle-period folding screens, each depicting an episode from the *Tale of Genji* (fig. 8).[53] The screens are said to have once belonged to the Enman-in, a subtemple of the giant Onjō-ji monastery in nearby Otsu. Enman-in was a *monzeki*, a monastery whose abbot was a prince of royal blood, and was thus closely linked to the imperial court.[54]

The right screen depicts an episode from the novel's fifth chapter, Young Murasaki

7. Tosa Mitsuoki, *Flowering Cherry Tree with Poem Slips*, c. 1660, one of pair of six-fold screens, color, ink, and gold on paper (142.5 x 293.2 cm)
Art Institute of Chicago

(Waka Murasaki). Genji, peeking through a brushwood fence, sees for the first time the young girl, Murasaki, who was to become his paramour. (She is shown dressed in white standing inside the apartment.) Employing a bold synthesis of Kanō and Tosa elements, Mitsuoki composed the landscape in a panoramic mode derived from Kanō Chinese-style imagery. He imbued the landforms and trees with a strong sense of vitality and energy, most notably in the stream that rushes down the hill toward the spectator. At the same time, the brilliant color and meticulous detail are characteristic of his father's miniature yamato-e style, and the apartment with the young children and their nurse is a faithful essay in Tosa imagery.

Perhaps Mitsuoki's most innovative treatment of a Genji theme is seen in a pair of screens now in the Tokyo National Museum.[55] Each screen illustrates an episode from the novel's seventeenth chapter, "Picture Competition" (e-awase), in which two princesses and their protectors compete for the favor of the emperor through their skill as painters and their taste as collectors. The right screen (fig. 9) shows Genji assisting Murasaki in choosing among albums and scrolls scattered on the tatami mats. The contest itself is shown in the left screen.

In a most extraordinary conception, Mitsuoki painted both scenes as though seen through narrow bamboo blinds. By depicting the brocade bindings of the blinds along the top and bottom edges of each panel of the folding screen, Mitsuoki created the sensation that the viewer is actually looking through the blinds into the room interiors. He reinforced that effect by depicting folding screens in the foregrounds as though they, too, are being seen from the rear and sides.

From as early as the twelfth century, Japanese court painters had been fascinated by the problem of depicting objects behind bamboo blinds. Mitsuyoshi (fig. 2) and Mitsunori had both done it on a relatively large scale, but no one had attempted so bold a treatment as Mitsuoki had here. The result, however, is almost surrealistic in its spatial ambiguity, for the system of linear perspective, which presupposes a bird's-eye view, clashes with the hyper-realistic treatment of the foreground blinds, which presupposes a head-on vantage point. As far as I know, this radical experiment was not repeated.

Mitsuoki's free-wheeling curiosity also caused him to adopt a kind of realism that had been stimulated by pictures brought by seventeenth-century Chinese immigrants to Japan. This is seen in a painting on silk depicting a bamboo plate filled with various ocean creatures—starfish, sea urchins, conch shells, bivalves, sea slugs, and oysters (fig. 10).[56] They are shown with a type of "haptic" realism that stresses the tactile, factual aspect of objects rather than the appearance of their surfaces.

8. Tosa Mitsuoki, Genji Espying Young Murasaki, c. 1660, one of pair of six-fold screens illustrating Tale of Genji, ink, color, and gold on paper (141.8 x 348.9 cm)
Wakino Ichirō collection, Kyoto (1955)
Photograph from Kokka 758 (May 1955)

9. Tosa Mitsuoki, *Genji and Murasaki Preparing for Picture Competition*, c. 1660, one of pair of six-fold screens illustrating *Tale of Genji*, ink, color, and gold on paper (85 x 252 cm)
Tokyo National Museum
Photograph from *Nihon byōbu-e shūsei*, vol. 5 (Tokyo, 1979), pl. 103

Mitsuoki's realist paintings, few in number and at variance with the traditional virtues of *yamato-e*, were not unprecedented. As mentioned above, the Tosa school produced innumerable quail paintings modeled on realistic Song Chinese examples. A pronounced strain of realism in contemporary Chinese painting had also attracted the Japanese, most notably Kanō Tan'yū.[57]

Mitsuoki, who seems to have given much thought to the subject of realism, stated in his 1690 painting treatise:

Among works of painting that delineate various kinds of objects, some are mediocre because they are exceedingly lifelike, and others are mediocre because they are not lifelike. If there is a painting which is lifelike and

which is good for that reason, that work has followed the laws of life. If there is a painting which is not lifelike and which is good for that reason, that work has followed the laws of painting.[58]

It is arresting to find so strong a Chinese flavor in a text that purports to justify the Tosa school as guardian of Japan's national painting style. Mitsuoki's treatise, like most Japanese essays in art theory, was strongly influenced by classical Chinese aesthetic doctrine, and restated the time-honored Chinese principle that the highest goal of painting was to capture the intangible spirit of an object. Mitsuoki held that artists must select details, leave things to the viewer's imagination, and combine verisimilitude with "lightness." "Lightness," in fact, was the crucial term in his treatise; he wrote that if the essence of painting can be reduced to a single term, it would be "lightness"—lightness in color, detail, and spirit. These efforts in art theory seem to have been inspired less by Mitsuoki's actual studio practice and more by the general aesthetic discourse, both Chinese and Japanese, of the period; "lightness" (*karumi*) had become a quality much desired in Japanese poetry.

Of a totally different aesthetic character—and further evidence of Mitsuoki's explorations far beyond the conventional limits of Tosa painting—is a brightly colored painting of a seated woman weeping (fig. 11).[59] The subject is identified as Takao, a legendary courtesan of the Yoshi-

10. Tosa Mitsuoki, *Sea Shells*, c. 1660, hanging scroll, ink and color on silk (32.6 x 48.2 cm)
Tokugawa Museum, Nagoya
Photograph from *Kokka* 287 (April 1914)

wara brothel district in Edo. Inscribed probably by Mitsuoki himself are poems derived from antique sources.[60] The Chinese inscription is a variant of a two-verse passage in the long poem, "Spring Scene," by the Tang master Du Fu (712–770). It may be translated:

The flowers,
  moved by the times,
    weep flowing tears.
The birds,
  suddenly startled,
    are reluctant to leave.

The other inscription, in flowing *hiragana* script, is a Japanese *waka* (poem of thirty-one syllables) by the classical poet Fujiwara Shunzei (1114–1204); it may be translated:

Omoiwabi	*Weary with longing,*
Mishi omokage wa	*Putting aside the memory*
Sate okite	*Of the face she gazed on.*
Koe sezarikemu	*To be without passion—*
Ori zo koishiki	*Is now her passion.*

The poems convey something of the drama of the legends of the courtesan Takao, said to have been murdered by a jealous lover.[61] The identification of the woman in this painting as Takao cannot be verified, for the courtesan had become so famous her name was appended without reason to many old paintings and woodblock prints of beautiful women. There is no question, however, that Mitsuoki's painting is related in style and subject matter to a large number of pictures of courtesans and dancers conventionally called Beauties of the Kambun Era (1661–1673; *kambun bijin*).[62] By the middle of the seventeenth century, Japanese painting workshops had begun depicting urban entertainment districts and their brothels, theaters, restaurants, wrestling arenas, and star performers—the so-called Floating World (*ukiyo*). Customers for these paintings were rich samurai, townsmen, and even courtiers who flocked to sample the urbane pleasures of the Floating Worlds of Edo, Kyoto, and Osaka.

Surprising as it may be to find a court artist's formal signature and seals on a painting of a prostitute, this is but a latter-day example of the Japanese court's interest in popular culture. Beginning in the early Heian period (795–897), the court

11. Tosa Mitsuoki, *Courtesan Said to Be Takao II*, c. 1660, hanging scroll, color and ink on silk (71.2 x 78.68 cm)
Inoue Tatsukuro Collection (1932)
Photograph from *Nihonga taisei* 2, pl. 90

had incorporated folktales and drama into its own literary culture; early Tosa artists painted handscrolls illustrating a type of folk narrative called "companion stories" (*otogi zōshi*). Mitsuzumi, who was Mitsuoki's teacher, worked in an idiom of genre painting—scenes of craftsmen and artisans—that flourished in the late middle ages.[63] Mitsunori did paintings of Kyoto citizens cooling off on a summer's night on platforms built over a river.[64] Mitsuoki himself painted a pair of large screens depicting everyday life of the capital, and he did a very lively narrative scroll of a popular festival at the Kitanō Shrine.[65] His son Mitsunari (1646–1710) showed even greater interest in this type of imagery.[66] Such diversity of subject matter is evidence of one of the major means by which the Tosa workshop was able to survive: its ability to adapt its thematic repertory to the interests of its patrons.

In 1681 Mitsuoki was given a conventional court honor, designation as *hokkyō* and given the religious name *Jōshō* (literally, "familiar brightness"). His son, Mitsunari, replaced him as *edokoro azukari*. In 1685 he was promoted to *hōgen*, and, adhering to a long-established custom among educated Japanese, Mitsuoki formally marked the last phase of his life by becoming a Buddhist lay-monk (*nyūdō*); nonetheless, he remained active as a painter.

Late years (1685–1691)

Tosa Mitsuoki continued to work in a dizzying variety of styles. Present-day critics have said that late paintings such as his illustration of chapter 20 of *Tale of Genji* (fig. 12) lack the energy and inventiveness seen earlier.[67] The conventionalized, languid character of this painting, however, may be less the result of Mitsuoki's advanced age and more the product of a kind of establishment academicism that appeared not only in Mitsuoki's work but also throughout the entire Kanō school as well.

This painting shows Genji and Murasaki, enraptured by the beauty of the snow in moonlight, watching children build a giant snowball. Combined in it are a number of separate stylistic tendencies: in the human figures and room interior, one sees the brightly colored *tsukuri-e* mode of court painting; in the pale delineation of the verandah, the *hakubyō* mode of Mitsuoki's father; and in the foreground pine tree as well as the overall scenic quality, the Kanō style.

As befit a traditional workshop head grooming his successor, Mitsuoki worked jointly with his son Mitsunari. In a conventional composition of quail and chrysanthemums, for example, the older man rendered the birds, the younger the flowers and grasses (fig. 13).[68] This was but one of dozens of quail paintings by Mitsuoki done in the Song Chinese academic idiom.[69]

12. Tosa Mitsuoki, *Genji and Murasaki Watch Children Make a Snowball*, hanging scroll, color and ink on silk (95.1 x 43 cm)
Nezu Museum, Tokyo
Photograph from *Kokka* 632 (June 1943)

13. Tosa Mitsuoki and Tosa Mitsunari, *Quail and Chrysanthemum*, c. 1690, hanging scroll, color, and ink on silk (dimensions unknown)
Collection unknown
Photograph from *Kokka* 54 (April 1894)

artists, *Tansei jakuboku-shū*, and a discussion of Chinese art theory, *Kosu-shū*. In 1678 Kanō Einō (1634–1700) completed his *History of Japanese Painting* (*Honchō gashi*), a vast biographical compilation that preserved much traditional artistic lore.[71] Though such treatises were intended primarily for workshop members and patrons, they soon passed into the general domain of educated persons.

Dating also from 1690 is Mitsuoki's ambitious set of three handscrolls illustrating the legends (called *Ōdera engi*) of

14. Tosa Mitsuoki, *Ōdera-engi-emaki*, 1690, detail of third handscroll in set of three, ink and color on paper (35.2 x 2144.6 cm), Sekiguchi Shrine, Osaka
Photograph from Murashige Yasushi, *Tosa-ha no kaiga* [exh. cat., Suntory Museum] (Tokyo, 1982), no. 27

15. Tosa Mitsuoki, *Ōdera-engi-emaki*, 1690, preparatory drawing, detail of third handscroll in set of three, ink on paper (33.3 x 1690.8 cm)
Collection unknown
Photograph from Murashige 1982, no. 28

A major product of his final years was his treatise, *Great Tradition of Japanese Painting*, in which he sought to create an historical and technical mandate for the Tosa school.[70] Divided into fifty sections, the treatise covers art theory, practice (preparing colors, affixing seals), and criticism (evaluating artists, saving his harshest judgments for Kanō painters).

Until the seventeenth century, Japanese artists had been disinclined to write about art history or theory—unlike their Chinese colleagues. By the end of the civil wars, however, Japanese intellectuals had developed a strong historical self-consciousness and they turned to China for historiographic models. The *Comprehensive National History* (*Honchō tsukan*) of Hayashi Razan (1583–1657), for example, reviewed the entire history of Japan and the status of the samurai class from a Confucian perspective. Mitsuoki's rivals in the Kanō school had responded to the same impulse to write history: Kanō Ikkei (1599–1662, also called Naizen) published a collection of biographies of Japanese

16. Tosa Mitsuoki, *Wang Zhaojun, Peacock, and Phoenix*, c. 1691, three hanging scrolls, ink and color on silk
Tiger Collection, Boston
Photograph: Harvard University Art Museums

the Sekiguchi Shrine in Sakai (figs. 14, 15).[72] Commissioned and donated to the shrine by the Senior Regent Konoe Motohiro (1648–1722), the three scrolls recount the deeds of famous Buddhist monks who taught there. The most striking aspect of this work is the fact that, at the end of his career, Mitsuoki returned to the narrative techniques of the forebear whom he greatly admired, Tosa Mitsunobu. The boldly simple color planes and attention to narrative detail are at variance with the meticulous miniature style of Mitsuoki

and his father; rather they reflect the Tosa style of almost two hundred years earlier.

Dated to his last year, 1691, is a brightly colored triptych showing a Chinese literary heroine, Wang Zhaojun (mid-first century B.C.), flanked by a phoenix and peacock (fig. 16).[73] The two birds are done in a decorative style derived from late Ming/early Qing professional painting. Paintings of this type were being brought to Japan by merchants and emigré Chinese monks of the Ōbaku (Huangpo) Zen sect. Mitsuoki's use of this florid idiom heralds

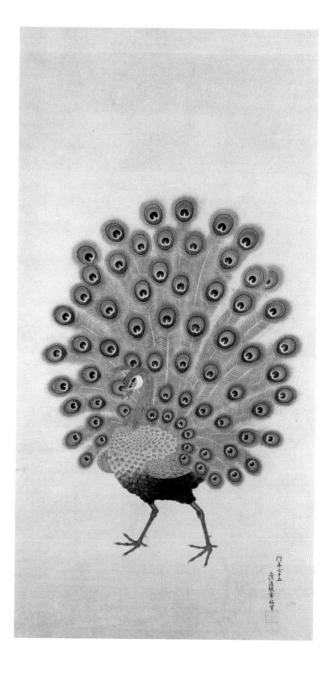

its considerable impact on Japanese painters in the eighteenth century, especially the Kyoto eccentric master Itō Jakuchū (1716–1800).

From his grounding in *tsukuri-e* techniques, Mitsuoki ventured into a great variety of artistic styles. In fact, traditional Tosa *yamato-e* comprises only a small portion of his surviving oeuvre, and his pluralism grew in part from that of Tosa predecessors who manifested the principle of stylistic independence discussed above: artists based in one style often explored others. Even his father, an arch-conservative, had painted scenes of everyday life. Tosa Ittoku had depicted birds in an ornate mode; and Mitsutsugu had done ink landscapes. In addition to such individual ventures, almost all Tosa artists had painted quail in the Song Chinese academic style, and had created monumental, brightly colored screens.

Mitsuoki was more adventurous than any other Tosa artist before him, but in reality no more so than his great rival Kanō Tan'yū. Such extreme versatility and intellectual curiosity were reflections of profound changes occurring in seventeenth-century Japan. Strong local cultures were appearing in the regional domains. Large cities were developing their own distinctive styles of literature, drama, music, and painting. Commoners were making vast fortunes in shipping and mercantile trade. Chinese and Western learning were inspiring new cultural ideals. New patrons and markets for artists were arising, and new stylistic systems were developing to meet the changing market.

Even though they worked in conservative government circles, Mitsuoki and Tan'yū innovated, borrowed, and made new stylistic combinations. By the beginning of the eighteenth century, the social and intellectual ferment had far outrun the power of the shogunal and imperial courts to define standards of national culture. Both courts lost their positions at the apex of cultural authority. The successors to Mitsuoki and Tan'yū, unable to escape the limits of their traditions, settled for the most part into bland repetitions of old formulas.

APPENDIX 1

Lesser Members of the Tosa Atelier in Sakai

Tosa Mitsutsugu (active c. late sixteenth century) was a member of Mitsuyoshi's atelier. Surviving works include an ink landscape painting in the Kanō manner depicting Monk Saigyō viewing Mount Fuji; also a pair of ink painting screens of tigers and dragons in the Ostasiatisches Museum, Cologne.[74]

Tosa Mitsuzumi (active c. late sixteenth–early seventeenth century) worked in Mitsuyoshi's atelier and is said to have taught Mitsuoki. Attributed to him is a detailed painting of the shop of a barrel maker that belongs to the popular idiom of artisan and craftsman imagery.[75]

Tosa Ittoku (active 1596–1615), said to be a pupil of Mitsuyoshi, painted quails, Genji album leaves. Door and ceiling panels (including one fantastic phoenix) at the Kita-in, Kawagoe, Saitama Prefecture, were commissioned by the monk Tenkai (1563?–1643), teacher of Tokugawa Ieyasu and one of the most influential religious leaders of the day.[76]

Tosa Hiromichi (1598–1670) was also called Tosa Mitsuhisa and Naiki; his parentage is unknown. He studied with Mitsuyoshi, became an assistant to Mitsunori and accompanied him when he moved to Kyoto. He emerged as a major artistic personality by 1625, when commissioned by Tenkai to come to Edo to paint an illustrated biography of Tokugawa Ieyasu, the *Tōshōgū-engi*; returned to Kyoto. With Mitsuoki he engaged in painting projects in the imperial palace in 1654; appointed *hōkkyō* in 1661; assumed Buddhist name Jokei; in 1662 ordered by Emperor Gosai to open new *yamato-e* workshop; started Sumiyoshi lineage of painters. Ordered by retired emperor Go-Mizunoo to copy surviving scrolls of great classic of court painting, *Yearly Events of the Court* (*Nenjū gyōji-emaki*) by late twelfth-century painter Tokiwa Mitsunaga.[77]

APPENDIX 2

Tosa Family and Workshop Genealogy

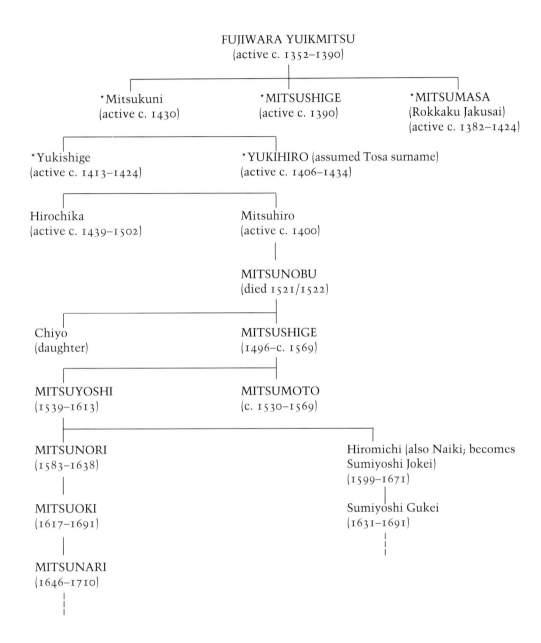

*Surname Fujiwara
Names of Painting Office heads (*edokoro azukari*) are capitalized
Genealogy adapted from Murashige Yasushi, *Tosa-ha no kaiga* [exh. cat., Suntory Museum] (Tokyo, 1982)

NOTES

I am most grateful to Naomi Noble Richard for editorial suggestions; to Sylvan Barnet, William Burto, Fukuhara Yasuko, Robert Mowry, William Samonides, and Wu Hung for advice and references.

All Japanese and Chinese personal names, including those of authors writing in English, appear in traditional fashion, family name first.

1. The first was Tokiwa Mitsunaga (active c. 1173–1190); the second was Tosa Mitsunobu (died 1521/1522). Mitsunaga was claimed by later Tosa artists as the patriarch of their lineage. He is credited with one of the great monuments of Japanese court painting, the sixty-scroll *Annual Events of the Court* (*Nenjū gyōji emaki*), commissioned by Emperor Go-Shirakawa. The surviving fragments of this project were copied by Tosa artists about 1661 (*Nenjū gyōji emaki*), Nihon emakimono zenshū, 2d ed., vol. 24, (Tokyo, 1978). For Mitsunobu, see below n. 24.

2. For surveys of painting of the Early Modern Era: Akiyama Terukazu, *Japanese Painting* (Lausanne, 1961), chaps. 7–9; William Watson, ed., *The Great Japan Exhibition: Art of the Edo Period, 1600–1868*, [exh. cat., Royal Academy of Arts] (London, 1981).

3. For social and political background, see John Hall et al, eds., *Japan before Tokugawa: Political Consolidation and Economic Growth, 1500 to 1650* (Princeton, 1981); Herschel Webb, *The Japanese Imperial Institution in the Tokugawa Period* (New York, 1968).

4. *Gyōsai gadan*, vol. 1 (Kyoto, 1877). The studio is that of Kanō Tōhaku II (?–1851), the seventh generation head of the Surugadai branch of the Kanō school.

5. Introductory bibliography in *Kanō-ha no kaiga* [exh. cat., Tokyo National Museum] (Tokyo, 1981). See also Shimizu Yoshiaki, "Workshop Management of the Early Kanō Painters, c. A.D. 1530–1600," *Archives of Asian Art* 34 (1981), 32–47.

6. Takamatsu Yoshiyuki, "Genre Representation of Tosa-school from the Beginning of the Early Modern Period: The Change from Mitsuyoshi to Mitsunori," manuscript prepared for Japan-America Workshop II; Los Angeles County Museum of Art, February 1989; Ariga Hoshimi, ed., *Gōka 'Genji-e' no sekai* (Tokyo, 1988); Miyajima Shin'ichi, *Tosa Mitsunobu to Tosa-ha no keifu*, Nihon no Bijutsu, no. 247 (Tokyo, 1986); Murase Miyeko, *Iconography of the* Tale of Genji (New York, 1983); Murashige Yasushi, *Tosa-ha no kaiga* [exh. cat., Suntory Museum] (Tokyo, 1982); Yoshida Tomoyuki, *Tosa Mitsunobu*, Nihon Bijutsu Kaiga Zenshū, vol. 5 (Tokyo, 1979); Baba Ichirō, ed., *Genji monogatari*, Taiyō special issue (Tokyo, 1976); Akiyama Terukazu, *Genji-e*, Nihon no Bijutsu, no. 119 (Tokyo, 1976); Kimura Tokue, *Tosa monjo kaisetsu* (Tokyo, 1935); *Nihonga Taisei*, vol. 2 (Tokyo, 1932).

7. Six panels of such portraits survive from the brush of a Tosa-related artist, Sumiyoshi Hiroyuki (1755–1831). Nihonga Taisei, 2, pl. 128; see below n. 29.

8. Wada Hidematsu, *Kanshoku yōkai* (Tokyo, 1927), 181–182.

9. *Eiga monogatari* (A Tale of Flowering Fortunes), trans. William and Helen McCullough, vol. 1 (Stanford, 1980), 92.

10. *Kokka* 14 (January 1890).

11. Miyajima Shin'ichi, "Jūyonseiki ni okeru edokoro azukari no keifu," *Bijutsu-shi* 22 (March 1973), 87–102.

12. Akiyama Terukazu, *Heian jidai sezoku-ga no kenkyū* (Tokyo, 1964), chap. 3.

13. Kimura 1935, 87. A *koku* (literally, "stone") equaled 180 liters of rice. This was the standard unit in the allocation of rice tax revenues and stipends. Kanō Tan'yū was allocated 200 *koku* by the military government.

14. Fujioka Micho, *Kyoto gosho* (Tokyo, 1956), 201–205; see below n. 49.

15. *Bukkyō Daijiten*, ed. Mochizuki Shinkō, vol. 5 (Tokyo, 1936), 1564, 4544–4545, 4589.

16. Akiyama 1961, 66–67, 165–167; Akiyama Terukazu, *Ōchō kaiga no tanjō: Genji Monogatari emaki o megutte*, Chūkō Shinsho, no. 173 (Tokyo, 1968).

17. Ueda Makoto, *Literary and Art Theories in Japan* (Cleveland, 1967), 139. See discussion of the *Honchō gahō taiden* below.

18. Artisan painting is often misleadingly called *Nara-e. Zaigai Nara ehon*, ed. Nara Ehon Kokusai Kaigi (Tokyo, 1981); Barbara Ruch, "In Search of Lost Treasures: *Nara ehon* Abroad," in *Zaigai shozō Nara ehon*, ed. Barbara Ruch et al. (Tokyo, 1979), 57; *Kokka* 813 (December 1959).

19. Karel Van Wolferen, *The Enigma of Japanese Power: People and Politics in a Stateless Nation* (New York, 1989), 8–9, 227–228.

20. Nakane Chie, *Japanese Society* (Berkeley, 1970), 58–59.

21. For detailed records of Ogata Kōrin, see Yamane Yūzō, *Konishi-ke kyūzō Kōrin kankei shiryō to sono kenkyū* (Tokyo, 1962). To my knowledge, one of the most complete sets of workshop records are those of the Ogata family, an offshoot of the Kanō school who served the lords of the Kuroda domain in Ōita, Kyushu. A total of 4,791 documents are reviewed in *Ogata-ke kaiga shiryō mokuroku*, ed. Fukuoka Kenritsu Bijutsukan, 2 vols. (Fukuoka, 1985).

22. Miyajima 1986, 78–80; Yoshida 1979, 137, 142, pls. 57–58, 85–88.

23. Doi Tsuguyoshi in *Edo no yamato-e: Sumiyoshi Jokei, Gukei* [exh. cat. Suntory Museum], (Tokyo, 1985).

24. Miyajima 1986; Yoshida 1979.

25. Premodern sources are summarized in *Honchō gashi*, comp. Kanō Einō (1634–1700), published 1678 (see Kasai Masaki, ed., *Honchō gashi* [Kyoto, 1985]); and *Koga bikō*, comp. Asaoka Okisada [1800–1856],

Ōta Susumu, ed., *Koga bikō* [Tokyo, 1904]); Tani Shin'ichi in *Bijutsu Kenkyū* 87 (March 1939); 100 (April 1940); 101 (May 1940); 103 (July 1940).

26. Paul Varley, *The Ōnin War* (New York, 1967).

27. For a detailed account of the Tosa family in Sakai: Kimura 1935, 87–126.

28. V. Dixon Morris, "Sakai: From *shōen* to Port City," in John Hall and Toyoda Takeshi, eds., *Japan in the Muromachi Age* (Berkeley, 1977), 145–158.

29. Takeda Tsuneo, *Shōhei-ga*, Genshoku Nihon no bijutsu, vol. 13 (Tokyo, 1967), pls. 27, 28; *Kokka* 1028 (November 1979); *Kokka* 1029 (December 1979).

30. Kimura 1935, 127–128.

31. *Sō-Gen no kaiga* [exh. cat., Tokyo National Museum] (Tokyo, 1962), nos. 49, 52; Werner Speiser, *Meisterwerke chinesischer Malerei aus der Higashiyama-Sammlung* (Berlin, 1958), pls. 1, 5, 6.

32. For sixteenth-century Tosa screen painting, see *Muromachi jidai no byōbu-e* [exh. cat., Tokyo National Museum] (Tokyo, 1989).

33. Murashige 1982, nos. 15, 16.

34. *Kokka* 749 (August 1954).

35. *Kokka* 736 (August 1953).

36. Shimizu Yoshiaki and John Rosenfield, *Masters of Japanese Calligraphy* (New York, 1984), 206–207, 250–258; Komatsu Shigemi, *Karasumaru Mitsuhiro*, 3 vols. (Tokyo, 1982).

37. *Kokka* 996 (December 1976).

38. Shimizu and Rosenfield 1984, 204–205, 212–215.

39. Naitō Akira, *Katsura: A Princely Retreat* (Tokyo, 1977).

40. *Suiboku bijutsu taikei*, vol. 4 (Tokyo, 1975), pls. 1, 12, 15, 27–30, 54, 60, 66.

41. Shimpō Toru, *Hakubyō emaki*, Nihon no Bijutsu, no. 48 (Tokyo, 1970); Charles Franklin Sayre, "Japanese Court-Style Narrative Painting of the Late Middle Ages," *Archives of Asian Art* 35 (1982), 71–81.

42. Murase Miyeko, *Japanese Art: Selections from the Mary and Jackson Burke Collection* (New York, 1975), no. 59; *The Freer Gallery of Art* 2 (Washington, 1972), ps. 35, 36.

43. Tokugawa Reimei-kai, ed., *Tokugawa Bijutsu-kan* (Tokyo, 1982), no. 41; chief among those writing inscriptions was Senior Regent Konoe Hidetsugu (died 1653).

44. *Kokka* 580 (March 1939); 583 (June 1939); 598 (September 1941); 606 (May 1941).

45. *Kokka* 390 (November 1922). Middle-period paintings of similar themes include a triptych of Confucius flanked by lion and peony, *Kokka* 440 (July 1927); and the Chinese poet Tao Yuan-ming, *Kokka* 118 (October 1899).

46. *Kokka* 911 (February 1968).

47. *Nihonga Taisei*, 2: pl. 89.

48. Ōta, *Koga bikō*, 3: 1050–1051

49. Payment records state that for colored paintings of human figures Tan'yū was paid 325 *momme* of silver (just over one kilogram) for each *tsubo* (3.31 square meters, or approximately one panel of a sliding screen); Tosa Hiromichi was paid 212.5 *momme*; Mitsuoki commanded only 144.5, the lowest stipend offered. Payments to the other Kanō painters averaged around 280 *momme*. Fujioka Michiō, *Kyoto gosho* (Tokyo, 1956), 201–205; Kono Motoaki, *Kanō Tan'yū*, Nihon no Bijutsu, no. 194 (Tokyo, 1982), 95–96.

50. *Kokka* 267 (August 1912).

51. Watson 1981, no. 17; *Nihonga taisei*, 2, pls. 92, 93. Collection of Sen Sōshitsu, Kyoto.

52. *Kokka* 789 (December 1957).

53. *Kokka* 758 (May 1955).

54. Enman-in, moreover, was to play a singularly important role in the history of painting a century later under the abbot Yūjō (1723–1773), patron of the brilliant Kyoto painter Maruyama Ōkyo (1773–1795). Ōkyo lived for a period at Enman-in and is said to have been much influenced by Mitsuoki's painting. Sasaki Jōhei, *Ōkyo and the Maruyama-Shijō School of Japanese Painting* [exh. cat., Saint Louis Art Museum] (Saint Louis, 1980).

55. *Nihon byōbu-e shūsei*, vol. 5 (Tokyo, 1979), pls. 25, 103, 104; *Nihonga taisei*, 2, pls. 98, 99.

56. *Kokka* 287 (April 1914). For other similar works by Mitsuoki: *Kokka* 61 (October 1894); Murashige 1982, nos. 45, 46.

57. Takeda Tsuneo, *Kanō Tan'yū*, Nihon bijutsu kaiga zenshū, vol. 15 (Tokyo, 1978), pls. 25, 27, 49–52; James Cahill, *The Distant Mountains: Chinese Painting of the Late Ming Period, 1570–1644* (Tokyo, 1988), p. 212.

58. Translation from Ueda 1967, 130.

59. *Nihonga taisei*, 2: pl. 90.

60. Du Fu, poem no. 10977 in *Tōdai no shihen*, ed. Kyoto University Institute for Humanistic Studies (Kyoto, 1964–1965); see Sydney Fung and S. T. Lai, *Twenty-five T'ang Poets: Index to English Translations* (Hong Kong, 1984), no. 2637; Fujiwara Shunzei, poem dated 1150, no. 1393 in the *Shin kokinshū*, *Shimpen Kokka Daikan*, 1 (Tokyo, 1985), 245. Translations courtesy of Fumiko E. Cranston.

61. A series of eleven courtesans named Takao worked in the Miura-ya brothel in the New Yoshiwara district in Edo. (Hereditary lineages prevailed in Japan's demimonde as well.) The first Takao died in 1660 after having retired to a nunnery. The second, said to be the subject of Mitsuoki's painting, was a farmer's daughter renowned for her beauty and talent as poet and calligrapher. She attracted a patron of the mighty Date family, lords of Sendai, who was rumored to have caused her murder while she was boating on the Sumida River. The story of her tragic death seems to have been false but was

widely believed at the time and later inspired a popular Kabuki play, *Takao's Repentence* (*Takao sange no dan*), first performed in 1744. Yoshida Teruji, *Ukiyo-e jiten*, vol. 2 (Tokyo, 1965), 163.

62. Yamane Yūzō, *Momoyama Genre Painting*, Heibonsha Survey of Japanese Art, vol. 17 (New York, 1973), 102–110, 163–177.

63. *Kokka* 102 (April 1888).

64. Murashige 1982, nos. 25, 26.

65. *Nihonga taisei*, 2, pl. 97.

66. *Nihonga taisei*, 2, pl. 111.

67. *Kokka* 632 (June 1943).

68. *Kokka* 54 (April 1894); *Nihonga taisei*, 2, pl. 67.

69. Mitsuoki adapted quail painting in one of his most imaginative middle-period compositions, a pair of large eight-fold screens showing the birds amid autumnal reeds and grasses against a low horizon line. Murashige 1982, no. 44; *Nihon byōbu-e shūsei*, vol. 6 (Tokyo 1978), pls. 88–89.

70. Sakazaki Shizuka, *Nihon no seishin* (Tokyo, 1942); partial English translation and analysis in Ueda 1967, 128–144.

71. See note 25 above.

72. *Kokka* 326 (July 1917); Murashige 1982, nos. 27, 28.

73. Murashige 1982, no. 40; for a similar painting see *Kokka* 559 (June 1937).

74. Miyajima 1986, fig. 91.

75. Tanaka Ichimatsu et al., *Kita-in shoku'nin zukushi-e byōbu* (Tokyo, 1979), pl. 12.

76. *Kokka* 102 (April 1888); note also a Chinese-style painting of Li Haijing (Rinnasei) inscribed by Hayashi Razan: *Kokka* 692 (November 1949).

77. Biography by Doi Tsugiyoshi in *Edo no yamato-e: Sumiyoshi Jokei, Gukei* [exh. cat., Suntory Museum] (Tokyo, 1985).

MARIANNA SHREVE SIMPSON
Freer Gallery of Art and Arthur M. Sackler Gallery, Smithsonian Institution

The Making of Manuscripts and the Workings of the Kitab-khana in Safavid Iran

As in other cultures both east and west, the making of a manuscript in Islamic Iran was a collective enterprise involving artists with various complementary skills engaged in a coordinated effort according to prescribed specifications, standards, and schedules. Even the most modest book required the sequential services of a papermaker, scribe, and binder, while a deluxe manuscript might be the handiwork of teams of calligraphers, illuminators, painters, and others working simultaneously. Persianate bookmaking activities in general, and deluxe manuscript production in particular, long have been associated with the *kitab-khana*, which literally means "book house," and which is translated most commonly as "library." Nowadays library universally refers to a place where books are gathered, stored, and preserved, and this certainly has been the primary meaning of *kitab-khana* for the past millennium.[1] Implicit in this definition is the notion of *kitab-khana* as "collection," that is, someone's private collection of books.[2] From at least the fifteenth century, however, the term *kitab-khana* was also used to signify a place for or at which books were made; thus, it is variously defined by modern scholars of Islamic art as a scriptorium, atelier, studio, or workshop.[3]

Although the existence of the *kitab-khana* has been accepted as a given, its history has not been treated in any systematic way within traditional studies of the Islamic and Irano-Islamic art of the book. Similarly, while the *kitab-khana*'s multiple identity as a library-cum-collection-cum-workshop has been taken for granted, interest in its actual organization and operation seems to have developed only in recent years.[4] We now are quite well informed about the workings of the *kitab-khana* established in the early fourteenth century outside the Il-Khanid capital of Tabriz by an endowment of the famous vizier and author Rashid al-Din.[5] Much more is also known about the *kitab-khana* in fifteenth-century Iran and its role in shaping the dynastic aesthetic of the ruling Timurid court.[6] In addition, new information and ideas have been presented about manuscript production and the *kitab-khana* during the subsequent Safavid period, as well as about parallel developments in the contemporary empires of Ottoman Turkey and Mughal India.[7]

Thus, even though a comprehensive account of the *kitab-khana* is still lacking, some parts of its history are becoming better understood. The piece of the story under consideration here is that which transpired in Safavid Iran (1501–1732), when the making of manuscripts occupied as much, if not more, energy than any of the other visual arts (except perhaps textiles) and the art of the book reached one of its highest levels of achieve-

ment. The aim is not to undertake a complete record of the *kitab-khana* in the sixteenth and seventeenth centuries. Instead it is first to lay out the range of evidence, both artistic and documentary, with which the Safavid *kitab-khana* may be examined; and second, to raise general issues about the function and structure of the *kitab-khana*, particularly its identity as a manuscript workshop, within Iranian culture as a whole. The intention is to set,

rather than solve, the problem, through the method of a specific case study.

This case study involves a richly illuminated and illustrated manuscript dated 963–972/1556–1565 that was made for a princely patron of the Safavid dynasty, Sultan Ibrahim Mirza (Freer Gallery of Art, 46.12).[8] The volume's text consists of seven poems (the *Haft Awrang* or Seven Thrones) written by Abd al-Rahman Jami, a celebrated author of the sec-

1. *Haft Awrang* of Jami, folio 38b, manuscript dated 963–972/1556–1565; opaque watercolor, ink, and gold on paper
Freer Gallery of Art, Smithsonian Institution, Washington (46.12)

2. *Haft Awrang* of Jami, folio 162a, manuscript dated 963–972/1556–1565; opaque watercolor, ink, and gold on paper
Freer Gallery of Art, Smithsonian Institution, Washington (46.12)

ond half of the fifteenth century. The Freer Jami, as it is frequently called, contains twenty-eight beautifully painted illustrations, of which two (folios 38b and 162a) are inscribed with variants of the phrase "birasm-i kitab-khana-yi Abu'l-Fath Sultan Ibrahim Mirza," meaning by order of the *kitab-khana* of Abu'l-Fath Sultan Ibrahim Mirza (figs. 1, 2). Expanded variants of the same phrase appear in three of the book's signed and

dated colophons (folios 83b, 139a, and 181a; figs. 3, 4, 5), with the prince's name preceded by titles and honorifics as, for example, "It has reached the frontiers of completeness by order of the *kitab-khana* of his highness, the lord, the world keeper, just in his works, the glorifier of rule, the world and religion, Ibrahim Mirza. May God protect his kingdom and sultanate."[9] Two other colophons (folios 46a and 272a; figs. 6, 7) also contain the

phrase "birasm-i/by order of" followed by honorifics and the name Sultan Ibrahim Mirza, albeit without mention of a *kitab-khana*. One painting (folio 132a; fig. 8) has an inscription band incorporated into the architecture that ends with the name of Sultan Ibrahim Mirza; the first part, obscured by a canopy, undoubtedly would have begun "birasm-i." The colophons in the Freer Jami also yield the names of five calligraphers as well as the dates and places they completed the transcription of various parts of the text. Each calligrapher signs himself with one, or more, standard formula, such as "the humble, sinning servant" and "the lowly, supplicant servant."[10] One of the five, named Muhibb-Ali (who copied two of the seven *Haft Awrang* poems), calls himself, in addition, the *kitab-dar*, that is, the head of the *kitab-khana*.[11]

This series of inscriptions provides a wealth of documentary information about the Freer Jami's origins—including when, where, for whom, and by whom it was done—which is almost without prece-

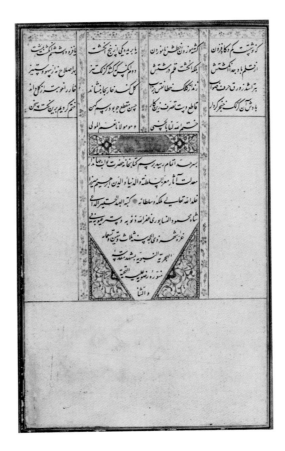

6. *Haft Awrang* of Jami, folio 46a, colophon dated Dhu'l-Hijja 963/October 1556; opaque watercolor, ink, and gold on paper
Freer Gallery of Art, Smithsonian Institution, Washington (46.12)

7. *Haft Awrang* of Jami, folio 272a, colophon dated Shawwal 972/May 1565; opaque watercolor, ink, and gold on paper
Freer Gallery of Art, Smithsonian Institution, Washington (46.12)

dent in the Islamic art of the book. Indeed, the roster of names (particularly that of Ibrahim Mirza), places, and dates is so absorbing that it is easy to bypass the ubiquitous introductory phrase—"birasm-i kitab-khana"—and to focus on the manuscript's internal chronology and patronage.[12] Such a perspective tends to overlook the equally compelling questions of how the manuscript was commissioned and how it was produced. "By order of the *kitab-khana*" suggests that the *kitab-khana* served as the vehicle or intermediary through which the patron's wish or need for a deluxe copy of Jami's *Haft Awrang* was realized. But what does it mean, in actual practice, when a calligrapher or painter states that his work was completed by order of a *kitab-khana*? Is he recording a request for services from, or rendered to, the *kitab-khana* as a book repository or art collection? Or is he documenting his participation in an artistic process that took place for or at the *kitab-khana* as a workshop or atelier? And what, if anything, does it signify

when the term *kitab-khana* is omitted and "birasm" is immediately followed, as in the first colophon of the Freer Jami (folio 46a), by a reference, in protocol form, to Ibrahim Mirza? Was the artistic process in this last case under the direct supervision of the patron, and was the artist here working directly for the patron, instead of for or at the *kitab-khana*?[13]

Any definition of the *kitab-khana*, particularly one that concerns its function and structure, must take account of such questions, however hypothetical they may be. To address them, some historical background about the manuscript made for Sultan Ibrahim Mirza may be necessary. The first and fifth colophons in the Freer Jami (folios 46a and 181a) are dated Dhu'l-Hijja 963/October 1556, the same year that Ibrahim Mirza took up the position of governor of the northeastern Iranian town of Mashhad. In both colophons the calligraphers—Malik al-Daylami and Shah-Mahmud al-Nishapuri, respectively—state that they completed their work in

Mashhad, and Shah-Mahmud specifies that his section of the *Haft Awrang* was completed "birasm-i kitab-khana." Thus, the *kitab-khana* of Sultan Ibrahim Mirza was already in operation by 963/1556, when, it might be added, the prince was about seventeen years old, and recently betrothed to be married, beside being a newly-appointed governor.[14] None of this was unusual at the time, and Ibrahim Mirza was by no means the first, nor last, member of his family whose name is linked with a *kitab-khana* or with a masterpiece of Iranian book art.[15] Shah Isma'il, the founder of the Safavid dynasty and Ibrahim Mirza's grandfather, had a *kitab-khana*, as did his oldest son and successor, Shah Tahmasp.[16] Ibrahim Mirza's father, Bahram Mirza, and uncle, Sam Mirza, also are associated with *kitab-khana*s. Later Safavid rulers with *kitab-khana*s include Isma'il II (ruled 1576–1578), Ibrahim Mirza's first cousin (and murderer), and Abbas (1588–1629), his first cousin once removed.[17]

Patronage of the arts of the book was not an exclusive prerogative of the Safavid family, nor did the kings and princes of this dynasty have a monopoly on the *kitab-khana* during the sixteenth and seventeenth centuries. Ismi-khana Shamlu of the Shaykhavand dynasty, a side branch of the Safavids in Ardabil, had a *kitab-khana*, as did at least two rulers of the rival Shaybanid dynasty that controlled Transoxiana in the sixteenth century.[18]

The evidence for the *kitab-khana* of Isma'il I, his progeny, successors, and rivals comes from a variety of sources, of which colophons, paintings, and illuminations inscribed "birasm-i kitab-khana" constitute a small but critical part.[19] The most extensive historical information for the *kitab-khana* from the early Safavid period through the first quarter of the seventeenth century appears in the *Gulistan-i hunar*, or Garden of Art, a biographical treatise written about 1596 by Qazi Ahmad, and in the *Tarikh-i alam-ara-yi Abbasi*, Iskandar Beg Munshi's chronicle of the reign of Shah Abbas.[20] These texts are supplemented by several royal decrees, edicts, and other documents pertaining to specific *kitab-khana*s

8. *Haft Awrang* of Jami, folio 132a, manuscript dated 963–972/1556–1565; opaque watercolor, ink, and gold on paper
Freer Gallery of Art, Smithsonian Institution, Washington (46.12)

including the well-known album preface by Dust-Muhammad.[21] In addition, an important—and largely underutilized—manual of Safavid administration, the *Tadhkirat al-Muluk*, which dates from the very end of the dynasty, documents earlier practices and procedures.[22] Finally, we have the memoirs and accounts of several Europeans who traveled in Iran, primarily on diplomatic missions and business ventures, during the seventeenth century.[23] Unfortunately, no single source contains an actual description of a *kitab-khana* as workshop, and any attempt to define this aspect of the *kitab-khana* from the available records involves the compilation of disparate, and sometimes inconsistent, bits of information. In addition, the type of information varies widely: in general, the sources for the first half of the Safavid period (that is, the early sixteenth through the first quarter of the seventeenth century) focus on individuals (patrons and artists), whereas the later sources emphasize Safavid governmental bureaucracy.

One point that all the sources, artistic and documentary, confirm is that in sixteenth-century Iran a *kitab-khana* belonged not to an artist, as was normally the case in Renaissance Italy, for example, but to a patron, who might be a king, a prince, or even a provincial noble. It is clear from the primary sources that a *kitab-khana* manifested and enhanced its sponsor's personal status and prestige. The sources further confirm that the *kitab-khana* was part of its patron's (usually, but not always, the ruler's) own household property, or *khassa*, as opposed to the official bureaucracy, the *diwan*, of a dynasty or court.[24] It was, in other words, a private concern. While there was certainly a dynastic tradition, perhaps even an expectation, among the Safavids (as there had been among the Timurids) of collecting and commissioning manuscripts, there was no such thing as a dynastic *kitab-khana* which functioned as an autonomous enterprise throughout the Safavid period.[25] That is to say, there seems to be no evidence that a *kitab-khana* as library and collection passed automatically and intact from father to son or from ruler to heir. And, although there could be some overlap in the personnel of the *kitab-khana* as workshop, the view that a princely patron inherited a staff of *kitab-khana* artists along with a kingdom has yet to be proven conclusively.[26] As a general rule, the sponsorship of a *kitab-khana* seems to have resulted from personal initiative, and the actual establishment of a *kitab-khana* was linked to an individual commission for a deluxe manuscript. A royal or noble patron desiring a volume of a particular text did not shop around for a workshop of proven reputation; he set up

his own *kitab-khana*. Completely dependent on an individual patron for its very existence, a *kitab-khana* likewise could be disbanded at its patron's will, as occurred around 1544–1545 when Shah Tahmasp lost interest in the arts of the book and allowed the artists working for his *kitab-khana* to leave the court and practice their art elsewhere, including in another country.[27]

Although private, the *kitab-khana* was not singular. From the detailed data in the *Tadhkirat al-Muluk* and several European accounts, we know that the *kitab-khana* in the later Safavid period was part of a series of *kar-khana*s, or workshops, over thirty in all, belonging to the royal household (*buyutat-i saltanati*).[28] A number of these *kar-khana*s served domestic functions of their owner's household, such as the kitchen (*ashpaz-khana*) and the barber shop (*salmani-khana*). Others, such as the goldsmiths' workshop (*zargar-khana*), produced luxury items.[29] The works of the *kitab-khana* may have fallen into the latter category. Another such *kar-khana* was the *naqqash-khana*, or painting studio, suggesting that painting (including presumably manuscript illustration) was an equal operation separate from all other aspects of manuscript production.[30]

The same sources that provide the general setting for the *kitab-khana* as part of a system of *kar-khana*s also delineate certain details of its organization and staff.[31] Each individual *kar-khana* was run by a *sahib jam'* (meaning roughly workshop master) and a *mushrif* (overseer), who were responsible for "estimating its needs, obtaining the necessary supplies of raw materials and fixing its internal arrangements."[32] These two officials reported to the *nazir-i buyutat*, the overall superintendent of the workshops. In addition, the workshop staff included a *bashi*, or chief, and *ustadan*, or master craftsmen, who directed the workshop's technical affairs and received their raw materials from the *mushrif*. While the recorded duties of each member of the workshop seem rather vague, a picture emerges of a staff hierarchy as well as of a distinction between what today might be called management (*sahib jam'* and *mushrif*) and labor (the *bashi* and *ustadan*).

More specific information about the duties of the *kitab-khana* managers can be gleaned from a pair of sixteenth-century decrees. The first, dating from the early 1520s, announces the appointment of the celebrated artist Bihzad as head of the royal *kitab-khana* at Tabriz.[33] It commands that "the rarity of the age, model of depictors, example of limners [i.e., illuminators], Master Kamal al-Din Bihzad . . . be appointed herewith to the post of superintendent and chief of the men of the royal *kitab-khana*—the scribes, painters, limners, rulers, fleckers, gold-leaf makers, and lapis lazuli washers, and the others who are attached to the aforesaid activities."[34] Next, all the court officers, including agents of administrative and fiscal affairs and the *kitab-khana* personnel in particular, are enjoined to recognize Bihzad as superintendent;[35] to perform all the tasks of the *kitab-khana* at his direction; to consider as official anything he signs or seals; and to follow everything he says concerning the *kitab-khana* activities and organization. The decree concludes with a final injunction: "And let them consider any and all that pertains to the aforesaid affairs, especially his affairs."[36] This is particularly interesting: just as a *kitab-khana* was the private property of a patron, so its affairs could be the personal business of the director. The second decree, dating some fifty years later (1575), concerns a similar appointment of one Hasan Muzahhib, that is, Hasan the illuminator, as director of the assembly of illuminators, scribes, bookbinders, painters, gold-leaf makers, and paper sellers of the "abode of the sultanate of Tabriz."[37] Although the term *kitab-khana* is not used in this decree (and in fact the *jama'at* or "assembly" here may refer to a bazaar guild),[38] the types of supervisory duties assigned Hasan Muzahhib were comparable to those borne by Bihzad. These included educating and training the staff and dismissing anyone who showed any impropriety.[39] Beside assigning duties, these decrees confirm that, again at least in the sixteenth century, the head of a *kitab-khana* was an artist and was appointed directly by the *kitab-khana* sponsor, who in the case of Bihzad and Hasan Muzahhib happened to be the reigning monarch.[40]

These two decrees are also useful as confirmation of the types of artists affiliated with the *kitab-khana*: *katiban* (calligraphers or scribes), *naqqashan* (painters), *muzahhiban* (limners or illuminators), *jadwal-kishan* (line drawers or rulers), *hall-karan* (gold-fleckers), and *sahhafan* (binders), along with others who prepared materials, including *zarkuban* (gold-leaf makers) and *lajvardi-shuyan* (lapis lazuli washers). Like the *kitab-khana* directors, these artists may also have received their appointments from the sponsor. According to the French jeweler Jean Chardin, who spent the years 1665–1669 and 1671–1677 in Iran, an artist or artisan of that period who wished to join a *kar-khana* would go first to the *sahib jam'* of the workshop of his craft with a sample of work in hand (usually something rather special) and a request. If the chief approved, the artisan was taken to the superintendent of all the workshops. On gaining the superintendent's approval, the candidate was brought before the king; if the king approved, he then fixed the artisan's wages and sustenance.[41] Once again the patron seems to have been directly involved in the employment process.[42]

Not all candidates were successful in their application for entrée into a *kar-khana* during the later Safavid period. For those who were, the conditions and terms of employment appear to have been quite favorable. First, *kar-khana* artists constituted a privileged class and had higher status than artists belonging to bazaar guilds.[43] Second, members of the *kar-khana* staff held lifelong employment, and each artisan had a letter of patent impressed with the king's seal, giving the amount of his salary (including food and "keep"); this amount was paid annually after a review (*san*) and was raised every three years.[44] In addition members of the *kar-khana* staff received free "social welfare" plus bonuses and presents for individual pieces of work or masterpieces.[45]

The privileges and benefits reported by Chardin for *kar-khana* artists in general of the seventeenth century accord with what we know about their sixteenth century *kitab-khana* counterparts in particular, and we have plenty of evidence for early Safavid artists receiving grants of land and pensions in addition to salary.[46] Indeed the status and stature that a *kitab-khana* artist could achieve seem often to have surpassed that of "mere" employee; and there are instances in the biographical and historical sources of artists described in such terms as "courtier" (*mulazim*) and "intimate" (*musahib*)—indicating a personal, as well as professional, relationship to a patron.[47] Occasionally artists were even allowed to sign themselves "al-Shahi," meaning of the king, another indication of high favor at a royal *kitab-khana*.[48] The evidence actually suggests, however, that artists with a fixed salary or long-term appointment with a single *kitab-khana* were in the minority, at least in the early Safavid period. Artists could, and did, move from one *kitab-khana* to another, and could even contribute to a project "birasm-i kitab-khana" without being on that particular *kitab-khana* staff.

The career of Shah-Mahmud al-Nishapuri—one of the Freer Jami calligraphers—is instructive in this regard. For about a twenty-year period, from roughly 1527 until the mid-1540s (or as Qazi Ahmad puts it, "all through the days of his progress and youth, of his growth and development"), Shah-Mahmud was a highly-regarded member of the *kitab-khana* of Shah Tahmasp, and was one of those permitted to add "al-Shahi" to his signature.[49] He also worked for the *kitab-khana* of Bahram Mirza.[50] Sometime after 1546, Shah-Mahmud left Tabriz, first for Ardabil and by the summer of 1551 for Mashhad, where, according to the *Gulistan-i hunar*, he received no patronage of any kind.[51] That is to say, during his later years Shah-Mahmud reportedly was not affiliated with a *kitab-khana*. Yet the calligrapher himself tells us that at the beginning of Dhu'l-Hijja 963/early October 1556 he completed the transcription of one of the seven poems of the *Haft Awrang* "by order of the *kitab-khana* of his highness . . . Ibrahim Mirza."[52] This suggests that artists could undertake

work for a *kitab-khana* without actually being on the *kitab-khana* staff. In other words, the personnel of a *kitab-khana* might include both "salaried" staff members and adjunct employees with one-time or short-term contracts. Rustam-Ali was another calligrapher of Shah-Mahmud's generation who moved from one *kitab-khana* to another: first he was affiliated with the *kitab-khana* of Bahram Mirza, then with that of Shah Tahmasp (where, like Shah-Mahmud, he signed himself Rustam-Ali Shahi), and finally with that of Sultan Ibrahim Mirza for which he copied one poem of the *Haft Awrang* in August 1556.[53] There are many other examples of Safavid artists who made similar "career shifts."

Two other aspects of workshop life as reported in the *Tadhkirat al-Muluk* deserve mention here, especially since they can be confirmed to an extent by earlier sources. First, between royal orders, *kar-khana* artists worked for themselves. This is interesting because it suggests that artists had autonomy even when under contract and perhaps were free to work for various patrons simultaneously. Second, although some artisans had to follow the court in its travels, they could easily obtain permission for home leave after six or twelve months.[54] Again this suggests a certain freedom of personal choice and professional movement. It also implies that the *kitab-khana* roster was probably rather fluid, and that the conditions of employment there were fairly flexible—which is exactly what the case of Shah-Mahmud al-Nishapuri, for instance, demonstrates.

From time to time, the question arises whether the *kitab-khana* as workshop ever occupied permanent quarters.[55] Chevalier Chardin notes with great precision how he passed along an *allée* at the palace of Isfahan and reached, at the top of a flight of stairs, several large *corps de logis* on all sides. These he identifies as the king's *magasins* or *galeries*, called *kar-khana*. The *kar-khana* on the right was the *kitab-khana*, a small room with deep niches along the lower walls where books were laid flat on top of each other according to size. Although he also mentions that the *kitab-khana* contained bookbinders and a librarian named Mirza Muqim, it seems clear that this space was primarily used for the deposit of books.[56] Writing in 1684, the German doctor Engelbert Kaempfer describes the *kitab-khana* similarly as part of the storage, rather than the workshop, facilities of the palace, remarking that nine to ten thousand volumes were kept there on boards (shelves) and in chests.[57]

Although these observations pertain primarily to the *kitab-khana* as library, they do not preclude the possibility that artists were at work somewhere on the *kar-khana* premises. Certainly there had to be a gathering place for all those artists whom Bihzad was said to have supervised at an early Safavid *kitab-khana*, and indeed, a document dated 964/1557 refers to Tahmasp's *kitab-khana* as a "place of assembly for all artists."[58] Yet such a remark is apt to have been more rhetorical than real, a way to flatter the monarch by suggesting that he had all the artists of the realm in his service—which certainly was not the case in 1557 when, in fact, several former members of Tahmasp's *kitab-khana* were working on a project for the *kitab-khana* of his nephew and son-in-law Sultan Ibrahim Mirza.

At this point it is useful to return to the young Safavid prince and the manuscript that serves as the case study of the Safavid *kitab-khana*, and particularly to information given in the colophons which is pertinent to the actual locus of a *kitab-khana*. As indicated at the outset, the text of this celebrated volume of the *Haft Awrang* was copied by five calligraphers who signed the eight colophons with the dates and places they completed their work. While the colophon dates range from 963–972/1556–1565, the colophons themselves are not arranged in chronological order—an apparent historical disjunction which can be explained by the manuscript's format and collation.[59]

Far more intriguing is the fact that three sections of the *Haft Awrang* were transcribed in Mashhad (the city in northeastern Iran where Ibrahim Mirza was governor), another part in Qazvin (the Safavid capital in northwestern Iran), and yet another in Herat (now in Afghanistan). One of the five calligra-

phers, Malik al-Daylami, who was responsible for the transcription of the *Silsilat al-dhahab*, a *Haft Awrang* poem in three parts, even states quite specifically that he completed the third part in the city of Qazvin, "after the initiation and writing of the greatest part of it [was done] in the illuminated, holy, sublime, sanctified, purified Mashhad."[60] Such a shift in venue might be the result of a move on the part of Sultan Ibrahim Mirza, in line with what the *Tadhkirat al-Muluk* says about some *kar-khana* artists having to follow the court in its travels. This, indeed, may explain why Muhibb-Ali, the *kitab-dar*, completed the transcription of one *Haft Awrang* poem in Mashhad in 964/1557 and another in 972/1565 in Herat,[61] since in that latter year his patron, Sultan Ibrahim Mirza, left Mashhad in order to take part in a military expedition aimed at quelling the seditious governor of Herat. According to the historical chronicles, the Safavid forces spent the winter in Herat after recapturing the city in the name of Shah Tahmasp.[62] Assuming that Ibrahim Mirza remained there with his fellow emirs, then it is likely that his retinue, including apparently Muhibb-Ali, would have stayed on as well.[63]

In the case of Malik al-Daylami we know that by 966/1559 he was recalled to the capital of Qazvin by Shah Tahmasp in order to provide inscriptions for a building being constructed in the palace complex.[64] At that time Sultan Ibrahim Mirza was still in Mashhad. The hundreds of miles then separating Malik al-Daylami and Ibrahim Mirza indicate that it was possible for an artist to continue working on a project commissioned by the *kitab-khana* (in this case, "birasm-i bayt al-kutub") of a patron residing in a distant part of the country.

The Freer Jami has been referred to elsewhere as a mail-order manuscript, partly on the strength of the physical evidence and partly on the strength of its internal documentation. It also has been suggested that the volume's text folios and perhaps even its illustrations could have been prepared virtually anywhere and sent to a central location for illumination and collation.[65] Presumably this

9. *Naqsh-i badi'* of Muhammad Ghazzali, folio 23b, manuscript dated Muharram 982/April–May 1574; opaque watercolor, ink, and gold on paper
Topkapi Saray Museum, Istanbul (R. 1038)

10. *Naqsh-i badi'* of Muhammad Ghazzali, folio 38a, manuscript dated Muharram 982/April–May 1574; opaque watercolor, ink, and gold on paper
Topkapi Saray Museum, Istanbul (R. 1038)

assembly point would have been Sultan Ibrahim Mirza's *kitab-khana*, where perhaps Muhibb-Ali, the *kitab-dar*, was the sole tenured appointee or employee during the many years required to prepare the *Haft Awrang*.[66] Only in 973/1565, at the very earliest, did the *kitab-khana* have to gear up to the level of production implied by Qazi Ahmad when he stated about Ibrahim Mirza that: "No sultan or khaqan possessed a more flourishing *kitab-khana* than that powerful prince."[67]

The bureaucratic system of *kar-khana*s described in later sources notwithstanding, almost everything that can be learned, deduced, or inferred about the *kitab-khana* as workshop suggests that it operated according to the circumstances, resources, and whims of individual patrons. A patron's resources would include, of course, monetary assets, and it may be precisely Ibrahim Mirza's lack thereof that explains why the transcription of the Freer Jami took nine years: the prince simply may not have been able to pay the

five calligraphers on a regular or timely basis. The case of Ibrahim Mirza also epitomizes the way a sponsor's political or social status could determine the scale of *kitab-khana* operations and his ability to assemble, maintain, and retain a *kitab-khana* staff. In the mid-1560s the prince was removed from his post as governor of Mashhad and sent in disgrace to the small town of Sabzivar, some one hundred and seventy kilometers west of Mashhad.[68] There he spent the next six to eight years isolated from provincial affairs and supported only by a modest allowance. That is not to say that he was totally penurious, nor that he had to abandon completely his bibliophilic and artistic interests. In fact, toward the end of this period of exile he commissioned an illustrated volume of a mystical love poem called the *Naqsh-i badi'* by the poet Muhammad Ghazzali Mashhadi (figs. 9, 10).[69] This manuscript was copied in Muharram 982/April–May 1574 "by order of the *kitab-khana* of his highness

Sultan Ibrahim Mirza in the city of Sabzivar by the poor [servant] Sultan-Muhammad Khandan."[70] Although perfectly respectable (indeed, its calligraphy is quite fine), the prince's *Naqsh-i badi'* cannot be compared, in terms of technical quality and artistic originality, with his *Haft Awrang*. The modest size of the codex and the simplicity of its illumination and even illustration certainly suggest that this work did not result from the kind of complex procedures required to produce the Freer Jami; furthermore none of the same artists seem to have been involved.[71] Clearly at this time the *kitab-khana* of Sultan Ibrahim Mirza had to settle for less than the best.

More than any other piece of evidence, the *Naqsh-i badi'* demonstrates the extent that the operations of a *kitab-khana* depended on the fortunes of its sponsor. Such a manuscript also makes the *kitab-khana* seem all the more ephemeral as a locus of artistic manufacture and belies the concept, which the textual sources tend to promote, of a *kitab-khana* as some kind of regular and regulated institution with a large, permanent staff. Certainly it would not be appropriate to speak of Sultan Ibrahim Mirza's *kitab-khana* as a "bibliophile academy," as it has sometimes been defined.[72] And while the manuscripts commissioned by patrons such as Shah Tahmasp may have been undertaken for and at continuously operational ateliers or studios, even their *kitab-khana* calligraphers, illuminators, painters, and binders were not necessarily working there at the same time, or even working in the same place. Although the critical phrase "birasm-i kitab-khana" may have set into motion an artistic process that culminated in a great masterpiece, the *kitab-khana* itself may have functioned more like a decentralized cottage industry than a unified atelier.

NOTES

I am grateful to Massumeh Farhad for invaluable assistance in the preparation of this article. The research and writing was completed in the fall of 1989 with subsequent additions to the notes.

1. Ali Akbar Dihkhuda, *Lughat-nama* (Tehran, 1336/1958), letter *k*, fasc. 1, s.v. "Kitab-khana" and "Kutub-khana." *Encyclopedia of Islam*, 1st ed. (Leiden and London, 1913–1938), s.v. "kitab-khana"; 2d ed. (Leiden and London, 1960–   ), s.v. "maktaba." These entries deal exclusively with the history of private and public libraries in the Islamic world. F. Steingass, *A Comprehensive Persian-English Dictionary* (New Delhi, 1973), s.v. "kitab-khana." Various synonyms for *kitab-khana* (and its plural *kutub-khana*) have been used in Persian, including *bayt al-kutub, dar al-kutub, khazanat al-kutub* and *makhzan al-kutub*; these phrases are of Arabic origin and also are translated as library. See Dihkhuda 1336/1958, letter *kh*, fasc. 6, s.v. "Khazana"; Josef von Karabacek, "Zur orientalischen Alterumskunde. IV—Muhammadanische Kunststudien," *Sitzungsberichte der philosophisch-historischen Klasse der K. Akademie der Wissenschaften* 172 (1912), 57–58; Sheila S. Blair, "Ilkhanid Architecture and Society: An Analysis of the Endowment Deed of the Rab'-i Rashidi," *Iran* 22 (1984), 76, 84–85. Wheeler M. Thackston, *A Century of Princes: Sources on Timurid History and Art* (Cambridge, 1989), 382; David James, *Qur'ans of the Mamluks* (New York, 1988), 260; C. Adle, "Entre Timurides, Mogoles et Safavides: Notes sur un *Châhnâmé* de l'Atelier-Bibliothèque Royal d'Ologh Beg II à Caboul," in *Art Islamique et Orientalisme*, ed. Étude Daussy-Ricqlès [sale cat., Drouot-Richelieu, 15 June 1990] (Paris, 1990), 138; C. Adle, "Autopsia, In Absentia: Sur la Date de l'Introduction et de la Constitution de l'Album de Bahram Mirza par Dust-Muhammad en 951/1544," *Studia Iranica* 19 (1990), 235–236. Also see below, note 19.

2. The acquisition of books for personal use began early in the Islamic world. A tenth-century vizier named Sahib Isma'il ibn Abbad had a library of 117,000 books in the town of Rayy. When offered a ministerial appointment in Bukhara, he is reported to have excused himself, saying: "I cannot live without books, and wherever I am I must have my library with me. It would take at least four hundred camels to transport my books, and I cannot get hold of so many." The vizier's collection later was endowed as what amounted to the public library of Rayy. Rukh al-Din Humayun-Farrukh, *Kitab va Kitab-khana-yi Shahanshahi-yi Iran*, 2 vols. (Tehran, 1347/1968), 2:6; Jan Rypka, *History of Iranian Literature* (Dordrecht, 1968), 147.

3. The earliest recorded use of the term seems to be in the celebrated *arzadasht*, a status report of a Timurid *kitab-khana* describing the work-in-progress of specific painters, calligraphers, illuminators, binders, and other artists (Istanbul, Topkapi Seray Library, H. 2153, folio 98a). The document begins: "Petition from the most humble servants of the regal library. . . ." The word itself is given as

kutub-khana. The author of the report, which probably dates to the 1420s, is believed to be Ja'far Tabrizi, head of the *kitab-khana* of prince Baysunghur Mirza. M. Kemal Özergin, "Temürlü sanatina ait eski bir belge: Tebrizli Ca'fer'in bir arzi," *Sanat Tarihi Yilligi* 6 (1976), 471–518. Recently the document has been translated into English by Thackston 1989, 323–327 (with commentary). It is also reproduced, discussed, and translated by Thomas W. Lentz and Glenn D. Lowry, *Timur and the Princely Vision: Persian Art and Culture in the Fifteenth Century* [exh. cat., Arthur M. Sackler Gallery and Los Angeles County Museum of Art] (Washington and Los Angeles, 1989), 159, 364–365 (here the Persian word for atelier is transliterated as *kitab-khana*), fig. 51. In a review of the Timurid exhibition and catalogue ("Washington and Los Angeles: Timurid Art," *Burlington Magazine* 131 [July 1989], 509), J. Michael Rogers states that the term *kitab-khana* was not used in contemporary (i.e., fifteenth-century) sources. Technically this is correct since, as mentioned above, the *arzadasht* employs the form *kutub-khana*, also cited by Rogers. *Kutub-khana* also was used by the calligrapher Ahmad ibn Abdullah al-Hijazi in a petition for employment written sometime after 854/1441–1442. See Thackston 1989, 330–332. It should be noted that the Timurid historian Mirkhwand (d. 903/1498) used *kitab-khana* with reference to the painter Mirak; see Assadullah Souren Melikian-Chirvani, "Khwāje Mirāk Naqqāsh," *Journal Asiatique* 276 (1988), 99 (where the term is rendered in French and in quotation marks as "maison de l'ecrit"). Dihkhuda 1958, (letter *k*, fasc. 1) does not note any difference in the use or meaning of *kitab-khana* and *kutub-khana*. An extensive disquisition on the orthography and etymology of *kitab-khana/kutub-khana* appears in Adle, "Entre Timurides," 1990, 138 and, "Autopsia," 1990, 235–236. It is likely that this discussion will add further fuel to the linguistic debate.

4. For a recent general discussion, see J. Michael Rogers, trans. and ed., *The Topkapi Seray Museum: The Albums and Illustrated Manuscripts* (London, 1986), chap. 2.

5. For the Il-Khanid period, see Blair 1984; James 1988, 127–131. Priscilla Soucek presented an important paper, "Manuscript Production at the Rab'-i Rashidi: A Documentary Study," at a colloquium on *The Islamic World after the Mongol Conquest* at Saint Anthony's College, Oxford, in 1980. Unfortunately, the proceedings of this conference have never been published. I am grateful to the author for sharing her unpublished study with me.

6. For the Timurid period, see: Lentz and Lowry 1989, chap. 3; Thomas W. Lentz, "Painting at Herat under Baysunghur ibn Shahrukh" (Ph.D. diss., Harvard University, 1969), 16–17, 23, 78, 122, 153, 238–239, 265–266, 272, 294–295, 481–488 (the *arzadasht*).

7. For the Safavid period, see Stuart Cary Welch, *A King's Book of Kings: The Shah-Nameh of Shah Tahmasp* (New York, 1972), 18–24; Stuart Cary Welch, *Persian Painting: Five Royal Manuscripts of*

the Sixteenth Century (New York, 1976), 11–27; Anthony Welch, "Painting and Patronage under Shah 'Abbas I," *Iranian Studies* 7: *Studies on Isfahan* 2 (summer-autumn 1974), 458–507; Anthony Welch, *Artists for the Shah: Late Sixteenth-Century Painting at the Imperial Court of Iran* (New Haven and London, 1976), esp. chap. 5; Stuart Cary Welch, *Wonders of the Age: Masterpieces of Early Safavid Painting, 1501–1576* (Cambridge, Mass., 1979), 14–15; Martin Dickson and Stuart Cary Welch, *The Houghton Shahnameh*, 2 vols. (Cambridge, Mass. and London, 1981), 1:8A–9B (general discussion of a royal atelier), 24A, 53A–B, 96A, 125B, 130A, 166B, 167A, 168A; Oleg F. Akimushkin, "O pridvornoi kitabkhane Sefevida Takhmasba I u Tabrize," *Srednevekovy Vostok. Istoriya, Kul'tura, Istochnikovedeniye* (Moscow, 1981), 5–20; Marianna Shreve Simpson, "The Production and Patronage of the *Haft Aurang* by Jami in the Freer Gallery of Art," *Ars Orientalis* 13 (1982), 97–99. Much of this recent work builds on two seminal studies by Ivan Stchoukine (*Les peintures des manuscrits safavis de 1502 à 1587* [Paris, 1959] and *Les peintures des manuscrits de Shah 'Abbas I à la fin des Safavis* [Paris, 1964]).

For Ottoman Turkey, when *nakkaşhane* was the functional equivalent to the Persian *kitab-khana*, see Esin Atil, ed., *Turkish Art* (Washington and New York, 1980), 140–141; Alan W. Fisher and Carol Garrett Fisher, "A Note on the Location of the Royal Ottoman Painting Ateliers," *Muqarnas* 3 (1985), 118–120; J. Michael Rogers and Rachel M. Ward, *Süleyman the Magnificent* (London, 1988), 120–124; Filiz Cagman, "Saray Nakkashanesinin Yeri Üzerine Düsünceler," in *Sanat Tarihinde Dogudan Batiya. Unsal Yucel Anisina Sempozyum Bildirileri. Sandoz Kültür Yayinlari* 11 (1989), 35–46; Esin Atil, *Süleymanname: The Illustrated History of Süleyman the Magnificent* (Washington and New York, 1986), 35–41; Esin Atil, *The Age of Sultan Süleyman the Magnificent* (Washington and New York, 1987), 29–36.

For Mughal India, see Milo Cleveland Beach, *The Imperial Image: Paintings for the Mughal Court* (Washington, 1981), 9–11; Michael Brand and Glenn D. Lowry, *Akbar's India: Art from the Mughal City of Victory* (New York, 1986), chaps. 3, 4, 5.

8. The manuscript figures in many general books about Islamic and Persianate painting, and in virtually all studies of the arts of the Safavid period. See, most recently, Simpson 1982, 93–119. This article is preliminary to a more detailed monograph, currently in preparation by the author; note 1 lists the principal scholarly references.

9. This is the beginning of the colophon on folio 181a. The seeming hyperbole is totally consistent with protocols commonly used for Iranian royalty and nobility, including members of the Safavid dynasty. Translations of all the Freer Jami colophons appear in Simpson 1982, 106; see also figs. 1–8. Slight revisions of these translations will be found in the Freer Jami monograph in process. The colophon on folio 83b uses the phrase *bayt al-kutub* instead of *kitab-khana*.

10. These phrases are the equivalent (in reverse, as it were) of the formulations of royal protocol and are not necessarily to be taken literally. For example, the calligraphers who transcribed the Freer Jami were not servants in the modern sense of the word; however, artisans were sometimes described in contemporary documents as *ghulam-i khassa*, or slave of the royal household. (See below, note 40, for a reference to one such "slave.")

11. When I first published the colophons and other inscriptions in the Freer Jami, *kitab-khana* was translated as library and *kitab-dar* as librarian. I now feel less confident about these translations, not for linguistic considerations but for their art-historical implications, and for the time prefer to leave *kitab-khana* and *kitab-dar* in the original Persian. The role of the *kitab-dar* will be discussed further below.

12. As evidenced in Simpson 1982, 106.

13. It should be noted, in the context of the problems posed here, that Adle ("Autopsia," 1990, 237) has questioned that "birasm-i kitab-khana" means the equivalent of "by order of the library." In addition, he takes issue with the assumptions that the owner of a manuscript with a *kitab-khana* inscription was automatically its patron, and that the *kitab-khana* specified in the inscription actually executed the manuscript. Adle cogently raises the distinction between ownership and patronage. It is easy to imagine, for instance, a rosette or *shamsa* inscribed "birasm-i kitab-khana" being added as an *ex-libris* at the front of a manuscript anytime after it had passed from an artistic atelier into someone's library. On the other hand, it could be argued that a "birasm-i kitab-khana" inscription carries greater "authority" as a document of commission when it is integral to a manuscript's decorative or pictorial program; that is, when it appears in a frontispiece, heading, text illustration, or colophon. In such instances (see note 19 below for a selected listing of sixteenth-century examples), "birasm-i kitab-khana" would seem to mean "by order of the library."

14. The chronology of this period of the prince's life is variously reported in the primary sources; the discrepancies and attempted clarification are presented in the author's forthcoming monograph on the Freer Jami (see note 8 above). This study also concerns the relationship between Ibrahim Mirza's commissioning of a deluxe manuscript and his new governmental responsibilities and marital status.

15. The Safavid tradition of patronage followed directly on, and was likely to have been directly inspired by, the rich legacy of princely patronage during the preceding Timurid dynasty. See Lentz and Lowry 1989, especially chapter 5.

16. Tahmasp was both Sultan Ibrahim Mirza's uncle and father-in-law (as of 963 or 964/1555 or 1557).

17. The artistic activities of the Safavids from Isma'il I through Isma'il II are outlined in Stchoukine 1959, 3–25. More detailed discussion is found in various publications by Stuart Cary Welch (see note 7 above), particularly Dickson and Welch 1981. For the later Safavids, see Stchoukine 1964 and Welch 1976.

18. For the Shamlus in general, see Barbara J. Schmitz, "Miniature Painting in Herat, 1570–1640" (Ph.D. diss., New York University, 1981), chap. 1; Riazul Islam, *The Shamlu Letters. A New Source of Iranian Diplomatic Correspondence* (Karachi, 1971). For Ismi-khan Shamlu, see Qazi Ahmad Qumi, *Gulistan-i Honar*, ed. Ahmad Suhayli-Khunsari (Tehran, 1359/1980), 124; Vladimir Minorsky, trans., *Calligraphers and Painters: A Treatise by Qazi Ahmad, Son of Mir Munshi* (Washington, 1959), 170.

For the Shaybanids, see Mukaddema Mukhtarovna Ashrafi-Aini, "The School of Bukhara to c. 1550," in Basil Gray, ed., *The Arts of the Book in Central Asia* (Boulder, Colo., 1979), 249–272; Dickson and Welch 1981, 1:241B, n. 25.

19. In addition to the *Haft Awrang* of Jami made for Sultan Ibrahim Mirza, sixteenth-century works bearing *kitab-khana* inscriptions include: the celebrated *Shahnama* made for Shah Tahmasp (formerly in the collection of Arthur B. Houghton and now sadly dispersed; the dedicatory rosette or *shamsa* is reproduced in S. C. Welch 1972, 78 and in Dickson and Welch 1981, 2:col. pl. 21, b/w pl. 4); the well-known album prepared by the artist Dust-Muhammad for Bahram Mirza (Topkapi Saray Library, Istanbul, H. 2154, the *shamsa* is inscribed "birasmi-i kitab-khana-yi shahryar Abu'l-Fath Bahram Mirza jam iqtidar," and reproduced in *Islamic Art* 1 [1981], fig. 1); a *Khamsa* of Amir Khusraw Dihlavi also made for Bahram Mirza (formerly in the Vever Collection and now in the Arthur M. Sackler Gallery, Washington, S86.0067–0068; all that survives is the double-page illuminated frontispiece with the same *kitab-khana* inscription as in the prince's album, reproduced in color in Glenn D. Lowry, *A Jeweler's Eye: Islamic Arts of the Book from the Vever Collection* [Washington, Seattle, and London, 1988] pl. 37); a *Sab'a Sayyara* of Nava'i dated 960/1553 and made for the Shaybanid ruler Abu'l-Fath Yar Muhammad Bahadur Khan, as per the "birasm-i kitab-khana" inscription on six of its illustrations (Bodleian Library, Oxford, MS Elliot 318; Basil W. Robinson, *A Descriptive Catalogue of the Persian Paintings in the Bodleian Library* [Oxford, 1958], cats. 972–982; reproduced in color in Alexandre Papadopoulo, *Islam and Muslim Art* [New York, 1979], pl. 55); a *Subhat al-abrar* of Jami illustrated for the Shaybanid ruler Abu'l-Ghazi Abdullah Bahadur Khan as per a "birasm-i kitab-khana" inscription on one of its paintings (al-Sabah Collection, Kuwait, LNS 16 MS; reproduced in color in Marilyn Jenkins, *Islamic Art in the Kuwait National Museum: the al-Sabah Collection* [London, 1983], 101); a *Tuhfat al-ahrar* of Jami made for the same patron in 971/1563–1564 (collection of Sadruddin Aga Khan, Geneva, MS 17; Anthony Welch, *A Collection of Islamic Art*, 4 vols. [Geneva, 1978], 4:63–65 and accompanying plates); a *Rawdat al-Muhibbin*, made for the same patron in 956/1549 as per "birasm-i kitab-khana" inscriptions on at least two of its illustrations (Salar Jung Museum, Hyderabad; M. S. Randhawa, "Rare Bukhara Manuscript: Raudat-ul-Muhibbin," *Arts and the Islamic World* 1 [Winter 1983–1984], 7–10 and cover). See also notes 50 and 70 below. It should be noted that comparable inscriptions in fifteenth-century manuscripts tend to

read "birasm-i khazana." There are several published references to such inscriptions, including, most recently, Lentz and Lowry 1989, cats. 138 and 139, figs. on 246 and 249. Earlier manuscripts are also apt to contain the "birasm-i khazana" formulation (or some variation thereof); see, for example, C. Rieu, *Supplement to the Catalogue of Persian Manuscripts in the British Museum* (London, 1895), cat. 392 (Or. 4392, dated 741/1340); James 1988, 239, cat. 46. Two extant manuscripts from the library of the Il-Khanid vizier Rashid al-Din (d. 1318) are stamped with a seal inscribed "mulk-i [or possibly vaqf-i] kitab-khana-yi Rashid." (See Francis Richard, "Muhr-i kitab-khana-yi Rashid ud-Din Fazl-ullah Hamadani?," *Ayande* 8 [1982], 343–346). Although this great bibliophile certainly commissioned manuscripts, including illustrated volumes, his seal may constitute a mark of ownership rather than actual patronage. It does represent, however, one of the earliest documented uses of the word *kitab-khana*. The shift from the term *khazana* in the fourteenth and fifteenth centuries to *kitab-khana* in the sixteenth remains to be investigated.

20. Qazi Ahmad 1359/1980; Minorsky 1959 (this translation is based on a redaction of the *Gulistan-i hunar* of c. 1601); Iskandar Bek Turkoman, *Tarikh-i alam-ara-yi Abbasi*, ed. Iradj Afshar, 2 vols. (Tehran, 1335/1956); Eskandar Beg Monshi, *History of Shah 'Abbas the Great*, trans. Roger M. Savory (Boulder, Colo., 1978).

21. M. Bayani, *Ahval va Asar Khushnivisan*, 3 vols. (Tehran, 1345–1348/1966–1969), 1:192–203; a new translation has been published by Thackston 1989, 335–350.

22. Vladimir Minorsky, trans. and expl., *Tadhkirat al-Muluk: A Manual of Safavid Administration* (London, 1943; repr., 1980). Minorsky based his translation on a manuscript in the British Museum (now British Library, Or. 9496). A table of contents for the Persian text precedes the English translation (37–39). The text itself is reproduced in facsimile, following the translation and commentary. This section is numbered separately; the printed page numbers appear on what would be the versos of the original manuscript. There seems to be a slight discrepancy between what one would expect to be the original foliation and the folio numbers given in the table of contents (e.g., the introduction begins on the verso of folio 1; this is cited in the table of contents as 1a or folio 1 recto).

23. Jean Chardin, *Voyages du Chevalier Chardin en Perse, et autres lieux de l'Orient*, 11 vols., ed. L. Langlès (Paris, 1811); Raphael Du Mans, *Estat de la Perse en 1660*, ed. C. Schefer (Paris, 1850; repr., 1969); E. Kaempfer, *Am Hofe des Persischen Grosskönigs (1684–1685)*, ed. W. Hinz (Leipzig, 1940).

24. Minorsky [1943]1980, 14, 29. Safavid administration was divided into a *khassa* branch, which was under the ruler's direct control and dealt with the administration of his property and household, and the *divan* or *mamalik* branch, in charge of the affairs of state and territory. Roger M. Savory, "The Safavid Administrative System," in *The Timurid and the Safavid Period*, vol. 6 of *The Cambridge History of*

Iran, ed. Peter Jackson and Laurence Lockhart (Cambridge, 1986), 351–353.

25. Thus the Safavid situation is in double contrast to that of seventeenth-century Japan, as discussed by John Rosenfield, where workshops were established and run by individual families of artists in a hereditary fashion and the Tosa family workshop served the imperial household (itself an unbroken lineage) over many generations. See John M. Rosenfield, "Japanese Studio Practice: The Tosa Family and the Imperial Painting Office in the Seventeenth Century" elsewhere in this volume.

26. S.C. Welch 1972, 22.

27. Dickson and Welch 1981, 1:45B; S.C. Welch 1972, 69–71; S.C. Welch 1976, 23; S.C. Welch 1979, 27; Akimushkin 1981, 13–14. A couple of Tahmasp's artists went from the Safavid court at Tabriz to that of the Mughals in India (via Afghanistan). For a succinct account, see Stuart Cary Welch, *Imperial Mughal Painting* (New York, 1978), 14–15; Jeremiah P. Losty, *The Art of the Book in India* (London, 1982), 75.

28. Minorsky [1943]1980, 29–30; Mehdi Keyvani, *Artisans and Guild Life in the Later Safavid Period: Contributions to the Social-Economic History of Persia* (Berlin, 1982), esp. 166–173. The relationship between commercial artisanal guilds and the private, princely *kar-khana* in Safavid Iran is a fascinating subject and worthy of much further consideration. (For guilds in general, see the invaluable article by Willem Floor in *Encyclopedia Iranica*, s.v. "Asnaf," with extensive references.) In the later Safavid period there definitely were independent bazaar guilds involved in book production, and the *kitab-khana*s sometimes obtained materials and sources from these commercial outfits.

It is also important to note that modern scholarship on the *kar-khana* has tended to create artificial order out of information scattered through various primary sources. Thus, for instance, Minorsky (135) and Keyvani (168–169), respectively, group the individual *kar-khana*s into eight and ten departments, each with a number of subdivisions. Keyvani (169) places the *kitab-khana* in a department of the library and the arts, and includes the bookbindery (*sahhafi*), paper factory (*kaghaz-sazi*), and book illumination (*tazhib-khana*) as subdivisions of the *kitab-khana*. His principal source is the narrative account of Engelbert Kaempfer, a German doctor in the service of the Dutch East India Company in the late seventeenth century, rendered by Keyvani in outline form. What Kaempfer (1940, 121) actually says is: "Dem Hofbuchwart sind die in der Hofbücherei tätigen Buchbinder, Linienzieher, Abschreiber, Vergolder usw. unterstellt." (For more on Keyvani's use of primary sources, see the trenchant review by Thomas M. Ricks in the *International Journal of Middle Eastern Studies* 18 [February 1986], 95–99.) The *Tadhkirat al-Muluk* presents information about the *kitab-khana* primarily in the form of payment records (Minorsky [1943]1980, 100, 135; Persian text 98 [possibly folio 98b] and 106 [possibly folio 106b]).

29. Minorsky [1943]1980, 29.

30. Kaempfer 1940, 122; Minorsky [1943]1980, 100, 135; Persian text 106 left (probably folio 107); Keyvani 1982, 169. The term *naqqash-khana* was used much less frequently than *kitab-khana* in Safavid Iran, at least in the sixteenth century: Dust-Muhammad lists all of Shah Tahmasp's calligraphers, portraitists, painters, and illuminators under the *kitab-khana* rubric (Thackson 1989, 347–349); and while Qazi Ahmad refers a dozen times to *kitab-khana*, only once does he mention a *naqqash-khana*. The differentiation between *kitab-khana* and *naqqash-khana* in the *Tadhkhirat al-Muluk* may signal a modification from the beginning to the end of the Safavid era in the nature of bookmaking activities, which in turn affected the function and structure of the *kitab-khana*. This is yet another of the many ancillary issues regarding the *kitab-khana* that requires further consideration and clarification.

31. Chardin, 1811, 7:329–334; Minorsky, [1943]1980, 48–49; Keyvani 1982, 167.

32. Keyvani 1982, 167.

33. This well-known decree appears in a collection of official and social correspondence compiled in the early 1520s by the historian Khwandamir and known as the *Nama-yi Nami*. See Mirza Muhammad Qazvini and L. Bouvat, "Deux documents inédits relatifs à Bihzad," *Revue du monde musulman* 26 (1914), 146–161; Thomas Arnold, *Painting in Islam* (Oxford, 1928; repr. New York, 1965), 150–151; Francesco Gabrieli, "Note miscellanée," *Rivista degli studi orientali* 16 (1936), 124–125; Muhammad Qazvini, *Bist Maqala-yi Qazvini*, 2 vols. (Tehran, 1332/1953–1954) 2:272–273; Lentz and Lowry 1989, 311–312. It is generally assumed, on the basis of the date of the decree (27 Jumada I 928/27 April 1522), that Bihzad's appointment was as the head of Shah Isma'il's *kitab-khana*. However, it has been recently pointed out that the same date appears on other documents with which the decree is grouped, so it may be misleading. Bihzad may not have arrived at the Safavid capital of Tabriz until after Isma'il's son Tahmasp became king in 930/1524. See Dickson and Welch 1981, 1:52B, 243A, nn. 6, 7; Lentz and Lowry 1989, 311–312.

34. The translation is by Wheeler Thackston, as published in Lentz and Lowry 1989, 311–312.

35. The word here is *kalantari*; given the context I equate the term with both *kitab-dar* and *bashi*. The gist of this part of the decree as given here is paraphrased from Thackston's translation in Lentz and Lowry 1989, 311–312.

36. Lentz and Lowry 1989, 312.

37. The original document, "Farman-i Shah Tahmasp dar bab-i Mulla Hasan Muzahhib," is in Tehran (Kitab-khana-yi Majlis-i Shaura-yi Milli, MS 606, 133–136); see Abdul Husain Nava'i, *Asnad va mukatabat-i tarikhi-yi Shah Tahmasp Safavi* (Tehran, 1350/1971), 24–26; Qazi Ahmad 1359/1980, 145–47 n. 1; Keyvani, 1982, 38.

38. The same term also appears in Ottoman registers (as *çema'at*) referring to the workshops of palace craftsmen. Rogers and Ward 1988, 124, n. 2. Here the word is translated as "group," and the authors comment that "the modern sense anachronistically suggests an organized society of craftsmen."

39. Nava'i 1350/1971, 25. Keyvani (1982, 81) would seem to have overinterpreted the rhetoric of the decree in stating that Hasan Muzahhib was to "take action against any artisan guilty of professional misconduct."

40. Toward the end of his life Shah Tahmasp appointed a calligrapher, named Mawlana Yusuf, a member of the royal household (*ghulam-i khassa*), as *kitab-dar*, and "committed to his charge the books contained in the royal library." Iskandar Beg 1335/1956, 174; Eskandar Beg 1976, 271; Arnold [1928]1965, 141. This position apparently was more akin to librarian (in the sense of a keeper of books) than workshop director.

41. Chardin 1811, 5:499–500; Keyvani 1982, 93.

42. It should be noted that here we are again in the realm of general administrative procedures, which may or may not correspond to actual practice.

43. Chardin 1811, 7:330–331; Minorsky, [1943]1980, 21; Keyvani 1982, 170–171. See also note 28 above.

44. Chardin 1811, 7:330–332; Minorsky [1943]1980, 21. The *Tadhkirat al-Muluk* (Minorsky [1943]1980, 100) specifies the salaries of the *sahib jam'*. Fifty *tuman* as the annual compensation for the *sahib jam'* of the *kitab-khana* may not be very meaningful today in absolute terms, but its value may be significant relative to the 30 *tuman* granted the *sahib jam'* of the *naqqash-khana*, and both *sahib jam'*s were paid on the high end of the scale, in the same range as the heads of other *kar-khana*s such as the treasury, the kitchen, and the stables. Compensation for the *sahib jam'* of the *kitab-khana* also included unspecified fees collected from other artisans, such as the block engraver (*basmachi*), gold-leaf maker (*zarkub*), paper maker (*kaghazgaran*), scissor maker (*migazgaran*), and gilder (*muzahhiban*). Minorsky has compiled salary figures for the *sahib jam'*s and *mushrif*s of all the *kar-khana* ([1943]1980, 135); these seem to be totals for all the personnel under the two principal *kar-khana* officers.

45. Chardin 1811, 2:110 and 7:332–333; Minorsky [1943]1980, 21.

46. For example, Qazi Ahmad 1359/1980, 123; Minorsky 1959, 170.

47. Qazi Ahmad 1359/1980, 139, 142; Minorsky 1959, 185, 188. Modern scholars also tend to employ the term "boon companion" (for example, Dickson and Welch 1981, 1:8B), possibly as an alternative for "intimate."

48. See below, notes 49, 53.

49. In his album's introduction (Topkapi Saray Library, Istanbul, H. 2154), Dust-Muhammad lists Shah-Mahmud first among "the scribes of the royal library who are renowned for their calligraphy." (See Thackston 1989, 347.) Manuscripts signed by Shah-Mahmud with the *nisba* al-Shahi include the celebrated *Khamsa* of Nizami dated 946–949/1539–1543

(British Library, London, Or. 2265; Norah M. Titley, *Miniatures from Persian Manuscripts* [London, 1977], cat. no. 315); and an unpublished Halnama (also called *Guy-u Chaugan*) of Arifi dated 953/1546 (Freer Gallery of Art, Washington, 35.18).

50. As evidenced by his signature in an undated poetic anthology made, according to the inscription in a heading on the opening text, "birasm-i kitab-khana Abu'l-Fath Bahram Mirza" (Topkapi Saray Library, Istanbul, R. 957). The manuscript is listed in Fehmi Edhem Karatay, *Topkapi Sarayi Müzesi Kutuphanesi. Farsça Yazmalar Katalogu* (Istanbul, 1961), cat. no. 898, without any mention of its patron. For more on this manuscript and other works made for the *kitab-khana* of Bahram Mirza, see Marianna Shreve Simpson, "A Manuscript Made for the Safavid Prince Bahram Mirza," *Burlington Magazine* 133 (June 1991): 376–384.

51. Qazi Ahmad 1359/1980, 87–88; Minorsky 1959, 135–136.

52. A more detailed discussion of Shah-Mahmud's career will appear in the forthcoming monograph on the Freer Jami.

53. Qazi Ahmad 1359–1980, 100; Minorsky 1959, 147; Thackston, 1989, 347. Rustam-Ali signed himself "al-Shahi" in several calligraphies incorporated into the Shah Tahmasp album in Istanbul (Istanbul University Library, F. 1422, folios 5a, 69a, 69b, 70b, and 77a). Further details of his life and oeuvre also will be given in the Freer Jami monograph.

54. Chardin 1811, 7:333; Minorsky, [1943]1980, 21.

55. This has been an issue of particular scholarly concern for the Ottoman *nakkaşhane*. See Atil 1986, 36; Fisher and Fisher, 1985; Cagman 1985.

56. Chardin 1811, 7:372–373. The exact meaning of some of Chardin's terms is not entirely certain. A *corps de logis* usually means a detached building; it is difficult to imagine several large buildings at the top of a staircase. *Magasin* and *galerie* are not necessarily synonymous; the former meaning storehouse or shop and the latter gallery. Chardin does gloss *kar-khana* (or as he transliterates it, "karkhone") as "*maison d'ouvrage*, parce qu'on y travaille pour le roi et pour sa maison."

57. Kaempfer 1940, 121. Wheeler Thackston has commented (1989, "Glossary," 382) that: "Although books may sometimes have been stored in the *kitabkhana*, they were generally kept in a *khizana* (treasury, storeroom)."

58. The document is a preface or introduction to an album mounted for Shah Tahmasp (Tehran, Kitab-khana-yi Majlis Shaura-yi Milli, MS 691, 393–403; this copy was transcribed in 1057/1647 by Muhammad Riza Wabd Hajji Tahmasp-Quli Beg). See Qutb al-Din Muhammad Yazdi, "Risala dar Tarikh-i khatt-u naqqashan," *Sukhan* 17 (1967), 666–676, especially 674 for the characterization of the shah's *kitab-khana*: "kitab-khana-yi humayun ka majma' majmu' hunarmandan rab' maskun ast."

59. This is discussed in Simpson 1982, 94–96, and further in "Codicology in the Service of Chronology: The Case of Some Safavid Manuscripts," *Les Manu-scrits du Moyens-Orient: Essais de codicologie et paléographie*, ed. F. Déroche (Istanbul and Paris, 1989), 133–139.

60. Folio 83b.

61. Folios 139a and 272a; Simpson 1982, 106.

62. Sharaf Khan Bidlisi, *Sharaf-nama*, ed. V. Velyamihov-Zernov, 2 vols. (Saint Petersburg, 1860–1862), 2:608–611; Eskander Beg 1978, 189–190. This information does not appear in the Persian edition of the *Tarikh-i alam-aray-i Abbasi*.

63. At least one Ottoman artist, Nasuh Matrakçi, seems to have traveled with Sultan Süleyman during military campaigns from the 1520s through the early 1560s. See Atil 1987, 84–86.

64. Qazi Ahmad 1359/1980, 94; Minorsky 1959, 142.

65. Simpson 1982, 97–98.

66. See Simpson 1982, 94–97 for various steps involved in the preparation of the manuscript and the length of time required to complete it.

67. Qazi Ahmad 1359/1980, 110; Minorsky 1959, 158.

68. Ibrahim Mirza's dismissal was apparently the result of his having disobeyed orders from the shah to assist in the rescue of his cousin, the crown prince, who had been trapped by enemy forces. This incident occurred in 974/1566–67. The most detailed account of this reversal in Ibrahim Mirza's fortunes appears in Afushta'i; Natanzi, *Naqavat al-Athar*, ed. Ishan Ishraqi (Tehran, 1328/1950), 48–51. A useful synopsis appears in Dickson and Welch 1981, 1:47B and 252A n.8.

69. Topkapi Saray Library, Istanbul, R. 1038; Karatay 1961, no. 787.

70. Colophon, folio 38a.

71. It is likely that most—if not all—of the artists (including scribes, illuminators, and painters) who worked on the Freer Jami left the employ of Sultan Ibrahim Mirza when he was "demoted" to Sabzivar. Only one artist, a painter named Shaykh-Muhammad, is recorded as having been in the service of Ibrahim Mirza in Sabzivar, and it is unlikely, on the basis of his known oeuvre, that he could have had a hand in the *Naqsh-i badi'*. See Marianna Shreve Simpson, "Shaykh-Muhammad," in *Persian Masters: Five Centuries of Painting*, ed. Sheila R. Canby (Bombay, 1990), 99–112.

72. Ernst J. Grube, *The World of Islam* (New York and Toronto [1966]), 143.

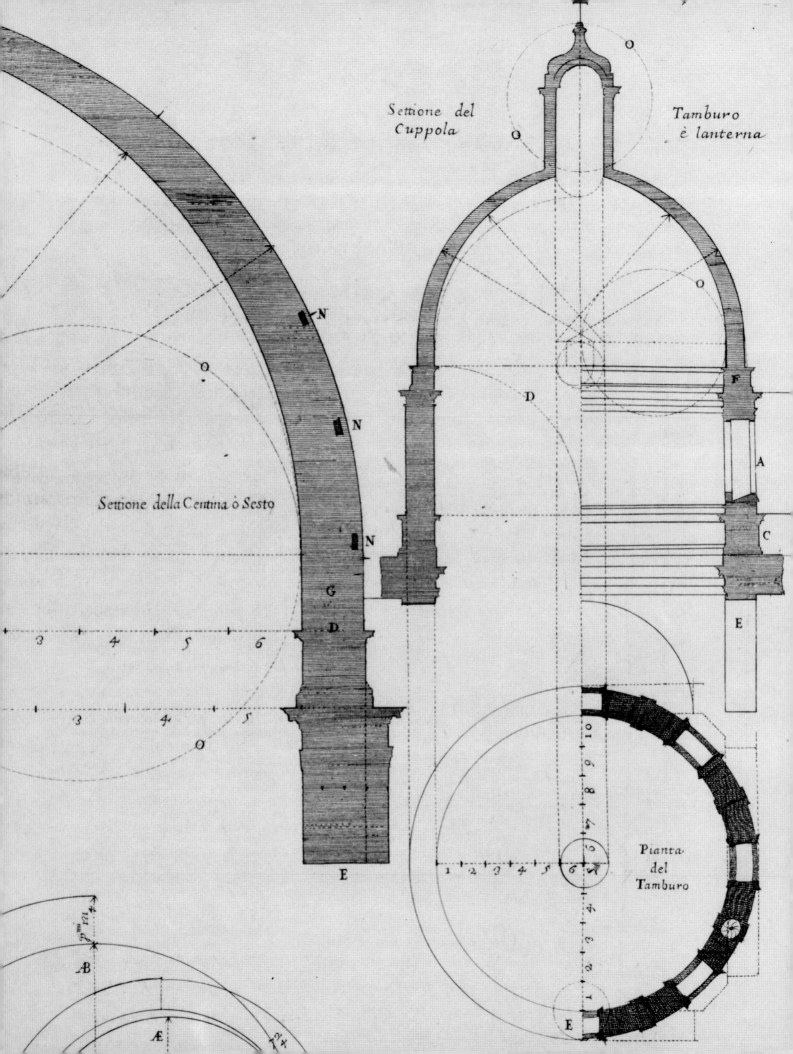

Settione del Cuppola

Tamburo è lanterna

Settione della Centina ò Sesto

Pianta del Tamburo

HELLMUT HAGER
Pennsylvania State University

Carlo Fontana: Pupil, Partner, Principal, Preceptor

Carlo Fontana merits our interest as the head of what was probably the most competitive architectural studio in Rome during the last quarter of the seventeenth and the beginning of the eighteenth century. Gian Lorenzo Bernini and Carlo Rainaldi had passed away before Fontana reached the acme of his career in the early 1680s, and while Mattia de' Rossi was able to attract some of the major commissions of that period, such as the Ospizio di Santa Galla and the original building complex of the Ospizio di San Michele,[1] Mattia never displayed the artistic talent of Carlo Fontana, and unfortunately died at the relatively young age of fifty-seven in 1695. Most of the work of Giovanni Battista Contini, the third major architect of Bernini's school, was restricted to the provinces.[2]

The exact date of Fontana's arrival in Rome is not known. He was born in 1638 in Rancate near Como, then in Switzerland. According to Lione Pascoli, most people in that region worked in the building profession and Fontana came to Rome as an adult with some experience in architecture, though Pascoli does not specify the level of his experience.[3] By contrast, a relative of Fontana stated that he arrived in Rome as early as age twelve, in 1650.[4]

It can be documented that Fontana's apprenticeship with Giovanni Maria Bolino (or Bolini), an *architetto-misuratore*, or project director, of high standing

to Virgilio Spada and Pope Alexander VII, began about 1653. At the time Carlo Fontana was preparing for his marriage to Caterina di Silvestro di Bianchi, Bolino testified as to Fontana's *stato libero* (that is, he was unmarried) on 10 January 1663. Bolino also mentioned that the young Fontana, then approximately twenty-two, had come from Tivoli ten years previously to visit him "per imparare l'esercitio d'Architettura," and since that time Carlo, now working as an architect, had never left Rome.[5] We can therefore be certain that Bolino was Fontana's first teacher in architecture and that Fontana began his formal training when he was approximately fifteen years old (not twenty-two as Bolino would have it!), which was quite typical. Bolino (c. 1587–7 November 1669) referred to himself in the above-mentioned document as *architetto di fabriche*.[6] A very competent director of building, he had the confidence of the highest-ranking patrons, although he was illiterate and signed his name with three crosses.

From Bolino Fontana received solid grounding in his profession, which along with expertise in hydraulic engineering, also acquired at an early date—though it remains unknown who instructed him in this aspect of his profession—prepared him for a field where practical talent seemed to have the best chances for success. The period after the death of Alexan-

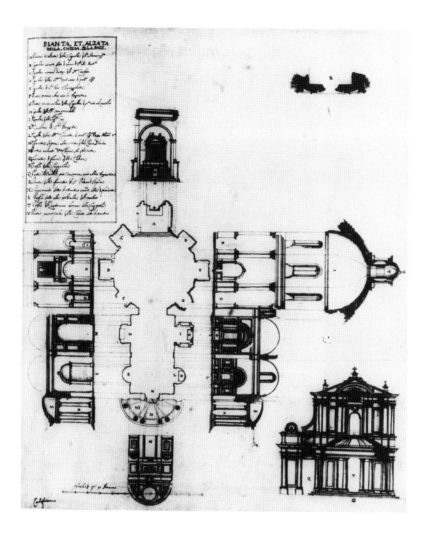

1. Santa Maria della Pace, Rome, survey drawing by Carlo Fontana, c. 1657, ground plan
Biblioteca Vaticana (MS Chigi P.VII. 9, fol. 75)

der VII, the greatest patron of urban architecture in baroque Rome, was after all one of economic difficulties.

Carlo Fontana, unlike most of his famous predecessors of the cinquecento, from Bramante and Baldassare Peruzzi to Michelangelo (whom he particularly revered), was not a so-called "artist-architect"[7] at first but rather an "engineer-architect" like his famous ancestor Domenico Fontana, who had moved the obelisks for Sixtus V (1585–1590). However, with additional training under the outstanding artist-architects in Rome, Pietro da Cortona and Bernini (while Alexander's architectural patronage was still at its peak), Carlo quickly developed into an artist-architect with the added advantage of his engineering background.

The choice of Bolino for his master was well considered. Virgilio Spada (in his list of Roman architects of 14 November 1657) referred to him as "vecchio misuratore pratichissimo, et stimato de' intiera fede" (very experienced, appreciated, and absolutely trustworthy project director and adjuster of artisans' accounts); he had collaborated with Cortona on the façade of Santi Luca e Martina from 1639 and was a special deputy of Alexander VII, responsible for the preservation of the houses surrounding the Piazza di Santa Maria della Pace.[8] It would appear that Bolino introduced his pupil to Cortona and they both assisted the great master in the commission for refurbishing Santa Maria della Pace (1657–1658). Bolino (then over seventy) was *misuratore* (project director or architect brought in to oversee artisans' accounts), and Carlo Fontana (not yet twenty) did the basic work of preparing the survey drawings of the church and cloister (figs. 1, 2).[9] The drawings are interesting because they show what kind of work was assigned to a young assistant; he measured the entire building and recorded every detail from the tombstones in the courtyard to the panels for the wall paintings and the organ loft. Fontana signed these drawings, an exceptional practice he followed throughout his life.

Fontana's first attempt at a project of his own appears in the longitudinal elevation drawing of the church (fig. 2), where he articulates the upper wall of the interior with fluted Corinthian marble pilasters and embraces the round-headed windows, to suffocating effect, with twisted columns, a device which, Herbert Kessler observed, was derived from the original decoration in Santa Maria Maggiore.[10] The attempt is not successful by any means, and except for an early inclination toward chromatic effects, it does not reveal promise for the development of the young draftsman. An example of the drawing skills he seems to have acquired in Cortona's studio is found in the survey drawing of Santa Maria della Pace (fig. 1) which shows in the lower right corner the elevation of Cortona's façade, where a three-dimensional effect is accomplished through shading. This level of accomplishment must have appealed to Bernini, who

accepted Fontana directly from Cortona's workshop, where Fontana had had his first experience with scenographically planned architecture, a concept important to his further development and his professional orientation.

Like Bernini's closest assistant, Mattia de' Rossi, Carlo Fontana was able to develop Bernini's sketches into highly finished drawings, as exemplified by the elevation drawing for the Chigi Palace in Piazza Santi Apostoli, where Fontana worked under Bernini from 1665 to 1667.[11] With the progress of the building Fontana's responsibilities increased to the extent that, in the second phase of the building campaign, direction of the work was left entirely to him. After 1666 Fontana was approving the *misure*, the workers' accounts.[12] Fontana became Bernini's project director in 1665 for the enlargement of the Chigi Palace in Ariccia (bought unfinished in 1661 from the Savelli family). The signed drawing was made by Fontana with two purposes in mind: adorning the area of the piazza and the church with gates and expanding the transverse rectangular piazza between the palace and the church with an exedra and a formal garden (fig. 3). Although parts of

2. Santa Maria della Pace, Rome, survey drawing by Carlo Fontana, c. 1657, section with Fontana's project for upper wall
Biblioteca Vaticana (MS Chigi P.VII. 9, fol. 70)

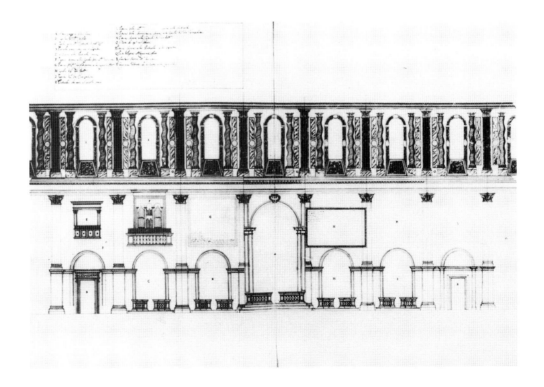

the master plan were finished about 1670, the expansion of the piazza was never carried out.[13]

The period of increasing responsibility in Bernini's studio during the mid-1660s coincides with Bernini and Mattia de' Rossi's involvement in projects for the Louvre, and with the first structures built to designs by Carlo Fontana himself, such as the façades of Santi Faustino e Giovita in the Via Giulia and the portico and façade of San Biagio in Campitelli (rededicated to Santa Rita by Alexander VII) that once stood at the foot of the Capitoline Hill near the *cordonata* and the stairway leading to Santa Maria in Aracoeli.[14]

In this period Fontana also was appointed to important offices instrumental in shaping the promising career that was beginning to develop in the orbit of Bernini. In 1664 Fontana became co-adjutor and successor-designate to Bernini as *misuratore e stimatore della Camera Apostolica*, the administrative authority responsible for building enterprises supported by the pope; and in 1666 Fontana was appointed *misuratore della Reverendissima Fabbrica di San Pietro*, which was the administrative unit that oversaw the adornment and maintenance of the basilica and the construction of the piazza of Saint Peter's.[15] Instituted by Julius II and traditionally headed by the cardinal *arciprete* of the basilica, its executive was the *economo generale della fabbrica*, a canon of Saint Peter's. The Cardinal Carlo Vespignani, who held this office in the latter part of the seicento, would play a major role in regard to Fontana's activities in and for the most important church in Christendom.

Before further discussing Fontana's development as a practicing architect, we should spotlight his relationship with Bernini—in whose studio he appears to have been by 1659—at a time when he was still working as a dependent of the great master. In his book on the Vatican basilica, published in 1694, Fontana writes that he was present when excavations for the foundations of the colonnades were made either for the north wing, in 1659, and/or for the south wing, in 1661.[16] Assuming that he was on the site already in 1659 not just as a curious observer but

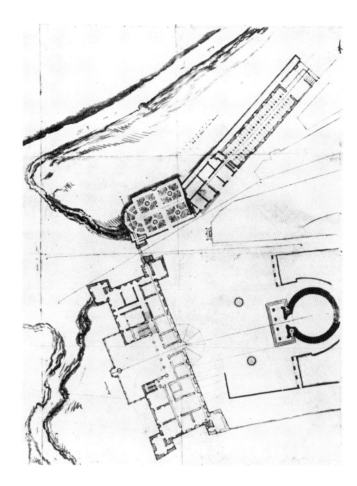

3. Carlo Fontana, project for the "Piazza di Corte," an expansion of the piazza between Chigi Palace in Ariccia and church, with addition of gates, exedra, and garden
Biblioteca Vaticana (MS Chigi P.VI.12) (c. 1665–1670)

as an assistant to Bernini, Fontana's statement would support the date 1659—first proposed by Heinrich Brauer and Rudolf Wittkower—as the beginning of his apprenticeship with Bernini.[17] This seems to be further supported by a diagram in Windsor Castle accompanied by a statement of Carlo Fontana that the drawing represents the scheme he used to erect the columns within a system of coordinates (on the south side of the piazza) on the oval perimeter.[18]

The architects mentioned in Fontana's book as having conducted the raising of the columns of the south wing of the colonnade are Marc Antonio de' Rossi (north side) and his son Mattia (south side) in conformity with a "regola facile e infallibile da loro pratticata,"[19] which appears to be the one he represented in his drawing—possibly redrawn with the intention of publishing it later in his work on the basilica.

Other drawings for the square that can be attributed with confidence to Fontana, preserved in the Chigi volumes in the Vatican Library, concern the pavement of the piazza. Under construction during the final period of Alexander VII's pontificate, it was eventually given priority over the project for the third arm, the *terzo braccio*.[20] One of these drawings (fig. 4) deserves special attention because it shows in a planimetric rendering Bernini's final idea for the third wing of the colonnades which has been moved eastward into the Piazza Rusticucci and is no longer curvilinear in shape, but straight, exactly as rendered in Bernini's penciled sketch of an elevation that shows the *terzo braccio* surmounted in the center by a clock-bell tower.[21]

This relocation of the projected third arm toward the east, well beyond the perimeter of the oval, was certainly in line with Fontana's own ideas for Saint Peter's Square; it tended to restore the emphasis on the axis perpendicularly directed toward the façade of the basilica, a major concern in Fontana's later enlargement plans for Saint Peter's Square (figs. 17, 18). This raises the question of whether Fontana shared in Bernini's experiments following abandonment of the earlier concept (published by Falda in

1665), which showed the *terzo braccio* on the curve of the oval.[22]

In conversations with Bernini, Carlo Fontana might have made his position known concerning the strong emphasis on the transverse axis: a situation that would divert the spectators' attention away from the church to the lateral curves of the colonnades when entering the piazza through a portico positioned on the same perimeter. This diversion would not occur if spectators passed through an intermediary space that would guide their view along the longitudinal axis directly toward the basilica and the Benediction Loggia. For Sant'Andrea al Quirinale the analogous problem was solved easily by means of the entrance vestibule, which, as the spectator enters the church, establishes an almost immediate visual contact with the altar. Aware of these difficulties, Fontana might have assisted Bernini in the experiments that led him to the rather radical modification of the earlier scheme. It is certainly conceivable that Bernini entrusted Fontana with the task of developing the penciled sketch of the *terzo braccio* into a formal project, which could also be the one Fontana later incorporated into his own proposals for the enlargement of Saint Peter's Square.

At that time Fontana was about thirty years old, and he must have felt ready to advance from assistant and pupil to partner. And—unlike Mattia de' Rossi, who always remained in a subordinate position—Fontana could be quite critical of his master's accomplishments. He considered the longitudinal oval more appropriate for the square of Saint Peter's, because it would have improved the visibility of the pope when he gave his blessing from the Benediction Loggia, a situation comparable to that of an ancient theater. Although Fontana admitted that Bernini could not utilize the longitudinal oval because of the location of the Vatican Palace, he published drawings to this effect in his book that made his own preference clear (fig. 5).[23] Whether he voiced his opinion while in Bernini's studio, we have no way of knowing.

We do know that Carlo Fontana did not hesitate to confront Rainaldi, with whom he competed from the early 1660s in the

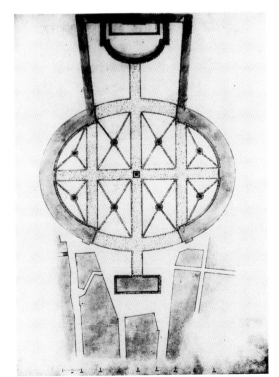

4. Saint Peter's Square, Rome, project attributed to Carlo Fontana for the pavement, c. 1665
Biblioteca Vaticana (MS Chigi P.VII. 9, fol. 15)

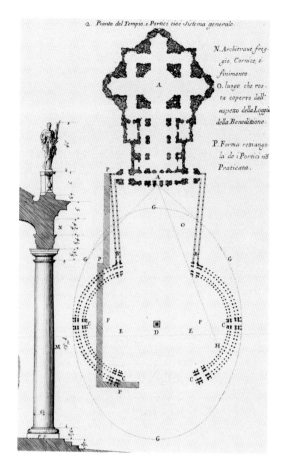

planning and construction of the twin churches, Santa Maria di Monte Santo and Santa Maria dei Miracoli on the Piazza del Popolo.[24] Whereas Rainaldi tended to emphasize the façade, relying on the impact of the open portico with free-standing tetrastyle colonnades, Fontana counted on the effect of high-rising drums and domes, inspired by the twin chapels of Sixtus V and Paul V in Santa Maria Maggiore. His pen and wash drawing (in the Archivio Segreto) must have challenged Rainaldi, who reacted with corrections defining a lower drum and dome.[25] Fontana was obviously on his way from assistant and partner to serious competitor. Although Rainaldi remained in charge of the twin churches until the death of Alexander VII (1667), Fontana immediately replaced him as the leading architect, and his project was accepted by Clemente Orlandi, patron of Santa Maria di Monte Santo, for the left of the two churches.[26] The completion of the church, its construction interrupted at the level of

the window sills of the drum, required a benefactor, and the Cardinal Girolamo Gastaldi established a legacy in October 1673 for the construction of both churches. Although Santa Maria di Monte Santo was initially constructed according to Fontana's plan, it might have been Gastaldi who created trouble for Fontana by calling in Bernini. The master objected to Fontana's attempt to make the longitudinal oval of the drum appear circular by strengthening the side walls, and he forced Fontana to return to the essence of Rainaldi's plan. He recommended, however, that the attic be replaced with a balustrade to increase visually the upward drive of the triangular pediment, similar to the ends of the colonnades in Saint Peter's Square (fig. 19). Fontana, on his way to independence and fame, was once more reduced to a subordinate role. He reacted by publishing his project in the form of an engraving and voicing his complaint in an inscription dedicated to Clemente Orlandi.[27]

If one finds these interactions among three studios strange, one might be even more perplexed to learn that Carlo Rainaldi was summoned again when the construction of Santa Maria dei Miracoli (the twin on the right) was resumed in 1675. However, this is not inconsistent with the manner in which rights of patronage were exercised in the period of Alexander VII. The Franciscan owners of the church intended to build Rainaldi's project, albeit with modifications, and it was not until the level of the drum was reached (1677) that for the second and final time Fontana succeeded Rainaldi in the commission and completed the building in 1681.

Despite the competition on the Piazza del Popolo, Fontana's career advanced steadily. His acceptance into the Accademia di San Luca in 1667 as *architetto di merito* implied the obligation to teach when called on (which happened in 1675) and allowed him to practice his profession with the official sanction of the academy. As early as about 1670 he was made *cavaliere*, by which time he must have established his own studio.[28] His first independent works, as mentioned above, date from about 1665.

5. Saint Peter's Square, Rome, engraving illustrating Fontana's ideas for the square on an oval ground plan
From Carlo Fontana, *Il Tempio Vaticano e sua origine* (Rome, 1694), 185

6. Santa Maria in Traspontina, Rome, site drawing of a project by Carlo Fontana for the high altar and choir screen; copy by Nicodemus Tessin the Younger, c. 1673
Nationalmuseum, Stockholm
(T.H.C. 1973)

7. Santa Maria in Traspontina, Rome, engraving after a project of c. 1674 by Carlo Fontana for the high altar
From Giovanni Giacomo de' Rossi, *Disegni di vari altari e Cappelle nelle Chiese di Roma* (Rome, n.d.)

The first foreign student to join Fontana's studio was Nicodemus Tessin the Younger (1654–1728). Arriving in Rome in 1673, he made contact with Fontana through the circle of Queen Christina, to which both Bernini and Fontana belonged; Fontana also built the Teatro Tordinona (1669–1671) for the queen.[29] At this time Fontana also undertook his first major design for the interior of a church, the Bernini-inspired high altar in Santa Maria in Traspontina, finished in 1674.[30] A drawing of an earlier project, which Tessin took home and is now in the Nationalmuseum, Stockholm (fig. 6),[31] is the result of Fontana's attempt to anticipate the effect of the projected altar in its setting. The *baldacchino* is represented beneath the surmounting arch of the choir entrance, and can be compared to the perspective sketches created by Francesco

Borromini for the setting of Bernini's *baldacchino* in Saint Peter's.[32] Tessin could have made the drawing for Fontana or he could have copied one made by Fontana. In any event, the outcome of the experiment was negative because the structure, terminated by a rather low pediment and angels with a Madonna medallion, appeared minuscule relative to the surrounding architecture. The deficiency was quickly remedied by Fontana, whose improved version culminates in a massive crown carried by angels who are placing it on the supporting columns. This unique motif sets the altar apart from Fontana's other works and is comparable only to Bernini's *baldacchino* above the high altar of Saint Peter's. That Fontana himself conceived the sculptural decoration is likely because of an intermediary project, an engraving (fig. 7), which shows addi-

tional theatrically animated angels carry-ing the venerated icon of the Madonna and Child.[33] Other projects deriving from the Traspontina altar, such as the one for King Pedro II's catafalque in San Antonio dei Portoghesi of 1707, exhibit similar profi-ciency.[34] The altar was constructed in a workshop established ad hoc in the ora-torio adjacent to the church,[35] where Fontana and the general of the order, Clemente Orlandi, could supervise the artisans and the sculptor, Leonardo Retti, working under Fontana's direction.

In Fontana's studio at that time Tessin learned his teacher's specialty (adopted from Bernini): the "orchestration" of all participating artists' shares—later includ-ing painters—into a complete work of art, an ability Fontana also developed through his experience as a stage designer. Early in his career he had worked in this capacity for the Chigi and Colonna families, as well as for Queen Christina.[36] This experi-ence, which stimulated the evolution of his artistic talents, enabled his studio to execute work that could not be handled with the same degree of success by more exclusively architectural workshops. Fon-tana's pupils benefited greatly from the master's flexibility.[37]

But who were Carlo's first Italian pupils and assistants, and what was their role in his studio? Pascoli lists first among Fontana's *scolari* Simone Felice del Lino, who appears in the Chigi documents as the author of the wooden models he made for the Villa in San Quirico d'Orcia (1679) and the Villa Versaglia ("Versailles") near Formello in 1681.[38] Pascoli records him also in the service of the Ottoboni family since the pontificate of Alexander VIII (1691), creating for them *diverse mac-chine*. In addition Pascoli mentions Del Lino as a good engraver and praises him as an excellent draftsman ("disegnava benis-simo"). As an engraver he assisted Carlo Fontana in 1674 in the publication of the above-mentioned project for the façade of Santa Maria di Monte Santo, and he par-ticipated in the production of Fontana's book on Saint Peter's in 1690.[39]

The role of the pupils in his studio, however, is difficult to define. The uni-form style of the surviving drawings, most of which date from the later period,[40]

8. Santa Maria del Popolo, Rome, Cappella Cybo as constructed by Carlo Fontana (1682–1684), longitudinal section
From *Disegni di vari altari . . .*

points to strict workshop discipline and the probability that Fontana, in contradis-tinction to his own work for Bernini, did the more important drawings himself. He seems to have relied on his students for the planimetric surveys, status quo ren-derings of buildings at the beginning of a commission, and practical help on the site. In the fall of 1672 and in 1673 when theatrical plays were performed in the large hall of the Chigi Palace in Ariccia, Carlo Fontana is recorded as arriving with two assistants (*giovani*), and as directing the work necessary for the erection of the stage and the scenery (presumably designed by Fontana himself).[41] Among artists mentioned is the painter Paolo Albertoni, who was still working for Fontana more than twenty years later on the decoration of the "drum" above the Baptismal Chapel in Saint Peter's (see below).

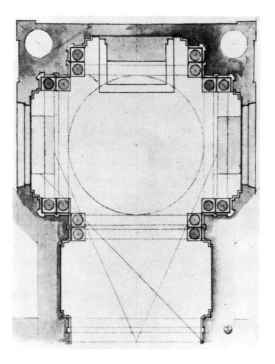

9. Santa Maria del Popolo, Rome, ground plan with sight lines for Cappella Cybo by Carlo Fontana, c. 1682
Uffizi, Florence (A 3188)

10. Santa Maria del Popolo, Rome, Cappella Cybo, high altar with painting by Carlo Maratti (finished by 1687)
From *Disegni di vari altari . . .*

Among the architecture students of the first generation who achieved prominence was Carlo Francesco Bizzacheri. Born in 1656, he may have trained under Fontana during the first half of the 1670s when the studio began to gain momentum. One of Bizzacheri's first works on his own account is the decoration of the Vivaldi Chapel in Santa Maria di Monte Santo, between 1677 and 1679. Bizzacheri is best known for the Cappella del Monte della Pietà (before 1699) and the convent building of San Luigi dei Francesi (1709–1712).[42] Of the same generation was Carlo Buratti (best known for his façade and transformation of the Duomo in Albano), who taught frequently at the Accademia di San Luca from 1698.[43] The connection with Domenico Martinelli (1650–1718) who, like Juvarra, had been ordained a priest before he became an architect, and who came into contact with Fontana about 1678, seems to have remained rather casual. Martinelli became independent quickly and was very active as a teacher of perspective at the academy (1683–1689), both before he began working in Vienna in 1690 and after his return in 1700.[44]

During the 1680s Carlo Fontana's genius for orchestrating the collaboration of artists from different workshops on his most complex projects was brought to full fruition. This period coincided with the completion of the chapel for Cardinal Marzio Ginetti (1671–1684) and saw the realization of Fontana's masterpieces: the façade of San Marcello al Corso (1682–1684) and the chapel for the Cardinal Alderano Cybo (c. 1680–1687).[45] For the Cappella Ginetti, Fontana not only designed the skeleton of the articulating columns, but also directed the sculptural decoration by Antonio Raggi (1624–1686). Raggi created Cardinal Marzio Ginetti's monument, the allegorical figures on top of the columns, and the altarpiece, *The*

Dream of Saint Joseph. Raggi must have been rather closely associated with Fontana's studio, because he also carried out the statuary decoration above the high altar in Santa Maria dei Miracoli, a group consisting of four flying angels carrying the venerated Madonna painting, as well as the busts for the funerary monuments of the Cardinal Girolamo Gastaldi and his brother Benedetto in the choir (c. 1677–1681).[46] At the same time, Fontana designed the sculptural decoration for the façade of San Marcello al Corso. The tondo above the portal, *San Filippo Benizi Renouncing the Tiara*, was again by Raggi, whereas the sculpture in the niches, *Pope Marcellus* (on the left) and *San Filippo Benizi* (on the right), was executed by Francesco Cavallini (c. 1683). Even twenty years later when the time came to execute the statues for the upper level (the allegories of *Faith* and *Hope*, and the *Beati Gioacchino Piccolomini* and *Francesco Patrizi*), Carlo Fontana chose the sculptor Andrea Fucigna, who accepted the commission.[47]

Cavallini served as Fontana's "sculptural executive" also for the decoration of the most accomplished of his complete works of art, the Cappella Cybo (figs. 8–10), where he had the advantage of constructing a chapel from the ground up but was limited by the site, which forced him to reduce three of the four arms of the Greek cross plan almost to a minimum. With the altar facing the entrance on the side aisle of Santa Maria del Popolo, there was no space left for an appropriate chapel. Fontana solved this seemingly intractable problem with the help of Carlo Maratti (1687), who created the missing space through pictorial illusion: the figures of the saints discussing the Immaculate Conception, which appears above them, are distributed on the platform and receding steps in such a way that the spectator is confronted by the illusion of a three-dimensional chapel. This effect suggests close cooperation between the two artists, who were equals in their respective professions. To avoid undesirable visual effects in his chapel, Fontana

11. Saint Peter's, Rome, Baptismal Chapel by Carlo Fontana, engraving with view of the interior
From Domenico de' Rossi, *Architettura Civile* 3 (Rome, 1721), pl. 50 (originally published by Carlo Fontana in *La Nobilissima Cappella del Fonte Battesimale nella Basilica Vaticana* (Rome, 1697)

employed coupled columns of brownish *diaspro di Sicilia* placed near the corners of the crossing, which enabled him to work with carefully controlled vistas.

Fontana's painstaking consideration of the visual conditions for the decorative elements in their respective settings can be demonstrated by his ground plan for the Cappella Cybo (fig 9). Diagonal lines emanating from the midpoint and the right corner of the entrance are intended to verify what could or should not yet be seen from certain vantage points: in particular, the reliefs of the Cardinals Lorenzo and Alderano Cybo by Francesco Cavallini (fig. 8), which guide the spectator's view toward the altar and Maratti's painting (fig. 10). The altarpiece also incorporates the lunette, usually reserved for a window, in order to complete the optical illusion.

Unfortunately, we are missing the sources that would provide the details concerning this harmonious interaction between artists of three different workshops, which was directed by Fontana and must be reconstructed only from circumstantial evidence. This *Gesamtkunstwerk* was completed by Maratti's former pupil Luigi Garzi (1638–1721), who painted the fresco of God the Father in the glory of angels.

The achievement of the Cappella Cybo may have encouraged the authorities of the Reverendissima Fabbrica of Saint Peter's to entrust Fontana with the remod-

eling of the Baptismal Chapel (1692–1698). This project required a similar coordination of workshops and an analogous amalgamation of artistic shares under the guidance of the architect, who had to provide the architectural framework for the integration of the various contributions (fig. 11). Maratti and his workshop associates Giuseppe Passeri and Andrea Procaccini were involved, as well as the sculptors Lorenzo Ottone, Jean Théodon, and Michel Maille (called "Michele Maglia"), who produced the models for the baptismal font, which was designed in all its details by Fontana and executed by the foundry workshop of Giovanni Giardini.[48]

To provide as much space as possible for Maratti's monumental painting of the *Baptism of Christ* in the center, and to create a setting for it comparable to that of the altarpiece in the Cappella Cybo (fig. 10), Fontana closed the preexisting semicircular window in the chapel. He then had to create a new light source, which he found in the outer wall of the basilica, above the chapel.[49] Its utilization, however, required an opening in the vault of the chapel and the creation of a "feigned drum," which was decorated by the painter Paolo Albertoni. This illumination from above, through an oculus like that of the Pantheon, provides the optimal condition for viewing Maratti's masterpiece. Such a solution was inherent in Fontana's repertory of architectural principles, including the location of windows in elevated positions.[50]

Fontana and Maratti, who on a personal level had become notorious enemies, were forced by the commission to work in partnership, which limited Maratti's jurisdiction to painting the three panels in conformity with Fontana's overall concept. All other parts of the decoration were Fontana's responsibility, including the production of the baptismal font (fig. 11).

In his late work, the Cappella Albani in San Sebastiano fuori le mura, Fontana again assumed responsibility for both the chapel's design and its decoration.[51] Here, as we learn from his design at the medal stage (1710, dedicated in 1712; fig. 12), the space allotted for the altar painting, similar to his device for the Baptismal Chapel

12. San Sebastiano fuori le mura, Rome, Cappella di San Fabiano (Albani), medal of 1710

at Saint Peter's, was to conform completely to the shape envisioned for the lateral paintings above the side entrances in the main space of the chapel. This plan combines ideas from the Cappella Cybo and from the Baptismal Chapel. The substitution of a niche containing Pietro Papaleo's statue of *Saint Sebastian* for that of the altar painting was probably a last-minute change made at the request of the patron, Clement XI. The pope had commissioned the chapel as a burial place for his brother Orazio, and wished to honor the patron saint of the church to which the Albani Chapel is attached. Papaleo (1642–1718) was nearly a contemporary of Carlo Fontana, whereas Giuseppe Passeri (1654–1714), who worked almost at the same time in the Baptismal Chapel and executed the painting of *Saint Silvester Baptizing the Emperor Constantine* in the Albani Chapel, was about half a generation younger than Fontana. Finally, Pier Leone Ghezzi (1674–1755), author of the painting of *Saint Fabiano and the Emperor Philip* (on the left in the same chapel), was even younger than Carlo's son Francesco, and belonged to the next generation.

Having briefly investigated Fontana's role as an overall designer and his interaction with artists from other studios, we can turn to the question of collaborators in Fontana's own studio at the height of his career (c. 1680–1700).

When he undertook his two major works of the 1680s, the façade of San Marcello al Corso and the Cappella Cybo, Fontana's closest pupil, his son Francesco, was about fourteen years old; when the two structures were complete in 1684, Francesco was about sixteen. This may well coincide with the period when Francesco, or his father, decided that he should become an architect, and he began his apprenticeship at the lowest level (*giovane*) in the studio. Francesco remained close to his father throughout his life, residing with his family (his wife, Caterina Santarelli, their son, Mauro, born in 1701, and two daughters) in Carlo's house[52] until he died of tuberculosis on 3 July 1708 at the age of forty in his villa at Castelgandolfo.[53]

Simone Felice del Lino, who executed the models for Fontana's Chigi villas in 1679 and 1681 and was praised so highly by Pascoli for his abilities as a draftsman, seems to have been present as Fontana's senior assistant until the end of the 1680s. If this is true, he would have been referred to in the terminology of the period as *architetto misuratore, architetto sovrastante,* or *architetto deputato,* and would have supervised the construction of buildings designed by his master.[54]

During the mid-1680s Carlo Fontana's nephew Girolamo also received architectural education from his uncle. Born in 1668, he was the son of Carlo's brother Francesco, also recorded by Pascoli as an architect, but whose activities are totally unknown. He may simply have been a builder, or perhaps he died early. In any event, Girolamo can be documented in Fontana's home in 1685 and 1687, which means that he was a member of the workshop at least during those years before he became architect to the Colonna family.[55] He finished the Sala Grande of their palace (as the successor of Antonio del Grande), and served as their stage designer on certain occasions about 1690. The position of *architetto della famiglia* carried high prestige, commensurate with the importance of the family. His major work is the façade of the cathedral in Frascati (1696–1701).[56]

Among the architects working for Carlo Fontana in the 1680s may have been Carlo Francesco Bizzacheri, who seems to have set up his own studio by 1680 when he presented his project for the convent of Santa Maddalena. Bizzacheri became *accademico di merito* in 1697.[57] Certainly Carlo Buratti was also present at this time; he helped Fontana with the repair of the Aqua Paola from the Lago di Bracciano, and received the commission for the façade of the cathedral in Albano, dated 1722. He had apparently assisted Fontana when he worked there for Cardinal Flavio Chigi in 1688/1689 to build the new sacristy and to embellish the interior with a new ceiling.[58] Other pupils of the period mentioned by Pascoli are Tommaso Mattei (died 1726), one of Fontana's most talented Italian students, who seems to have built the Cappella Montioni in Santa Maria di Monte Santo in 1687 after a design by Fontana.[59] Mattei had begun to work independently in 1680 when he built the bell tower for the church of Lanuvio near Genzano. He was almost certainly independent before 1693 when he built his most accomplished work, the Chiesa del Miracolo adjacent to the church of Santa Cristina in Bolsena. Like Fontana, he was also involved in the production of temporary architecture;[60] however, he was not accepted into the academy as *accademico di merito* before 1706.

Alessandro Specchi (1668–1729), who belongs to Francesco Fontana's generation, seems to have trained under Carlo more or less simultaneously with Francesco, and began to work for Carlo Fontana when he was occupied with the book on Saint Peter's. The first payments for the engravings Specchi executed after Fontana's drawings are registered in 1690,[61] but the actual work may have been done at least in part a few years earlier.[62] Specchi's association with Fontana continued through the 1690s and beyond, but he seems to have had a studio of his own before he received the commission for the Porto di Ripetta (1703–1705).[63]

Born in the same year as Francesco, Lucas von Hildebrandt (1668–1745) was born in Genoa as the son of an officer in the Austrian army and an Italian mother. He reached Fontana's studio about 1690 and studied under him until he went to Vienna before the turn of the century.[64]

Close in age was another architect who came to Rome from Bamberg just before the end of the seicento, Johann Dientzenhofer (1663–1726),[65] who, like Juvarra after him, seems to have had a particularly close relationship with Francesco before being appointed *Stiftsbaumeister* in Fulda in 1700.[66] To the list of Fontana's pupils from the North we can now add the name of a Frenchman, Giles-Marie Oppenord (1672–1742), who sojourned in Rome from 1692 to 1699. As Gil Smith has suggested, Oppenord was drawn to the studio of Fontana rather than the French Academy in Rome, then in a state of severe crisis.[67]

Members of Fontana's workshop during the 1690s—the period of the Baptismal Chapel in Saint Peter's—certainly included Filippo de Romanis, recorded in 1714 as having worked for Fontana for twenty years,[68] and probably also Romano Fortunato Carapecchia (active 1681–1741), who at the beginning of the settecento executed for Fontana the Casino Vaini on the Janiculum before going to Malta in 1715.[69] An album of drawings for his own projects (with the latest possible dates of between 1689 and 1704) is preserved in London.[70]

During the 1690s Francesco Fontana began to come into his own. *Accademico di merito* at the Accademia di San Luca since 1694, he began to teach there in the same year, while his father was *principe* (1693–1699), and he participated actively in the first centennial celebrations of 1695–1696.[71] After the expiration of Carlo's tenure as head of the academy, Francesco became first the associate of the new president, Carlo Maratti, then "acting president" (*viceprincipe*) in October 1703 and again in 1706 when Maratti's health began to fail.[72]

As he matured Francesco seems to have conducted a kind of associate studio, and with relative independence he developed congenial, though clearly distinct, design concepts. For the rebuilding of Santi Apostoli, inspired by Sant'Ignazio, he carried the so-called "Roman gravity" style almost to an extreme, yet this church concludes the cycle of the major Roman basilicas at the beginning of the settecento in a very competent and dignified fashion. The commission apparently went directly to Francesco in 1702, and we do not know why his father received only the comparatively modest one for the portico and façade of Santa Maria in Trastevere at the same time.[73] The new Pope Clement XI, as Pascoli says, probably made increasing use of the services of Francesco, knowing that Carlo was aging.

Again as recorded by Pascoli, Carlo developed a project followed by a model for the rebuilding of the Abbey Church in Fulda, which later achieved the status of cathedral. Nevertheless, the strong planimetric similarity between the church as it stands now and Francesco's basilica of Santi Apostoli in Rome points to the latter as the author of the scheme.[74] It also points to the relative independence Francesco had achieved from his father's work by then, without jeopardizing their close personal and professional relationship, also mentioned by Pascoli. The close connection between their studios may account for Pascoli's error in attributing the design for Fulda to Carlo.[75] During this period Francesco would have prepared himself to assume his father's business and combine the two studios, had he not been struck by illness. Pascoli's report suggests that Carlo Fontana was a broken man after the death of his son in 1708. Called on to finish Francesco's basilica of Santi Apostoli (still under construction in the choir and apse), he was overcome by emotion on entering the church.[76]

Francesco's cousin Girolamo, who died even younger, at age thirty-three in 1701, had at least seen his major work completed, the façade of the Cathedral of San Pietro in Frascati, including part of the sculptural decoration.[77] Here again the question must be raised: why was Girolamo appointed over his famous uncle? The answer is probably connected with the patronage of the Colonna family, for whom Girolamo worked.[78] His job consisted in completing an unfinished façade with only one bell tower. The extant wooden model, which shows a double-storied front articulated by columns and flanked by three-tiered bell towers, may be considered representative of those models known to us only through sources and documents. They served not only as working models, but also to inform and persuade customers. Like Fontana's drawing for the façade of San Marcello al Corso, this model is complete with the statuary decoration, executed in part by sculptors with whom Carlo Fontana had worked on other occasions (Vincenzo Felice, at Santa Maria in Traspontina, Santa Maria in Trastevere, and Santo Spirito dei Napolitani; and Andrea Fucigna at the façade of San Marcello al Corso).

Since the façade, except for the statues, was complete in 1700 in time for the Holy Year, Girolamo had been able to accomplish something denied his uncle, who in anticipation of the *Anno Santo* had participated in an inconsequential competition for the façade of San Giovanni in Laterano, known mainly through Andrea Pozzo's engravings made *fuori competizione*. Were it not for a drawing by James Gibbs

(1682–1754), who came from Scotland to train under Carlo Fontana from 1705 to 1708, the knowledge of Carlo's entry in this competition would be lost.[79]

At the time James Gibbs arrived in Rome, Girolamo's studio no longer existed, and that of Francesco was involved in the enormous task of rebuilding Santi Apostoli. Concurrently, Francesco was also acting director of the Accademia di San Luca. Among his many obligations as director were the architectural competitions of the *Concorsi Clementini*, institutionalized by Clement XI in 1702,[80] which Francesco not only supervised, but also inspired with the themes he provided. At his side was his father, whose official role at the academy had become *primo consigliere* in architecture. We know from Carlo's correspondence that at the beginning of the eighteenth century he was suffering from gout—a common disease among architects in Rome, which had troubled Carlo Maderno among others. The condition certainly made Fontana more dependent on assistants, about whom we are better informed in this late period than at the height of his career. Fontana's studio in this phase included, as before, Filippo de Romanis, as well as Matteo Sassi (architect and *misuratore*, who was born in 1648 and could have served him over an extensive period), and Nicola Michetti (c. 1678–1758), whom he "inherited" from his son and who played a prominent role in Carlo's studio during his last years. Carapecchia, already mentioned, had been delegated to the Casino Vaini project.

When Clement XI made a concerted effort in 1703 to improve his native town of Urbino and to embellish some of its buildings under Carlo Fontana's direction, the names of Francesco Bufalini (from Urbino, and known in Rome as a draftsman for many of the engravings for the *Insignium Romae Templorum Prospectus* of 1684), Filippo Barigioni (born 1672 in Rome), and Alessandro Specchi are mentioned in various capacities on the project.[81]

At this time Fontana's illness did not prevent him from producing some of the finest drawings of his career—projects for the Fontana di Trevi and the catafalques for the Emperor Leopold I (1705) and King

Pedro II of Portugal (1707).[82] Fontana also remained a forceful leader and continued to direct his studio, where the *giovani* mentioned by Filippo Juvarra's biographers seem to have been highly receptive to his teaching. When Juvarra arrived in Rome in August 1704 (probably for the feast of the Assumption), Fontana's studio was the most remarkable architectural school in Rome, and it is not surprising that the talented young aspirant sought training there.[83]

Fontana by that time had finished the Casa Correzionale for juvenile delinquents (1702–1704), for which he executed the drawings himself, and was beginning expansion of the Ospizio di San Michele, a project begun in 1708. This illuminating project[84] demonstrates how the aging architect alone was able to confront a committee of three cardinals ("protectors")—Spada, Sacripante, and Spinola—who opposed it. They criticized its magnificence, costliness, and the fact that it would hide the original structure built under Innocent XI (by Mattia de' Rossi, 1686–1689). Despite their requests and threats reiterated between 1708 and 1711, Fontana presented no new overall plan. When he approached one of Fontana's *giovani*, Leonardo Libri, chief administrator of the Ospizio, seems to have obtained no more than a kind of survey drawing. But Fontana established a working relationship with Cardinal Spada and succeeded in managing the execution of the extension project by giving ad hoc instructions to the workmen. He was also able to determine the organization and articulation of the entire river front, which is the main façade, even though construction was interrupted at the time of his death and completed much later in the eighteenth century. Instead of continuing Mattia de' Rossi's scheme, which he had been ordered to do, Fontana managed to submerge it—at least the exterior view—within his own comprehensive design. Fontana conducted the affairs of the Ospizio despite illness until the end of 1713. After his death on 6 February 1714, a successor had to be appointed for the completion of the project. Among the several possible choices—Matteo Sassi, referred to as *misuratore*; Filippo de Romanis,

mentioned as having worked with Fontana over the past twenty years, and who had replaced him on occasion during the last three years of his life; and Nicola Michetti, called *suo architetto*—Michetti was chosen.[85]

The Ospizio di San Michele is a most telling example of Carlo Fontana's vitality and circumspection as the leader of his workshop; he left a legacy that his successors could not ignore, even over an extended period of time.

Although Fontana has been justly recognized for the leadership qualities manifested in his own workshop, as well as for his capacity to interact with other artists and their workshops with the goal of creating a unified work of art, he was not entirely without competitors. Most notable among them was Antonio Gherardi (1644–1702), though even he was not able to synchronize three artistic media as successfully.[86]

Any discussion of Fontana and his workshop would be incomplete without consideration of his teaching. When Fontana assumed the role of "preceptor," he undertook a function close to his heart and much in harmony with his personality. We need only remember Pascoli's famous, rather sarcastic remark that Fontana spoke very well but that he would have spoken even better had he talked less about himself and his own works. Considering this statement relative to Fontana's documented activities, one concludes that Fontana must have felt a constant drive to instruct. That he did so successfully is borne out by the great number of his foreign students and by their distinguished careers. Similarly, that Fontana consistently attracted top students makes us curious as to what Fontana taught and what made his teaching so attractive.

The biographers of Filippo Juvarra mention the *giovani* assembled in the workshop when Juvarra arrived in 1704.[87] A "studio dei giovani" is again described in Carlo Fontana's house (i.e., the one in which he is recorded from 1706) after the death of his grandson Mauro (17 July 1767), who had lived there. Mauro had enjoyed a not undistinguished architectural career, achieving the rank of *principe* of the Accademia di San Luca (1762–

1763).[88] In Mauro's time, the studio for the students was equipped with "Un Tavolone da Studio longo palmi undeci e largo cinque con Quattro Tiratori serature e Chiavi, Piedi torniti e sue traverse. . . ." and "Quattro Sedie d'appoggio all'antica coperte di Vacchetta con spaliere dorate e braccij dritti." There was also "una credenza di noce con tre Sportelli, Serratura e Chiave con diversi Spartimenti dentro per Scritture. . . ." The room was decorated with paintings of such subjects as a Madonna and Child, Annunciation, Saint Gregory, Resurrection, and others (artists unidentified), and also with architectural projects and *vedute* mentioned but not specified (except for *Prospetto della Dogana di Terra*, a Roman temple remodeled by Francesco Fontana, 1694–1705). The room described is reminiscent of the *Sala di studio* in the no-longer-extant building of the Accademia di San Luca.[89]

The "studio dei giovani," however, should be distinguished from the adjoining workspace used by the architect himself. Fontana's studio, referred to in the inventory as the "stanza dello studio del defonto," contained a desk with five small drawers, two tables, and in a more spacious area "above the *studiolo*," among other furniture, seven chairs described "con fusti torniti" and mentioned as "assai vecchie, ed antiche," suggesting that the ambience remained that of Carlo's time. The decoration (in addition to three unidentified portraits, two male, one female) consisted of drawings (probably the original projects) representing Carlo Fontana's works: the Palazzo Montecitorio, the façade of San Marcello al Corso, the Baptismal Chapel of Saint Peter's, again Francesco Fontana's Dogana di Piazza di Pietra, the Porto di Ripetta, and other diverse "Vedute di Architettura in Prospettiva con Vetro avanti, e Cornice negra"—in short, an appropriate display of instructional material. Directly related to the architectural profession were the three drawing boards of different sizes: "Tre telari da disegnare, uno grande, altro mezzano, et altro piccolo, con suoi fusti, Righe, e Squadre."[90]

Fontana's book on the Vatican basilica provides valuable information that enables us to reconstruct his studio curriculum, which included all aspects of architectural planning and realization from the building of foundations to the composition of trusswork for roofs and the construction of domes. Although his other books are important (the *Utilissimo Trattato delle Acque correnti*, 1696, and the book on the Palazzo Montecitorio, 1694 and 1708), the *Templum Vaticanum* is particularly useful as a source for Fontana's teaching. Commissioned by Innocent XI through the authority of the Reverendissima Fabrica di San Pietro in 1680 for the purpose of instructing laymen as well as professionals internationally, the text was meant to address the recently questioned stability of the dome of Saint Peter's and the suitability of the basilica as a model for architectural inspiration. At the time of its publication Mattia de' Rossi, successor to Bernini, was still the leading architect of the Fabbrica. Fontana's status had remained that of *misuratore*, an office he had held since 1666, until he achieved in 1697 the highest office an architect could hold in the service of the Fabbrica of Saint Peter's.[91]

Despite Fontana's strong connections with the Accademia di San Luca and his impact on its development as chief administrator in 1686 and 1693–1699, most of his formal teaching seems to have taken place in his personal studio (in his home near the Forum of Trajan), or in an office established temporarily in the vicinity of a major construction project.[92] Surprisingly, he is recorded only once as a teacher at the academy, as early as 1675, when he was asked to teach the basic architecture course (on Sundays and holidays), which ran from spring through the fall.[93] Teaching in his personal studio corresponded to an established practice that prevailed until the later eighteenth century throughout Europe.

On the other hand, the organization of the architectural competitions at the academy, which were divided into three classes, reflects not only the three levels of teaching and learning at the Accademia but also the three degrees of perfection pursued during apprenticeship in the architects' personal workshops.[94] The beginner first acquired drafting skills, which were tested in the competitions

13. Il Gesù, Rome, view of the exterior

14. Sant'Andrea della Valle, Rome, dome, view of the exterior

of the third class at the Accademia by copying famous buildings. Carlo Fontana attached particular importance to this practice, as we know from his famous conversation with Juvarra, whom he advised to draw buildings of the classical tradition (in spite of the newcomer's exceptional draftsmanship).[95] Fontana did this with the clear intention of channeling his students' talents in the direction of his own architectural convictions.

A pupil who had acquired advanced standing in his architectural education and was in full command of drawing skills would be sufficiently qualified to enter the competitions of the second class at the academy, which required the demonstration of proficiency in developing building ideas on a given theme of moderate difficulty. The theme usually required a project complete with ground plan, elevation, and section. An apprentice at this level would certainly be able to work in partnership with his master and to direct construction on the site. He could also be employed as *architetto misuratore* or offer his services to patrons for jobs of a limited size such as houses, small churches, or small palaces. This was about the level Fontana had reached when he worked with Bernini on the Chigi Palace in the

Piazza Santi Apostoli and subsequently in Ariccia, a period that saw his first independent structures: the façade and portico of San Biagio in Campitelli (Santa Rita) and the façade of Santi Faustino e Giovita in Via Giulia.

It was expected that a participant in a competition of the first class could design and produce projects on an urban scale. A first-prize winner was eligible for promotion to the rank of *architetto di merito*, thereby acquiring full membership in the academy. Carlo Fontana was awarded this status in 1667 when he was twenty-nine years old and had already begun to work independently. Since the academy had established a rule in 1680 that the minimum age for this honor was thirty,[96] we have a point of reference for the typical age when an apprentice became independent, ready to train students and to establish a workshop or studio.

Returning to our earlier question: why was Carlo Fontana's teaching so appealing that more pupils were apprenticed to him than to any other architect in Rome? It is probably safe to assume that it was his method of instructing through examples of carefully selected built architecture. The monument most important to him was without question Saint Peter's, which he considered unmatched even by the most revered structures of antiquity—the Pantheon in Rome and the Temple of Solomon in Jerusalem. To Fontana and the commissioners of his book it was unsurpassable, and therefore most suitable as a model for the training of young architects—a kind of "academy," as it is actually referred to in the documents of the Reverendissima Fabbrica.[97]

As an example of the correct building method for foundations, he could refer to the bell towers of Saint Peter's, explaining as he does in his book the proper method by which Bernini's ill-fated structure could have been saved.[98] Obviously inspired by Martino Longhi's published proposal of 1645, Fontana felt that the problem of Saint Peter's static stability in a swampy area could have been solved by constructing a new platform beneath the foundations, to be supported by *passonate*, or piles, rammed into the ground and buttressed laterally by a system of niches and arches.[99]

What Fontana had to say about the trusswork construction for the roof can be gleaned from the chapter on the roof of old Saint Peter's.[100] To begin with, he recommended that so important a part of the building as the roof never be left to the *meccanici*, ordinary craftsmen, who in his opinion were capable only of applying the rules they had learned. Fontana reported that the roof of old Saint Peter's was in such good condition that the material could be reused for the roofing of the Palazzo Farnese. He admired the construction of the trusswork, which consisted of a single vertical king post without braces connected with the tie beams and the collar. This system differed from the usual method of construction with a pair of queen posts above the tie beam. Fontana employed this latter system himself in 1695 for the construction of the new Teatro Tordinona, though he did not fail to alert his students and readers to possible problems that might result in a sagging roof.[101]

Considering the construction of domes and their visibility from both inside and outside a church, Fontana mentioned, among others, two particularly problematic examples. On one hand, the dome of

Vignola's Gesù finished by Giacomo della Porta (fig. 13) pleases the viewer from within because the dome is of moderate height. Seen from the outside, however, the dome appears too low, and further, the octagon of the drum is bisected by the gables of the roof. On the other hand, Fontana mentions Carlo Maderno's dome of Sant'Andrea della Valle (fig. 14), which is satisfactory from outside because of the remarkable height of the drum and dome. From the inside, however, the observer under the crossing will be disappointed

15. Saint Peter's, Rome, section through the crossing and dome
From *Il Tempio Vaticano*, 331

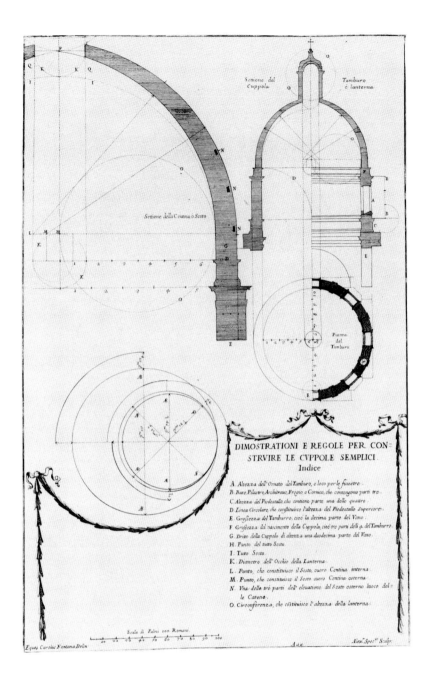

DIMOSTRATIONI E REGOLE PER CON-
STRVIRE LE CVPPOLE SEMPLICI.
Indice

because the height appears excessive. To avoid this dilemma, Carlo recommended the double-shell construction, as exemplified *par excellence* by the dome of Saint Peter's (fig. 15), and employed by himself in his Cappella Cybo (fig. 8), where he very consciously considered the spectator standing in the Piazza del Popolo.[102]

In cases where the double shell was not appropriate—as, for example, when the walls of the supporting structure were not strong enough to carry its weight—Fontana had rules for obtaining aestheti-

cally pleasing proportions (fig. 16) with the single-shell dome. They are straightforward and easy to follow.[103]

According to Fontana the height of the drum was to be determined by its radius and the dome was to have a stilted form further to be increased vertically by using a cylindrical wall, called "dritto della Cupola" ("G"), whose height equaled one-sixth of its semidiameter. The strength of the wall of the drum was to correspond to one-tenth of the diameter. Three-quarters of the thickness of the drum wall was con-

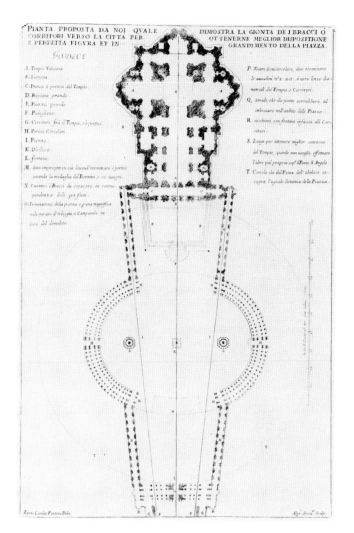

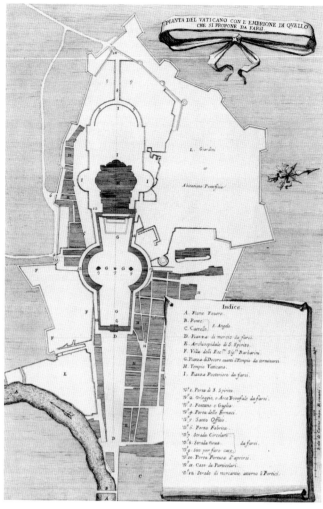

sidered adequate for the shell of the dome where the profile begins to curve.

As a rule regarding the "strength of materials," Carlo Fontana suggested the following: the thickness of the wall of the drum (one-tenth of its diameter) would be sufficient only if brick were used and the mortar were of high quality. If stone, or *tufo*, had to be employed instead, and the mortar were inferior in quality, one-ninth of the diameter was recommended to achieve the necessary strength for the wall of the drum.

His geometrical rules for the construction of the dome are also easily comprehended, and were drafted in a way that could be directly applied by his students. The interior and exterior profiles of the dome that Fontana presented as a model (fig. 16) were determined by the semidiameter, which was to be increased by one-sixth and one-twelfth respectively, to

draw the contour from the points "L" (inner shell) and "M" (outer shell); they are located on the dotted line that separates the dome from the cylindrical wall underneath it ("G"). The height of the lantern was again established by the radius of the dome. To ensure static stability Carlo Fontana advised the use of iron chains on three levels ("N") within the lower third of the outer shell. Such *regole*, handy rules of thumb, were very much appreciated by his students, and they reveal Fontana as a representative of artisanship within the architect's profession. Essentially based on tradition and experience, Fontana's pedagogical method seems to have fallen behind the kind of instruction then available at the Académie Royale d'Architecture in Paris. Fontana's contemporary there was Gabriel Philippe de la Hire (1640–1718), who published his *Traité de Mécanique* in 1695. When, half a

17. Saint Peter's Square, Rome, Carlo Fontana's first project for the enlargement
From *Il Tempio Vaticano*, 230

18. Saint Peter's Square, Rome, Carlo Fontana's second project for enlargement of the square and development of the area
From *Il Tempio Vaticano*, 231

century later, Giovanni Poleni was called (1743) by Benedict XIV from Padua to reexamine the question of the static stability of the dome of Saint Peter's, he expressed little esteem for Fontana's *regole*, but he admired in De la Hire the ability to "integrate geometry and the science of mechanics for the benefit of architecture."[104]

Notwithstanding the limitations of his approach, Carlo Fontana was able to establish beyond doubt that the dome of Saint Peter's was statically sound, and Poleni followed Fontana (fig. 15) in suggesting the use of iron chains (in addition to those already employed at the time of construction) for additional safety.[105] There is no better attestation to the validity of Fontana's teaching in Rome during his time.

Fontana must also have placed strong emphasis on urbanism in his instructional program. This assumption is underscored by his two famous plans for the square of Saint Peter's (figs. 17, 18). The trapezoidal Piazza Retta in front of the basilica is virtually repeated on the site of the former Piazza Rusticucci, and in Fontana's plans the obelisk again occupies a place at the midpoint of the perpendicular axis, as it did in the Circus of Nero. Here it bears a strictly Christian connotation, recalling the martyrdom of Saint Peter, in whose honor the basilica was originally erected by the Emperor Constantine.

In the second project Carlo Fontana pursued his urban aspirations further, to complete—rather radically—the reorganization of the entire Borgo area, envisioning the clearing of the Spina. Fontana also considered such practical aspects as that of commerce in his location of shops for the pilgrims near the Castel Sant'Angelo, and the flow of traffic to a newly established piazza behind the apse of the basilica. From there a new street would have guided the traveler out of the Vatican area through the Porta Pertusa to the highway leading to the seaport of Civitavecchia.[106]

Other considerations were of even greater importance to Fontana: the razing of the Spina made it possible to view Saint Peter's from what Fontana regarded as the optimal point: the Ponte Sant'Angelo. Central to his planning was the aspect of Christian triumph already indicated by the allusion to the Circus of Nero and the ipso facto increased emphasis on the obelisk. Approaching the piazza from the Ponte Sant'Angelo, the pilgrim would have been confronted first by a "triumphal arch of the Christian faith," the *terzo braccio* created by Bernini in his last known drawing related to this project.[107] Fontana moved the third arm further down, however, even beyond what once was the Piazza Rusticucci, in the direction of the Tiber. To the pilgrims moving toward the goal of their journey, the third arm would have stood out as a screen protecting the square in front of the basilica, a secondary but prominent vantage point which, for Fontana, was in carefully considered subordination to the preeminent vista of the dome of Saint Peter's.

In the years following Fontana's death, his concept of the *Arco trionfale della Fede Cattolica* experienced a revival in the form of an academic exercise, prescribed in 1716 by Clement XI himself for the students at the Accademia di San Luca. The *soggetto* called for a triumphal arch in honor of a *condottiere vittorioso* who had defended the Christian faith, a theme that made obvious reference to the specific political problem of that year: the Turks had again mobilized their forces against the West. The functional analogy with the triumphal arches erected for the emperors of ancient Rome is even more immediate than in the structure Carlo Fontana projected, which was more of a monument to the victory of Christianity over paganism. The winner of the first prize, Giuseppe Marchetti, adopted from Fontana the device of a superstructure in the center, treated not as a tower but as a receptacle for a sculptural group of the *Ecclesia triumphans*. Correspondingly, instead of a pediment, the structure is crowned by a triumphant carriage guided by an allegorical figure of the *Ecclesia militans*.[108]

The theme and the approach to its resolution could hardly have been more in line with one of Fontana's major concerns: the adaptation of ancient motifs and their utilization in a persuasive demonstration of the insuperability of the Christian faith.[109]

A further and particularly eloquent source for Fontana's kind of urban planning in the service of the rehabilitation of ancient monuments and sizes related to the history of the Christian faith is his book on the Colosseum, completed a few years after the publication of the *Templum Vaticanum*, but published posthumously in 1725. Here, in the manner of his suggestions for the development of the Borgo, Fontana added to the description and reconstruction of the Flavian amphitheater his famous proposal for a church in the arena, accompanied by explanatory texts (fig. 20).

This project for an ecclesiastical building in the Colosseum was first commissioned soon after the Holy Year of 1675 by Innocent XI (then still a cardinal). Interrupted by the war against the Turks, Fontana only resumed the project in anticipation of the Holy Year of 1700. This project was an excellent way to teach his students how a pagan monument enclosing the site of early Christian martyrdom could be consecrated to the Christian faith by constructing a church as a monument to the *Ecclesia triumphans*.[110] It was also appropriate for a demonstration of the church's proportional relationship to its environment: Fontana adopted the tier system of the amphitheater to that of the church, characterized by a ratio of 1:1:1.

Of particular importance to Fontana, as former stage designer, was the scenographic effect. The spectator's first impression of the church building in its setting would have been an overall frontal view framed by the entrance arch. Centrally located on the longitudinal axis of the Colosseum, the opening is part of the arcade with which Carlo intended to embrace the arena to create a kind of forecourt or square facing the projected church. It is evident that he wanted to apply his earlier idea for the oval piazza of Saint Peter's (fig. 5) to a different location, one propitious to the longitudinal oval. This arrangement would have placed the church on display like the set piece in a stage design against the backdrop of the curved amphitheater; the remains of the high screening wall would have provided the ideal setting for the drum and dome of the church, flanked by its bell towers.

As a result, the subject matter of Fontana's "course in architecture" might

be designated not simply "urbanism" but more specifically "urban scenography"— certainly no other architect of that period would have been better equipped to teach it than the former assistant to Bernini, except perhaps Carlo's son Francesco. Since Fontana believed the best vantage point for the church of Saint Peter's would have been near the Ponte Sant'Angelo, it is reasonable to conclude that the most favorable view of the projected church in the Colosseum would have been from beneath the entrance arch, directly opposite it, where the circular building would vigorously thrust forward from the concavity of its surroundings. The choice of this primary viewing point connects this

19. Piazza del Popolo, Rome, view from the Porta Flaminia

project directly with the twin churches of the Piazza del Popolo, whose axes converge under the entrance arch of the Porta Flaminia (fig. 19), where the traveler from the north receives his first contact not only with the two churches flanking the Corso, but also with the city of Rome at large.[111] The project for the church in the Colosseum, viewed in the same way, is probably the best indicator of Carlo Fontana's indebtedness not only to Cortona and Bernini, but also to Carlo Rainaldi with whom he had competed earlier. Analogously, Fontana's façade for San Marcello al Corso had been specifically conceived for the spectator standing at the midpoint of the concentric curves on which the concave movement of the

façade had been based.[112] The strict consistency of Fontana's development is also evident in his last, but unexecuted, project for San Marcello al Corso, which had twin bell towers not unlike those in his church project for the Colosseum (fig. 20).

There is still one further aspect to "professional survival skills" under adverse circumstances that Fontana's students could observe in their master, who used the instrument of publication to promote and commemorate his projects. This he did as early as 1674 with his above-mentioned façade design for Santa Maria di Monte Santo and later with his reconstruction proposal of the Ponte Rotto according to a new scheme (1692). Also, the publication of his projects for the

20. Carlo Fontana, project for a church to be built in the Colosseum
From *L'Anfiteatro Flavio* (The Hague, 1725)

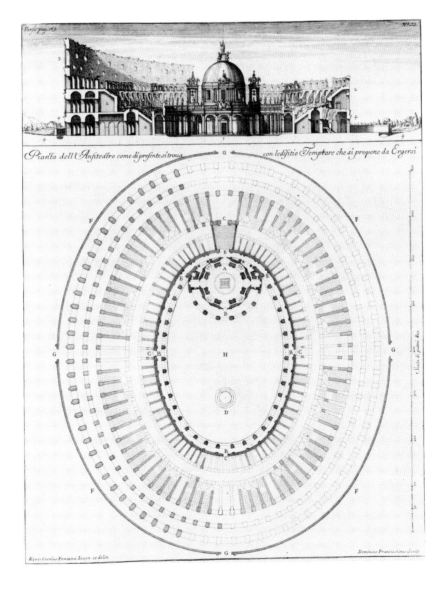

expansion of Saint Peter's Square and the urbanization of the Borgo Area (1694), as well as his design ideas for the Curia Innocenziana (1694 and 1708), the plans for the regularization of the Tiber curve near Sant'Andrea in Via Flaminia (1696), the overall plan for the remodeling of the Baptismal Chapel in Saint Peter's in 1697 (then nearly finished), and eventually publication of his project for a church in the Colosseum, which, as we saw, appeared only posthumously in 1725, were all undertaken with essentially the same intentions in mind.[113]

While these attempts at advertising are themselves worthy of note since they seem to anticipate developments which came into frequent practice during the later nineteenth century,[114] they were of little effect in his lifetime and even caused him difficulties when he used the medium of publication as an outlet to make his conflicts with colleagues public. Publication of the "Discorso sopra le cause delle innondazioni del Tevere" in 1696 resulted in a memorable backlash when Fontana's opponent, the Dutch engineer Cornelis Meyer, whose case had also been brought to public attention, promptly demonstrated that Carlo Fontana was wrong.[115]

21. Filippo Juvarra, tomb design for Carlo Fontana, c. 1730
Museo Civico, Turin (vol. 3, fol. 2, dis. 2)

22. Filippo Juvarra, drawing of a cenotaph for Francesco Fontana and his coat of arms, c. 1708
Biblioteca Nazionale, Turin (vol. 59/4, fol. 100)

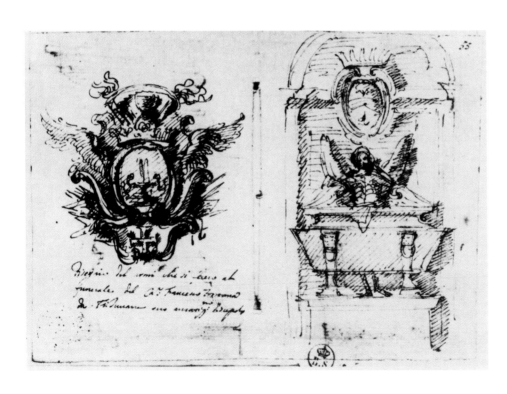

The impact of Fontana's writings deserves further attention as does the growing use during the eighteenth century of published architectural drawings for the diffusion of building ideas and instructional purposes.[116]

In the final analysis, what made Carlo Fontana a much sought-after teacher seems to be a combination of factors. At the most elementary level he offered solid basic training for the architectural profession rooted in his comprehensive experience in matters of building technology; engineering played an essential role in all his designs and thinking. Well appreciated by his apprentices was certainly his already-mentioned ability to convey information, which he "packaged" into hard and fast rules applicable to any situation. Fontana was equally adept at creating aesthetically convincing effects that he coordinated with other artists to a precise degree rarely matched at that time in Rome. He provided his students with examples and rules for proper proportions and, in his chapels, introduced them to the delicate task of establishing chromatic harmony through the appropriate choices of materials available for purposes of incrustation and articulation. In this case his students could best learn from the examples he had created himself.[117]

In particular, Fontana's unusually broad approach to historical architecture—from antiquity as well as from the then-modern tradition of the Renaissance and baroque —which he relied on and recommended as a resource for the handling of architectural problems as well as for inspiration, did not fail to make its impact on students from abroad like Nicodemus Tessin the Younger and Fischer von Erlach, for whom historical architecture became subject matter in its own right. Fontana's preoccupation with architectural forms of the past came to the fore when he began to investigate Solomon's temple in Jerusalem, the Pantheon, and the Circus of Nero, as well as the Vatican and Montecitorio areas of Rome, which he attempted to reconstruct.

Although there is undoubtedly more to be said about the organization and operation of Fontana's studio, it is possible to obtain an informed view of Carlo Fontana

as a teacher—and his son Francesco as well—and the quality of instruction in their studio from one of their most prominent students: Filippo Juvarra.[118] Juvarra provides this in the inscription on his design for a monument to Carlo Fontana (fig. 21) which refers to his former master with the respectful dedication: "Cav. Carlo Fontana celebre architetto morì in Roma 1712 [sic] disegnio per memoria." Juvarra expressed similar feelings of appreciation and strong personal affection for Carlo's son when he inscribed the drawings for a cenotaph and the coat of arms (fig. 22) for Francesco's funeral as follows: "Disegnio del armi che si fecero al funerale del Ca:e Francesco Fontana da Fi. Juvarra suo amatissimo discepolo."[119]

Naturally Carlo's death in 1714, followed by Juvarra's departure from Rome in the same year, left Rome devoid of an exceptionally attractive and influential teacher, and brought about the demise of a workshop that had established a direct link across the long stretch from the Roman high baroque to the early settecento. In that workshop the students who had come from abroad, as well as those who went abroad for employment, experienced their introduction to, or their advancement in, the architectural profession—Nicola Michetti, Romano Carapecchia, and Tommaso Mattei. Those architects who stayed in Rome—Alessandro Specchi, Carlo Francesco Bizzacheri, Carlo Buratti—either through their own workshops or through the Accademia at large practiced with solid professionalism and maintained standards that enabled the next generation of architects to assume the reins at the beginning of the 1720s. John Pinto has referred to these architects as the "heirs of Carlo Fontana": Luigi Vanvitelli, Ferdinando Fuga, Alessandro Galilei, and Nicola Salvi, all of whom accepted their historic mission and accomplished a revival of the seventeenth-century full baroque with the same vigorous and versatile manifestations that had characterized the Roman seicento—a period that had left so much of its legacy in the able hands of Carlo Fontana and his remarkably efficient workshop.

NOTES

1. Allan Braham and Hellmut Hager, *Carlo Fontana: The Drawings at Windsor Castle* (London, 1977), 11.

2. On Giovanni Battista Contini's activities see Alessandro del Bufalo, *G. B. Contini e la tradizione del tardomanierismo, nell'architettura tra '600 e '700* (Rome, 1982); and Hellmut Hager, "Giovanni Battista Contini," in *Dizionario biografico degli Italiani* 28 (Rome, 1983), 515–522.

3. Lione Pascoli, *Vite de' pittori, scultori ed architetti moderni*, 2 vols. (Rome, 1730–1736), 2:542–549.

4. Ugo Donati, *Artisti ticinesi a Roma* (Bellinzona, 1942), 264; see 264 n. 3 for Carlo Fontana's year of birth (which Pascoli gave as 1634) but the relative, Padre Sisto Sassi, who wrote about Fontana's family in 1697, established beyond doubt (as 22 April 1638) through the baptismal records. As to Fontana's arrival in Rome recorded by Sassi as early as 1650, see Donati, 264 nn. 2, 3.

5. Archivio del Vicariato di Roma, *Testamenti e matrimoni*, Ufficio I, notaio Bernardinus de Sanctis (dal 24 dicembre 1661 al 22 dicembre 1663). Giovanni Maria Bolino's statement is entered 10 January 1663. Fontana's marriage to Catarina Anastasia, daughter of Silvestro di Bianchi, took place about two weeks later, 23 January 1663, in the parish of Santa Maria in Via (Archivio del Vicariato di Roma, *Matrimonium Liber*, 1643–1680). For this and the other information from the Archivio del Vicariato used in this paper, I am grateful to Maria A. Sportelli-Hager.

6. Giovanni Maria Bolino died 7 November 1669 and was buried in Santa Maria in Vallicella (Archivio del Vicariato di Roma, San Stefano in Piscinula, *Liber Mortuorum*).

7. About the development of the architect's profession in Italy since the Renaissance see Leopold Ettlinger, "The Emergence of the Italian Architect during the Fifteenth Century," and Catherine Wilkinson, "The New Professionalism in the Renaissance," in *The Architect, Chapters in the History of the Profession*, ed. Spiro Kostof (New York, 1977), 96–123 and 124–160, respectively. For the period under examination see in particular: Bruno Contardi e Giovanna Curcio, eds., *In Urbe Architectus, Modelli Disegni Misure. La professione dell'architetto Roma 1680–1750* [exh. cat., Museo Nazionale di Castel Sant'Angelo] (Rome, 1991) (with biographies of virtually all architects who were active in Rome during the late baroque).

8. For Bolino's professional position and activities see Minna Heimbürger Ravalli, *Architettura, Scultura e Arti Minori nel Barocco Italiano* (Florence, 1977), 46 n. 36, 261, 274, 301 n. 24; Hans Ost, "Studien zu Pietro da Cortonas Umbau von S. Maria della Pace," *Römisches Jahrbuch für Kunstgeschichte* 13 (1971), 244–245 (elevation after Bolino, fig. 12); Karl Noehles, *La Chiesa dei SS. Luca e Martina nell' opera di Pietro da Cortona* (Rome, 1970), 345–346 doc. 70, 353–354 docs. 102 and 103; Furio Fasolo, *L'Opera di Hieronymo e Carlo Rainaldi* (Rome, 1961), 346, 364. For the collaboration between Bolino and Mattia de' Rossi on Bernini's project, see: Anna Menichella, *Mattia de' Rossi, Discepolo prediletto del Bernini* (Rome, 1985), 18, 19, 61, 62–64, 83, 84, 86, 87.

9. Eduard Coudenhove-Erthal, *Carlo Fontana und die Architektur des römischen Spätbarocks* (Vienna, 1930), 17–19; Ost 1971, 244–257.

10. Personal communication with Herbert Kessler, Johns Hopkins University, on the occasion of the symposium dedicated to "The Artist's Workshop," at the Center for Advanced Study in the Visual Arts, National Gallery of Art, Washington, 11–12 March 1989, with reference to Richard Krautheimer, Spencer Corbett, Wolfgang Frankl, *Corpus Basilicarum Christianarum Romae*, vol. 3 (Città del Vaticano, 1967), 51, figs. 50, 52, 53.

11. Heinrich Brauer and Rudolf Wittkower, *Die Zeichnungen des Gianlorenzo Bernini* (Berlin, 1931), 1:127–129; Vincenzo Golzio, *Documenti artistici sul Seicento nell'Archivio Chigi* (Rome, 1939), 6, 29, 31, 34, 36–69; Coudenhove-Erthal 1930, 24–26; for a recent investigation into the planning and building history and an assessment of Fontana's role, see Elisabeth Sladek, "Der Palazzo Chigi-Odescalchi, Studien und Materialien zu den frühen Bauphasen des 16. und 17. Jahrhunderts," *Römische Historische Mitteilungen* 27 (1985), 439–503.

12. For the organization of the work on the building site during the seventeenth century in Rome, see "Baubetrieb und Arbeitsleben" in Gerhard Eimer, *La Fabbrica di S. Agnese in Navona, Römische Architekten, Bauherren und Handwerker im Zeitalter des Nepotismus*, 2 vols. (Stockholm, 1970–1971), 1:210–243 (see note 54 below).

A *misuratore* can be either (like Bolino) a subordinate but professionally highly skilled architect who does *not* direct building on his own account but works dependently with others (comparable to a project director on the site in modern terminology); or like Fontana for many years at Saint Peter's in Rome and elsewhere, *any* architect asked to check the artisans' accounts.

Of particular importance was the *capomaestro muratore*, the master mason responsible for the construction. Next followed the *scarpellini* (stone carvers), carpenters, and plumbers who submitted their own accounts, which were all reviewed by the leading architect or his deputy, the *architetto deputato*, functioning also as *architetto misuratore*; this was Fontana's de facto position not only at the Palazzo Chigi in Piazza Santi Apostoli but also at Ariccia, where he seems to have been subordinate to Mattia de' Rossi when the Church of the Assumption was built (see note 13).

13. Brauer and Wittkower 1931, 1:122–126; Giovanni Incisa della Rocchetta, "Notizie sulla fabbrica della chiesa collegiata di Ariccia, 1662–1664," *Rivista del R. Istituto Archeologia, Storia e Arte* 1 (1929), 349–377; Renato Lefevre, *Il Bernini ad Ariccia e la "Piazza di Corte" dei Chigi* (Rome, 1981), 33–62.

14. For these churches see Coudenhove-Erthal 1930, 20–22; Hellmut Hager, "Le facciate dei SS. Faustino e Giovita e di S. Biagio in Campitelli (S. Rita) a Roma. A proposito di due opere giovanili di Carlo Fontana," *Commentari* 23 (1972), 261–271.

15. For Fontana's career in this period see Braham and Hager, 1977, 7–14; for the history and organization of the Fabbrica see Niccolò del Re, "La Sacra Congregazione della Reverenda Fabbrica di San Pietro," *Studi Romani* 17 (1969), 288–301; Peter Rietbergen, "A Vision Come True: Pope Alexander VII, Gianlorenzo Bernini, and the Colonnades of Saint Peter's," *Mededelingen van het Nederlands Instituut te Rome* 44/45 (1983), 121–129; Helga Tratz, "Werkstatt und Arbeitsweise Berninis," *Römisches Jahrbuch für Kunstgeschichte* 23/24 (1988), 422–427. Alessandra Anselmi, Gli architetti della Fabbrica di S. Pietro, in: *In Urbe Architectus*, 272–280.

16. Carlo Fontana, *Il Tempio Vaticano e la sua origine* (Rome, 1694), 188; the foundation stone was already laid 28 August 1657: see Brauer and Wittkower 1931, 1:74–83; for a survey of chronology see Timothy K. Kitao, *Circle and Oval in the Square of Saint Peter's* (New York, 1974); Rietbergen 1983, 144–146; Menichella 1985, 17–18.

17. Brauer and Wittkower 1931, 1:82, 87. The proposition by Timothy Kitao that Carlo Fontana was totally excluded from participation in the project of Saint Peter's Square does not seem to be tenable in its absolute form. See Timothy K. Kitao, "Carlo Fontana Had No Part in Bernini's Planning for the Square of Saint Peter's," *Journal of the Society of Architectural Historians* 36 (1977), 85–93.

18. Braham and Hager 1977, 38–39.

19. Fontana 1694, 285.

20. Brauer and Wittkower, 1931, 1:64–102; Rudolf Wittkower, "Il terzo braccio del Bernini in Piazza San Pietro," *Bollettino d'Arte* 34 (1949), 129–134; Maurizio and Marcello Fagiolo dell'Arco, *Bernini, una introduzione al gran teatro del Barocco* (Rome, 1967), *scheda* 166; Hellmut Hager, "Progetti del tardo barocco romano per il terzo braccio del colonnato della Piazza di San Pietro," *Commentari* 19 (1968), 299–314; Kitao 1974, 49–51; 55–56.

21. The pavement plan in the Vatican (fig. 3) published by Kitao (1974, fig. 79) as a drawing of Bernini's workshop, and a second pavement plan (fig. 73 in Kitao) are both attributable to Carlo Fontana, whose handwriting can be recognized in the figures of the *palmi romani* scale. For the sketched elevation of the *terzo braccio* by Bernini, see Brauer and Wittkower 1931, 1:87, pl. 64. Rather than intentionally plagiarizing Bernini's project, however, Fontana seems to have published the elevation drawing (or an elaboration thereof) that Bernini apparently ordered from him when he worked as his assistant.

22. Kitao 1974, fig. 36.

23. Kitao 1974, 74–76, fig. 13; Hellmut Hager, "Osservazioni su Carlo Fontana e la sua opera del *Tempio Vaticano* (1694)," in proceedings of the conference, Centri e Periferie del Barocco (Rome, Accademia dei Lincei, 1987), in press.

24. For the increasing conflict between Carlo Fontana and Carlo Rainaldi on this project see Hellmut Hager, "Zur Planungs- und Baugeschichte der Zwillingskirchen auf der Piazza del Popolo," *Römisches Jahrbuch für Kunstgeschichte* 11 (1967/1968), 212–239, with further bibliographical references.

25. Hager 1967/1968, 209, fig. 152. The drawing (among other drawings and documents from the Archivio Segreto Vaticano) was introduced into the discussion about the planning history of the twin churches with the correct attribution to Carlo Fontana by Vincenzo Golzio, "Le Chiese di Santa Maria di Montesanto e di Santa Maria dei Miracoli a Piazza del Popolo in Roma," *Archivi d'Italia*, vol. 8 (1934), 122–148.

26. First published by Rudolf Wittkower, "Carlo Rainaldi and the Roman Architecture of the Full Baroque," *Art Bulletin* 19 (1937), 248, fig. 10; Hager 1967/1968, 209, fig. 154.

27. For the text of the inscription, dated 20 March 1674, see Hager 1967/1968, 240 n. 98.

28. Braham and Hager 1977, 8, 10–12. Carlo Fontana with his wife, Caterina de' Bianchi, and their growing family lived from 1664 to 1678 in a house in the Strada Alessandrina in the parish of Santa Maria in Campo Carleo (near the Forum of Trajan), with the possible exception of the years 1666–1669, for which there is no mention of them in the records of the Stati d'Anime of the Archivio del Vicariato di Roma (Parrochia di Santa Maria in Campo Carleo). From 1672 Carlo is referred to with the title *cavaliere* and from 1676 as *Illustre cavaliere*. We are again without information about his residence between 1678 and 1684 (see notes 52 and 88 below). For a view of the no-longer-extant church of Santa Maria in Campo Carleo and the Via Alessandrina, see Giuseppe Vasi, *Delle Magnificenze di Roma* 6 (Rome, 1756), pl. 102.

29. Per Bjurström, "Feast and Theater in Queen Christina's Rome," *Analecta Reginensia* 3 (1966), 88–112. For the history of the Teatro Tor di Nona see further: Sergio Rotondi, *Il Teatro Tordinona, Storia, progetti, architettura* (Rome, 1987); Bianca Tavassi La Greca, "Carlo Fontana e il Teatro di Tor di Nona," in *Il Teatro a Roma nel Settecento*, 2 vols. (Rome, 1989), 1:19–34.

30. For Fontana's altar compare Claudio Catena, *Traspontina: guida storica e artistica*, Rome [1956], 51–55.

31. Ragnar Josephson, *Nicodemus Tessin* (Stockholm, 1930), 1:52–55, pl. 50. It is known through an explicit statement by Tessin of this period that he made drawings under the supervision of Carlo Fontana (see note 36 below).

32. Heinrich Thelen, *Zur Entstehungsgeschichte der Hochaltar-Architektur von St. Peter in Rom* (Berlin, 1967), 56–57, 63–64; Thelen, *Francesco Borromini, Die Handzeichnungen* (Graz, 1967), 79–82, cat. C, 68–70.

33. Giovanni Giacomo de' Rossi, ed., *Disegni di vari altari e Cappelle nelle Chiese di Roma* (Rome, n.d.), pl. 27. (Modern edition by Anthony Blunt, Westmead, Farmborough, Hunts, England, 1972.)

34. Allan Braham, *Funeral Decoration in Early Eighteenth Century Rome* (London, 1975), 22–25; Braham and Hager 1977, 98–103, fig. 212.

35. Catena [1956], 53–57. Leonardo Retti (or Reti) from Lombardi, who had trained under Ercole Ferrata and collaborated with Antonio Raggi, was working from Fontana's drawings when he created the no-longer-extant statues on Innocent XII's triumphal arch of 1692 in Rome (Coudenhove-Erthal 1930, 122 n. 216, fig. 34; Rudolf Wittkower in Thieme-Becker 28 [1934]: 189). Further on Retti's career and his professional activities, see David Bershed, "Leonardo Reti and the Restoration of Statuary in the Villa Aldobrandini in Frascati," *Antologia di Belle Arti* 5, 1981, 204–210.

36. Bjurström 1966, 58–112. Bjurström refers to a statement by Nicodemus Tessin of 3 August 1673 that he made the designs for Queen Christina's theater under the supervision of Carlo Fontana. Compare Bjurström, *Den Romerska Barockens Scenografi* (Lund, 1977), 80. For Carlo's activities as a stage designer, see also Pietro Ruschi, "Due 'inventioni' di Carlo Fontana per una festa in casa Fürstenberg," *Bollettino d'Arte*, 65 (1980), 75–80.

37. Also of high value was Carlo's historical approach to architecture, which obviously influenced Fischer von Erlach, who was in Rome from c. 1671 to 1686. For an outline of Fischer's sojourn in Rome see Hans Sedlmayr (who emphatically denies the yet to be more thoroughly investigated possibility of Fontana's influence), *Johann Bernhard Fischer von Erlach*, 2d ed. (Vienna, 1976), 20–29; Hans Aurenhammer, *J. B. Fischer von Erlach* (London, 1973), 18–20, 153. Compare Hellmut Hager, "Osservazioni su Carlo Fontana," in press.

38. Golzio 1939, 149–187, 229–237.

39. Hager, "Osservazioni su Carlo Fontana," in press.

40. Braham and Hager 1977, 19–23.

41. Golzio 1939, 240. *Giovane* means beginning apprentice in a studio (see note 87 below).

42. Compare Nina A. Mallory, "Carlo Francesco Bizzaccheri (1655–1721), with an annotated catalogue by John Varriano," *Journal of the Society of Architectural Historians* 33 (1974), 27–47; Marina Carta, "Carlo Francesco Bizzaccheri e la Cappella del Monte di Pietà," *Bollettino d'Arte* 65 (1980), 49–50; Carta, "Il muro di cinta di Villa Aldobrandini a Frascati: Un monumento della produzione artistica di Carlo Francesco Bizzaccheri," *Bollettino d'Arte* 67 (1982), 89–96.

43. *Architectural Fantasy and Reality: Drawings from the Accademia Nazionale di San Luca in Rome, Concorsi Clementini, 1700–1750*, intro. Hellmut Hager [exh. cat., Museum of Art, Pennsylvania State University, University Park and Cooper-Hewitt Museum, New York] (New York, 1981–1982), 4.

44. *Architectural Fantasy and Reality*, 1981–1982, 4. For more on Domenico Martinelli see Giambattista Franceschini, *Memorie della Vita di Domenico Martinelli, sacerdote Lucchese e insigne architetto* (Lucca, 1772); Hans Tietze, "Domenico Martinelli und seine Tätigkeit für Österreich," *Jahrbuch des Kunsthistorischen Instituts* 13 (1919), 1–46; and especially the recent monograph about the architect by Hellmut Lorenz, *Domenico Martinelli und die österreichische Barockarchitektur* (Vienna, 1991), 9–11.

45. Compare Luigi Salerno, in Emilio Lavagnino et al., *Altari barocchi in Roma* (Rome, 1959), 157–161; Francis H. Dowley, "Some Maratti Drawings at Düsseldorf," *Art Quarterly* 20 (1957), 163–179; Hellmut Hager, "La cappella del Cardinale Alderano Cybo in Santa Maria del Popolo," *Commentari* 25 (1974), 47–61; Hager, "Un riesame di tre cappelle di Carlo Fontana a Roma," *Commentari* 27 (1976), 252–289.

46. Hager 1967/1968, 274–276, figs. 199, 202, 203.

47. Hellmut Hager, "La facciata di San Marcello al Corso. Contributo alla storia della costruzione," *Commentari* 24 (1973) 61–65; Hager "A proposito della costruzione della facciata di San Marcello al Corso e delle traversie collegate al compimento della decorazione scultorea dovuta ad Andrea Fucigna," *Commentari* 29 (1978), 201–216. The statues of the upper register have been traditionally (though erroneously) given to Francesco Cavallini. Compare Laura Gigli, *San Marcello al Corso*. Le Chiese di Roma illustrate (Rome, 1977), 35–40, and Anthony Blunt, *Guide to Baroque Rome* (London, 1982), 78.

48. Francis H. Dowley, "Carlo Maratti, Carlo Fontana, and the Baptismal Chapel in Saint Peter's," *Art Bulletin* 47 (1965), 57–81; Hager 1976, 264–267.

49. Braham and Hager 1977, 43, 45, nos. 35–37, figs. 9–12; Hager 1976, 267, figs. 17–19.

50. Fontana 1694, 303.

51. For the Cappella Albani see Hager 1976, 267, 270–278.

52. From 1685 to 1696 Carlo can be documented with his family (which included his son Francesco, born in 1668, but in 1687 his wife, Catarina, is not recorded) in the house called Casa Manucci located in Isola 20 and "in faccia la n[ost]ra chiesa," that is, opposite the church of Spirito Santo (number 114 on the map of Nolli, 1748). Exceptions are the year 1690 when the house is described as empty and, possibly in 1691, a year for which information is missing. The church belonged to the parish of San Lorenzo ai Monti, also near the Forum of Trajan. In 1697 this house must have become the property of Carlo Fontana because it is described from that year and thereafter as the "Casa del Cavalier Fontana." But until 1706 he apparently lived elsewhere, because other names are recorded for residents. In 1706 Carlo returned with his family, among them his sons, Gaspare, a priest, and Francesco with his wife Caterina Santarelli and three children (including the future architect Mauro, born in 1701). See Archivio del Vicariato di Roma, Stati d'Anime, San Lorenzo ai Monti. Compare note 28 and note 88.

53. The property of Francesco Fontana, who, beside the villa in Castelgandolfo, owned a three-story house opposite the church of Santa Maria in Carlo Carleo; another one, also of three stories and opposite the church of Sant' Eufemia, included *casette* and *vigne*. But the inventory in the Archivio di Stato di Roma (Not. Uff. 32, Petrus Antonius Quintilius 332), kindly communicated to me by Marcello del Piazzo, makes no reference to a "studio." Only Francesco's instruments are entered in the register of his possessions, among them, as one might expect, several compasses, in part specified as "un compasso grande di ottone con punta di acciaio di Giacomo Lusuergh, or un compassetto di Giacomo Lusuergh. Further mentioned are "un tiralineo di acciaio usato, un toccalapis con stelletta dall' altera parte, un semicircolo di ottone, un altra squadra di ottone, un istrumento per gli ouati," and a "Calibro di ottone per fistole e quadre."

54. For the hierarchies in the architectural profession in Rome, the modes of remuneration, and studio practices, see Eimer 1970–1971, 1:58, 61, 81, 86, 210, 212, 224, 296, 428, 443, 491, 644–646. See our notes 12 and 41. For the career of Simone Felice del Lino, see Mario Bevilacqua, "Documenti per il Tardo Barocco Romano: Casa Panizza e l'opera dell'architetto Simone Felice Delino," in *Palladio* 3 (1989), 133–142.

55. Archivio del Vicariato di Roma, Stati d'Anime, San Lorenzo ai Monti. Girolamo is recorded as twenty years old in 1685 and twenty-two in 1687, which corresponds to his age as established by Leonello Razza, *La Basilica Cattedrale di Frascati* (Frascati, 1979), 125 n. 14. Girolamo died on 27 September 1701 when he was "approximately" thirty-three years old. In September his name appears along with that of his uncle and others on "perizie" and "misure" concerning the watterconduct of the Acqua Felice. See document transcripts of the period which are attached with a set of original drawings to the copy of Francesco Fontana's *Relazione dello stato Vecchio, e Nuovo dell' Acqua Felice* (Rome, 1696), in the Bibliotheca Hertziana in Rome (Raro, gr. Dr. 453-2960, fols. 19–21 v.)

56. Bjurström 1977, 96–110; Razza 1979, 114–126; Hellmut Hager, "Girolamo Fontana e la facciata della cattedrale di San Pietro a Frascati," *Commentari* 28 (1977), 273–288.

Girolamo's brother, Carlo Stefano, seems to have trained with Carlo Fontana at an unspecified date before he participated in the Concorsi Clementini of 1703, 1704, and 1705 (always winning second prize). *Abate* and beneficiary of San Giovanni in Laterano, he practiced the architectural profession with a considerable degree of competence (see Donati 1942, 378–380; for the Concorsi Clementini of 1704 see Bernadette Balco, and of 1705, Susan S. Munshower in *Architectural Fantasy and Reality*, 1981–1982, 17–29 and 30–42, respectively). However, Carlo Stefano still relied strongly on his uncle when he used the ground plan of Carlo's project for a casino in the Veneto (1689) as the inspiration for his submitted church project when he became *accademico di merito* in 1721. He died in 1740. See Werner Oechslin,

Bildungsgut und Antikenrezeption des frühen Settecento in Rom. Studien zum römischen Aufenthalt Bernardo Antonio Vittones (Zurich and Freiburg im Breisgau, 1972), 111, 175 n. 4; Braham and Hager 1977, 107–109, figs. 232–239.

57. For the façade drawing Bizzacheri presented to the Accademia di San Luca on the occasion of his promotion to the rank of *accademico di merito*, and which seems to have been drawn with the front of a major Roman basilica in mind, see Mallory 1974, 38, 45, pl. 16; Hellmut Hager, "On a Project Ascribed to Carlo Fontana for the Façade of San Giovanni in Laterano," *Burlington Magazine* 117 (1975), 106, 111, fig. 58.

58. Golzio 1939, 255; the refurbishment of the interior and the new façade may therefore have been commissioned from him by Cardinal Fabrizio Paolucci upon the recommendation of Carlo Fontana. For these works executed between 1715 and 1722 see G. del Pinto, "La Basilica Costantiniana di Albano," in *Ricordi della riapertura della cattedrale basilica Constantiniana di Albano* (1913), 37, 44.

59. Hager 1967/1968, 254, 245, figs. 78, 179.

60. Andrea Adami, *Storia di Volsena, antica metropoli della toscana*, 2 vols. (Rome, 1734–1737). The author of the present paper plans to return to the topic of this church on another occasion. Christian Elling, *Rome: The Biography of a City: Its Architecture from Bernini to Thorvaldsen* (Tübingen, 1975), 72, 101; Armindo Ayres de Carvalho, *Joao V e a arte do seu tempo*, 2 vols. (Mafra, 1962).

61. Hager, "Osservazioni su Carlo Fontana," in press. In 1689 Specchi illustrated the libretto for an opera with engravings of the stage settings. See Elling 1975, 71.

62. Specchi also did the engravings for Carlo Fontana's *Utilissimo trattato delle acque correnti* (Rome, 1696).

63. Braham and Hager 1977, 151–152; Tod A. Marder, "The Porto di Ripetta a Roma," *Journal of the Society of Architectural Historians* 39 (1980), 28–56.

64. Coudenhove-Erthal 1930, 140–141; Bruno Grimschitz, *Johann Lucas von Hildebrandt* (Vienna, 1959), 8, 171, 201.

65. For Johann and the Dientzenhofer family of architects, see Heinrich Gerhard Franz, *Bauten und Baumeister der Barockzeit in Böhmen* (Leipzig, 1963), 55.

66. Hellmut Hager, "Johann Dientzenhofer's Cathedral in Fulda and the Question of Its Roman Origins," in *Light on the Eternal City: Observations and Discoveries in the Art and Architecture of Rome*. Papers in Art History from Pennsylvania State University 2 (University Park, 1987), 189–230.

67. Gil Smith in "Gilles-Maria Oppenord in Italy," presented at the meeting of the Society of Architectural Historians, Montreal, April 1989.

68. For the activity of Filippo de Romanis at the

Accademia di San Luca in Rome, see essay 2 by Bernadette Balco, in *Architectural Fantasy and Reality*, 1981–1982, 17–29. See also note 69.

69. The first known work by Romano Fortunato Carapecchia is a palace design with which he won first prize in the Concorso Accademico of 1681 at the Accademia di San Luca. See Paolo Marconi, Angela Cipriani, Enrico Valeriani, "Archival Notes Concerning the Architectural Drawings of the Seventeenth Century, Preserved in the Saint Luke Academy in Rome," in *Architectural Fantasy and Reality*, 1981–1982, app. 167, where this date is confirmed. For the Casino Vaini before 1703 see Coudenhove-Erthal 1930, 109, 112, figs. 43, 44, 131; Braham and Hager 1977, 177. Further on Carapecchia see Jo Tonna and Dennis de Lucca, *Romano Carapecchia: Studies in Maltese Architecture* 1 (Malta University Press, 1975); John Pinto, *The Trevi Fountain* (New Haven, 1986), 72–73.

70. Braham and Hager 1977, 177.

71. For this event and a comprehensive assessment of the role played by Carlo and Francesco Fontana in the shaping of the curriculum and the structure of the academy, see the publication by Gil Smith, *Diplomacy by Design: The Earliest Competitions in Architecture at the Accademia di San Luca, and the Late Baroque Discourse between Rome and France* (Architectural History Foundation), forthcoming.

72. Luigi Pirotta, "Francesco Fontana sostituto di Carlo Maratta nel Principato dell' Accademia di San Luca," *L'Urbe* 31 (1988), no. 2, 16–21; Carlo Pietrangeli et al., *L'Accademia Nazionale di San Luca* (Rome, 1974).

73. Emma Zocca, *La basilica dei SS. Apostoli in Roma* (Rome, 1959), 59–65; Braham and Hager 1977, 77–79, 177–178.

74. Hager 1987, 189–194.

75. Coudenhove-Erthal 1930, 144–145, who referred to Pascoli, was unaware of the fact that a model had been sent from Rome in or before 1706, whereas Frieda Dettweiler, *Die Stuckarbeiten im Dom zu Fulda und ihre Meister* (Frankfurt am Main, 1928), 1 n. 1, who published the document related to the payment for the transportation of the model, had no knowledge of the information provided by Lione Pascoli.

76. When Francesco Fontana died in 1708, Carlo was seventy years old. Even though Carlo is known to have worked until shortly before his death (6 February 1714), he confessed that he was suffering from gout as early as 1703. Since Clement XI, as Pascoli reports, tended increasingly to make use of Francesco's services, the assumption is almost unavoidable that by 1708 Francesco, under normal circumstances, would have been the future heir of his father's studio. A similar situation prevailed in the Rainaldi studio. At age forty Carlo Rainaldi (1611–1691) began to replace his father Girolamo (1570–1655) when in 1651 he followed him in his office of "Architetto del Popolo Romano" (Girolamo was then approximately eighty years old). Carlo Rainaldi then began plans for Sant'Agnese in Piazza Navona. However, documentary information concerning the connections between their studios is missing. See Eimer, *La Fabbrica di S. Agnese in Navona*, 1:58–59.

Braham and Hager 1977, 177–178, fig. 472. A drawing in the collection at Windsor Castle shows a perspective view of Santi Apostoli while under construction, looking along the arches of the nave toward the entrance. We recognize the supporting centering under the first arch and, above the main cornice, a scaffolding for the workmen occupied with the window underneath the vault penetration. Similar supporting devices are visible in other places on the site, where about twenty-five workmen can be counted. Windlasses, crowbars, blocks and pulleys, and other instruments for construction can be seen in this rare view that allows us to witness the progress of building during the early settecento. For a detailed representation of such machinery see Carlo Fontana *Il Tempio Vaticano*, 124–126, and plate on 127. For further information on the subject of the tools and equipment used for the construction of buildings, see the volume *Castelli e Ponti* (Rome, 1743), dedicated to Maestro Niccola Zabbaglia (1664–1750) and furnished with numerous engravings of the devices employed.

77. Razza 1979, 119–121; Hager 1977, 281–286.

78. The *governatore* of Frascati who commissioned the façade was also a member of the Colonna family (Monsignor Carlo Colonna) and had assumed office shortly before Girolamo was called in; Razza 1979, 114–118.

79. For the training of James Gibbs in Rome under Carlo Fontana, see Bryan Little, *The Life and Work of James Gibbs (1682–1754)* (London, 1955), 19–25; Terry Friedman, *James Gibbs* (New Haven and London, 1984), 36–38, fig. 13.

80. Gaetana Scano, "Insegnamento e Concorsi," in Pietrangeli et al. 1974; see also Hager, introduction, as well as entry 2 on 1704 by Bernadette Balco; entries 3 and 4 on 1705 by Susan S. Munshower; entry 5 on 1706 by William Eisler, and entry 6 on 1708 by Christine Challingsworth, in *Architectural Fantasy and Reality*, 1981–1982, 5–6, 17–74.

81. Braham and Hager 1977, 15, 184–190.

82. Braham and Hager 1977, 16, 89–103.

83. For the establishment of the date of Juvarra's arrival in Rome see Mary Myers, *Architectural and Ornament Drawings: Juvarra, Vanvitelli, the Bibiena Family, and Other Italian Draughtsmen* [exh. cat., Metropolitan Museum of Art, New York] (New York, 1975), 30; Henry A. Millon, *Filippo Juvarra: Drawings from the Roman Period, 1704–1714*, part 1 (Rome, 1984), xviii–xix, no. 48.

84. Hellmut Hager, "Carlo Fontana e l'ingrandimento dell' Ospizio di San Michele. Contributo allo sviluppo architettonico di un'istituzione caritativa del Tardo Barocco Romano," *Commentari* 26 (1975), 344–359; Braham and Hager 1977, 137–150.

85. Braham and Hager 1977, 141. Michetti succeeded Fontana also in the coordinated project of the Curia

Innocenziana, a mammoth undertaking begun in 1694 with Mattia de' Rossi and continued by Fontana alone after Mattia's death in 1695. For Michetti's training and career see John Pinto, "Nicola Michetti (c. 1675–1758) and Eighteenth-Century Architecture in Rome and Saint Petersburg" (Ph.D. diss., Harvard University, 1976).

86. Gherardi's major works are the Cappella Avila in Santa Maria in Trastevere (1680), and the Cappella di Santa Cecilia in San Carlo ai Catinari, where the overall design is the work of an artist who is essentially a painter-architect. However, the degree of integration of architecture, painting, and sculpture, though very remarkable, is not quite as sophisticated as Fontana's works. Above all, there is a certain lack of cohesion in the Cappella Avila where Gherardi enforces overly sharp foreshortening perspective on the observer in the lower part of the chapel, conceived in Borrominian style with the free movement of the Berninian angels carrying the columnar *tempietto*. The latter has been deliberately forced into the structure of the encasing lantern to create a kind of "dimmer" effect for the light, and the completeness of the whole is not convincingly achieved. Similarly, in the Cappella di Santa Cecilia, the motif of the truncated dome and the view into a light chamber with music-making angels certainly commands respect for its high scenographic quality and its remarkable impact on German eighteenth-century architecture (Abbey Church at Weltenburg by Cosmas Damian Asam). But again the relationship with the chapel architecture is problematic because of the predetermined strong verticality, which forced the artist to impose a sharply angled perspective on the spectator. Therefore—contrary to almost all Fontana's chapels—one cannot perceive the architecture of the chapel and its much more theatrical decoration as a complete work. For a comprehensive investigation into the works of Antonio Gherardi (who, born in 1638, was an exact contemporary of Carlo Fontana), see Thomas Pickrel, "Antonio Gherardi, Painter and Architect of the Late Baroque in Rome" (Ph.D. diss., University of Kansas, 1981); Pickrel, "Maglia, Theodon, and Ottoni at San Carlo ai Catinari: A Note on the Sculpture in the Chapel of Santa Cecilia," *Antologia di Belle Arti* 23/24 (1984), 27–37. For his "influence" on the Abbey church in Weltenburg see Henry-Russell Hitchcock, *Rococo Architecture in Southern Germany* (London, 1968), 27, pls., 22 and 24.

87. The "*giovani*" in Fontana's studio are mentioned in the *Vita* of Juvarra by an unknown author and first published by Adamo Rossi (see n. 12). See Vittorio Viale, *Mostra di Filippo Juvarra* (Messina, 1966), 31. See also Salvatore Boscarino, *Juvarra architetto* (Rome, 1973), 101, 107–109; Millon 1984, xvi–xvii; Hellmut Hager, "Il significato dell' esperienza juvarriana nella 'scuola' di Carlo Fontana," *Atti del Convegno dell' Accademia delle Scienze* (Turin, 1979; repr. Rome, 1985), 63–98. For the competition between Juvarra and Carlo Stefano Fontana in the Concorso Clementino of 1705, see Susan S. Munshower in *Architectural Fantasy and Reality*, 1981–1982, 30–42.

88. Mauro had become *accademico di merito* in 1758, rather late in his career. The two mandatory *dono* drawings that he submitted showed a project for the extension of the Confessio in San Giovanni in Laterano (Archivio Storico dell' Accademia di San Luca, MS 51, fol. 114v, 116v, 117, 118). Two years later, in 1760, he withdrew these drawings and replaced them with five others for a sepulchral monument (Archivio Storico dell' Accademia, MS 52, fol. 6v). He was elected *principe* in December 1761 and confirmed for a second period of office in November 1762 (Archivio Storico dell' Accademia, MS 52, fols. 28, 29, 42v). For details concerning Fontana's house, see notes 28 and 52 above.

89. The "studio dei giovani" is described in the "Inventario dei Beni" of Carlo Fontana's house, then inhabited by his son Francesco and his grandson Mauro, subsequent to the description of the studio used by Mauro Fontana. Archivio di Stato di Roma, Not. Cap. Uff. 13, Andreolus vol. 606, folios 310v–313. Mauro's wife, Antonia Sabatini, died in 1760 (Coudenhove-Erthal 1930, 130). The house also contained (probably from the time of Carlo Fontana, whose son Gaspare was a priest) a rather simply furnished chapel with "Un altare di legno amovibile con sua Predella, e Paliotto di ferandina di tutti colori guarnito di seta gialla. . . ." The major decoration consisted of "un Quadro di testa rappresentante la Madonna SS. ma col Bambino con Cornice negra a due Ordini d' Intaglio dorata, e suo Baldacchino sopra di Tela dipinta à guazzo con Cascatina attorno di Nobilità Verde. . . ." the whole being valued at six *scudi*. Further mentioned are "Un Cristo e Piedestallo di pero tinto negro" and "un piccolo Reliquiario inargentato con Reliquia di S. Vincenzo Ferreri," which were not evaluated because Mauro Fontana had willed them "al Sig. Curato Gallo" (fols. 321v–322 of the inventory). For the study facilities in the Accademia di San Luca see Hager, introduction, *Architectural Fantasy and Reality*, 1981–1982, 6.

90. ASR, Not. Cap. Uff. 13, Andreolus vol. 606, "Inventario dei Beni di Mauro Fontana," folios 305v–310v. The library of the Fontana family of architects consisted of two major categories—architecture and history, mentioned in summary fashion at the end of the inventory (fol. 341v). The *Libri di Architettura* were estimated to have a value of 16 *scudi* and the *Libri d'Istorie diverse*, 20 *scudi*.

91. On the title page Fontana identifies himself as *architetto deputato*, the usual designation for an architect who had received a special assignment but did not have full decision-making power. This restriction did not apply to his book, which required the imprimatur granted in 1692 (that it did not contain anything against the Faith and Morals) and the permission of Innocent XII, which was almost denied because the Pope was afraid that mention of the amount of money spent on the construction (which Carlo Fontana had attempted to estimate) could be used as an argument by the Protestants in favor of their cause (see Braham and Hager 1977, 35). About the offices and functions of the *architetto della fabbrica* and the *soprastante* within the struc-

ture of the R. Fabbrica di S. Pietro, see Tratz 1988, 422–424; Alessandra Anselmi, "Gli architetti della Fabbrica, 272–280.

92. For the ad hoc establishment of such an office at a time when Sant'Agnese in Piazza Navona was under construction, see Eimer 1970–1971, 81, 213, 224, 296, 491; and for an investigation into the facilities available to the Fabbrica di San Pietro at the time of Bernini, see Tratz 1988, 424–427.

93. Hellmut Hager, in *Architectural Fantasy and Reality*, 1981–1982, 4–5; Hager, "The Accademia di S. Luca in Rome and the Académie Royale d'Architecture in Paris: A Preliminary Investigation," *Projects and Monuments in the Period of the Roman Baroque.* Papers in Art History from Pennsylvania State University I (University Park, Pennsylvania, 1984), 131.

94. For a complete presentation of the surviving material and its organization see Paolo Marconi, Angela Cipriani, and Enrico Valeriani, *I disegni di architettura dell'archivio storico dell'Accademia di San Luca*, 2 vols. (Rome, 1974). For a correction of dates erroneously added during the eighteenth century to some late seicento *concorsi* drawings, see Marconi, Cipriani, Valeriani, in *Architectural Fantasy and Reality*, 1981–1982, app. 66–167.

95. See note 87 above.

96. See Ann Percy, "Castiglione's Chronology: Some Documentary Notes," *Burlington Magazine* 109 (1967), 672–677.

97. See Hager, "Osservazioni su Carlo Fontana," in press.

98. For his demonstration see Fontana 1694, pls. on 267 and 293.

99. Further on Longhi's treatise see John L. Varriano, "The Roman Ecclesiastical Architecture of Martino Longhi the Younger" (Ph.D. diss., University of Michigan, Ann Arbor, 1970), 85–88. Additional bibliographical references and discussion of this subject in Hager, "Osservazioni su Carlo Fontana," in press.

100. Fontana 1694, 97, pl. on 99.

101. Fontana 1694, 101–103, pl. on 105.

102. Hager 1974, 58. For the planning and building histories of the domes of the Gesù and Sant'Andrea della Valle see Richard Bösel, *Jesuitenarchitektur in Italien (1540–1773)* (Vienna, 1985), 167–169; Howard Hibbard, *Carlo Maderno and Roman Architecture, 1580–1630* (Pennsylvania State University Press, University Park and London, 1971), 151–152.

103. Fontana 1694, 361–364, pl. on 367.

104. Giovanni Poleni, *Memorie istoriche della gran cupola del Tempio Vaticano e de' danni di essa, e de' ristoramenti loro* (Padua, 1748), 31–33 n. 57.

105. Fontana 1694, pl. on 331; Poleni 1748, 410–424, nos. 572–603, pl. K, fig. 26.

106. Coudenhove-Erthal 1930, 90–97; Coudenhove-Erthal, "Römisches Stadtbaudenken zu Ende des Seicento," *Festschrift für Hermann Egger* (Graz, 1933), 95–103; Hager 1968; Kitao 1974, 62–64; *Le*

statue berniniane del Colonnato di San Pietro, ed. Valentino Martinelli (Rome, 1987).

107. Brauer and Wittkower 1931, 1: pl. 64; Kitao 1974, fig. 68.

108. Wolfgang E. Stopfel, "Triumphbögenentwürfe des 18. Jahrhunderts im Archiv der Accademia di San Luca in Rom," *Kunstgeschichtliche Studien für Kurt Bauch zum 70. Geburtstag von seinen Schülern* (Munich and Berlin, 1967), 241–252.

109. Further evidence for the paramount role of urbanism in the teaching of the two Fontanas, Carlo and Francesco, derives from additional competition topics at the Accademia di San Luca. Of particular interest is the theme for the first class of the Concorso Clementino of 1706, which Francesco had devised as a design for a piazza in the center of a metropolitan area. Unfortunately the entries of the participants on this fascinating topic are lost.

110. Michela di Macco, *Il Colosseo. Funzione simbolica, storica, urbana* (Rome, 1971), 82–89; Hellmut Hager, "Carlo Fontana's Project for a Church in Honour of the 'Ecclesia Triumphans' in the Colosseum, Rome," *Journal of the Warburg and Courtauld Institutes* 36 (1973), 319–337.

111. According to Richard Krautheimer, *The Rome of Alexander VII, 1655–1667* (Princeton, 1985), 131–140, the "official" itinerary began (as exemplified by Queen Christina's procession in 1655) with the experience of the Piazza del Popolo and terminated beyond the square of Saint Peter's in the Vatican basilica, in front of the Baldacchino facing "framed" by the columns of the High Altar, the Cathedra Petri.

112. Hager 1973, 65–66.

113. Compare Hellmut Hager, "Le opere letterarie di Carlo Fontana come autorappresentazione," in *In Urbe Architectus*, 155–203.

114. This aspect is emphasized in the current research of Mary N. Woods. See "Imagining the American Architect" in Abstracts and Program Statements 1993, First Annual Conference of the College Art Association, 3–6 February 1993.

115. Hager, "Le opere letterarie," 177–187.

116. Simona Ciofetta, "Lo Studio d'Architettura Civile edito da Domenico De Rossi (1702, 1711, 1721)," in *In Urbe Architectus*, 214–228.

117. Fontana's predilection for the contrast of African *verde antico* marble used for the incrustation of walls with articulating columns in light brown *diaspro di sicilia* or bands and frames in yellow marble, particularly manifest in the Cappella Cybo, had been taken to heart by his son Francesco for the interior of the church of Santi Apostoli, and could still be observed during the 1730s in Antonio Derizet's church of Santissima Nome di Maria al Foro Trajano, where Carlo Fontana's grandson Mauro was assigned the task of decorating the interior of the chapel for the main altar.

118. For a systematic investigation into the question of the subjects taught by Fontana's pupil Filippo

Juvarra and the circumstances of teaching at the academy in the early eighteenth century, see Henry A. Millon, "Filippo Juvarra and the Accademia di San Luca in the Early Eighteenth Century," in *Projects and Monuments in the Period of the Roman Baroque*. Papers in Art History from Pennsylvania State University 1 (University Park, 1984), 12–26. For an attempt to assess the influence of Carlo Fontana on Filippo Juvarra see Hager, "Il significato dell' esperienza juvarriana nella 'scuola' di Carlo Fontana," *Studi Juvarriani, Atti del Convegno dell' Accademia delle Scienze* (Turin, 1979/1985), 63–98; Hager (with Allan Braham), monograph on Carlo Fontana, in preparation.

119. L. Rovere, V. Viale, A. E. Brinckmann, *Filippo Juvarra* (Turin, 1937), 46, 133, pl. 132. *Montecitorio, Ricerche di Storia Urbana*, ed. Franco Borsi et al. (Rome, 1972), pl. 14.

DAVID B. BROWNLEE
University of Pennsylvania

Victorian Office Practice and Victorian Architecture: The Case of Sir Gilbert Scott

In the course of a few years, almost exactly at the midpoint of the nineteenth century, British architecture was transformed. Inaugurated during this period was the corporally and chromatically powerful architecture that is often called "High Victorian," which replaced the gentler, picturesque vocabulary that had survived from the eighteenth century. The new architecture developed its power in response to the great challenges that it was asked to meet: its visual language was strong enough to address the clamorous modern world, and its underpinning philosophy undertook nothing less than a reconciliation of the urgent demands of modern Britain with all the beguiling attractions of an increasingly well-understood past. As if these were not accomplishments enough, everything was done at a vast, new scale. This change in scale is central to the topic now under consideration, for it profoundly affected the way that architects did business; invented to serve these new needs was the modern multipartner office: the modern "artist's workshop."[1]

One of the first places where this new way of doing business was implemented was at the same time the place where many leading features of the new style and its ideology were being invented: the office of George Gilbert Scott in the late 1840s. Although Scott (1811–1878) is associated with more than one thousand commissions, he is probably best known as the architect of several large buildings in London—the hotel at Saint Pancras Station, the Government Offices in Whitehall, and the Albert Memorial.[2] Between 1844 and 1850 he created an office large enough to undertake such vast work and one capable of inventing a design vocabulary with which to do it. These were closely related phenomena.

The mainstays of Scott's office during this fertile period of expansion and exploration were three immensely talented men, all of them in their early twenties: George Edmund Street (1824–1881),[3] William White (1825–1900),[4] and George Frederick Bodley (1827–1907).[5] Together, Scott, Street, White, and Bodley could claim to possess at least half of the best talent of High Victorian architecture, and among them, they were responsible for more than three thousand commissions.

Within Scott's office almost all the varied aspects of High Victorianism were born, and it seems likely that one of the new style's most salient traits—its resistance to formal definition and periodization—is due in part to the type of multidesigner architectural practice that Scott created. Unfortunately little detail can be reported about Scott's office in the 1840s, although it is probably safe to project backward much of what is contained in the memoirs of Thomas Graham Jackson, who was there as a student in 1858–1861 when the establishment was even bigger. Jackson recalled:

Scott's office was a very large one. Counting pupils, salaried assistants, and clerks, I think we were twenty-seven in all. I was put to work in the first-floor room at the back with six others; there were about a dozen more in two rooms on the second floor; the ground-floor front room, which served also as the waiting-room, was the sanctum of Mr. Burlison, the head man, who made the estimates and surveys. Scott's own room was the ground-floor back, and farther back still were the writing clerk and the office-boys. The front room first floor was let to a Mr. Moriarity, a barrister, a mysterious person whom we never saw. Of Scott we saw but little. He was up to the eyes in engagements and it was hard to get him to look at our work. I have seen three or four men with drawings awaiting correction or approval grouped outside his door. The door flew open and out he came: "No time to-day!"; the cab was at the door and he was whirled away to some cathedral where he would spend a couple of hours and then fly off again to some other great work at the other end of the kingdom. Now and then the only chance of getting instructions was to go with him in the cab to the station. I see that I wrote at the time, "What a fine thing it is to be so busy"; but looking back from my present standpoint I find nothing in such a career to envy, and much to wonder at. It need hardly be said that it is an impossibility really to direct so large a staff as Scott's; but the work had of course to be done somehow.[6]

The work was in fact done by delegation. In 1841 Scott had hired two reliable men, John Burlison and John Drayton Wyatt, both of whom advanced to positions of responsibility and stayed with him for more than twenty-five years. Burlison, as mentioned by Jackson, was the head of the office and in charge of its administration and a wide range of nondesign matters, carried out by correspondence clerks in the office and by surveyors and clerks of the works who were hired for each construction project. Wyatt was the chief draftsman, directing the work of the several drafting rooms, each of which had its own head.

This hierarchy seems to have existed in embryonic form in the 1840s, when Scott, Street, White, and Bodley worked together. Street and White, like many of the other

1. George Gilbert Scott, Saint Mary Magdalene, Flaunden, Hertfordshire, 1838

especially talented young architects who worked for Scott in later years, operated from a special position. They were not there as draftsmen or administrators or as permanent employees of any stripe; indeed they served for only five and two years respectively before setting up on their own. Like Scott himself, they exercised substantial authority over design work—each was demonstrably responsible for particular projects—and could call on the office staff for assistance. Bodley, by contrast, was one of the half-dozen articled pupils in the office during the 1840s who paid a premium for the instruction they received (300 guineas a year in Jackson's time); and as they advanced, they began to help with the work of the office. The relationship among these four men is by no means easily diagrammed, but an examination of the works produced by the Scott office during their time together suggests that it consisted of a lively mixture of independence and collaboration, within which the nature of High Victorian architecture was defined both by their ideas and their working methods.

To understand what happened, it is first necessary to reinvestigate the character of Gilbert Scott's work. History has remembered him as a prodigious organizer, a genial latitudinarian in both religion and art, a muddled architectural thinker, and a minor designer. There is a series of oft-repeated stories about Scott, one of which tells of him arriving at a rural railway station on one of his frequent one-day dashes from London to inspect work in progress. He springs from the carriage with a purposefulness that dissolves after a moment into embarrassment as he makes his way to the telegraph clerk. There he dispatches a message back to his office, inquiring, "Why am I here?"[7] Another such tale has him arriving at the remote construction site of a church and taking the clerk of works aside for an earnest consultation. It is several minutes before the poor clerk can interrupt, saying, "You know, Mr. Scott, this is not your church; this is Mr. Street's, your church is farther down the road."[8] These anecdotes bespeak the modus operandi of his huge practice.

Scott's earliest works did not appear to compensate with architectural originality for their author's distractedness. His first church, of 1838 at Flaunden, Hertfordshire, was a preaching box built for his clergyman uncle (fig. 1). The design treated the congregation as an ordinary audience, setting some of them up in a gallery, and provided no separate chancel for the proper conduct of ritual; it was just the kind of building then earning the con-

tempt of the leading architectural radicals: Welby Pugin and his protestant allies in the Cambridge Camden Society (later renamed the Ecclesiological Society). Before Flaunden, Scott and his first partner, an erstwhile joiner named William Moffatt, had specialized almost exclusively in building workhouses, as mandated under the Poor Law Amendment Act of 1834; that experience had taught them to build cheaply and in great volume, but it had not prepared them for the rigors of artistic debate.[9]

Not all of Scott's subsequent ecclesiastical work from the late thirties and early forties was as primitive as Flaunden, however, and while most of this creditable work was in a very restrained Early English manner, sometimes his relative naïveté led him into new territory. Such was the essay in the Romanesque that he produced at Norbiton in 1841–1842, an adventurous design when compared to the orthodoxy of prevailing taste (fig. 2). But he should have known better than to send a batch of these designs off for review by the Cambridge Camden Society, for the stinging lash of their reviewer, James M. Neale, fell cruelly on them.[10] By the time the criticism appeared in print, however, Scott was penitent, and he seems to have accepted the acerbic words with something like gratitude. His epiphany came

2. George Gilbert Scott, Saint Peter, Norbiton, Greater London, 1841–1842

while reading Augustus Welby Northmore Pugin in 1841: "I suddenly found myself like a person awakened from a long feverish dream, which had rendered him unconscious of what was going on about him."[11]

His awakening had almost immediate effect, and by 1842–1844, when he rebuilt the big church of Saint Giles, Camberwell, after a fire, his work had changed dramatically.[12] He took the precaution this time of having the design vetted first by the Cambridge Camden Society, which he joined that year, and the result was an exterior picturesquely expressive of the internal liturgical functionalism that they required (especially the provision of a large, separate chancel). It was also rendered in their favored style—that stemming from what was called (not humorously) "the later days of early Middle Pointed"—that is, the English Decorated Gothic of circa 1300. With such work Scott made himself first respectable and then important, and his practice expanded rapidly under the support of the quasi-official arbiters of ecclesiastical taste. In 1845–1855 his office received fifty commissions for new churches and seventy for restorations, but in the midst of this prosperity Scott changed directions. It was then that High Victorian architecture first put on its public face.

The inspiration for this transformation seems to have come from abroad. Until this time the Gothic Revival in England had been a strenuously nationalist affair, with the Houses of Parliament still regarded, patriotically, as its central monument. But in 1843 the Nikolaikirche in Hamburg burned, and in 1844 Scott entered and won the competition for its reconstruction. His church still raises its spire above the Aussenalster—a monument to the new internationalism of British architecture.[13]

Significantly Scott made the design a German one, rushing to tour the Gothic architecture of Germany in advance of submitting his entry. (Previously his foreign travel had consisted of one night spent in Calais.) What he learned is most easily seen in plan (fig. 3): in the shape of the choir and, even more strikingly, in the axial placement of the single western tower, a hallmark of such quintessential monuments of German Gothic as the cathedral of Freiburg-im-Breisgau. While Scott apparently did this in order to win the support of Germany's Gothic nationalists, his interest in foreign architecture for its own sake was growing, fostered by his new connections to the rival of the Cambridge Camden Society, the Oxford Society for Promoting the Study of Gothic Architecture, which he had joined in 1843. The Oxonians' view of style was rather more liberal than the Cantabrigians', straying earlier and later than Middle Pointed and venturing outside of England as well; their eclecticism was more in keeping with Scott's earlier, naïve experimentation.[14]

3. George Gilbert Scott, Nikolaikirche, Hamburg, 1844–1883, plan, c. 1845
British Architectural Library, London

By 1849 Scott could give words—some of the first words—to the High Victorian sensibility that grew out of this kind of thinking; he called for the

. . . amalgamation of all which is really beautiful and intrinsically valuable in the hitherto attained developements of pointed architecture [specifically including Continental Gothic, too]; and, while we take one period as our nucleus or groundwork, the engrafting upon it of all the essential beauties of the earlier or later periods . . . and fusing of the whole into a style essentially one, yet capable of greater variety of expression than can be commanded, single-handed, by any developement yet attained.[15]

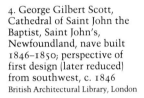

4. George Gilbert Scott, Cathedral of Saint John the Baptist, Saint John's, Newfoundland, nave built 1846–1850; perspective of first design (later reduced) from southwest, c. 1846
British Architectural Library, London

5. George Gilbert Scott, Cathedral of Saint John the Baptist, Saint John's, Newfoundland, nave built 1846–1850; section through north porch and details of ribs, probably by George Edmund Street, c. 1847
British Architectural Library, London

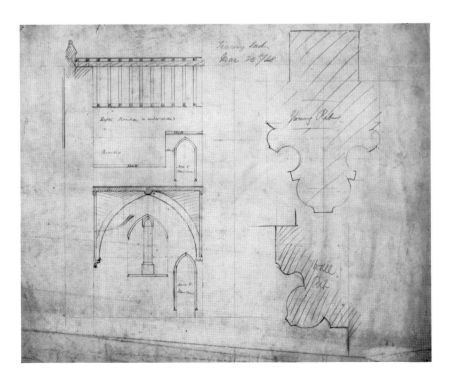

The concept of "development"—the organic process that reconciled diverse forces and connected history to the present—was a deliberate borrowing from the terminology then current in Oxford.

The excitement of this new style was just emerging in the fall of 1844, when Scott returned from Germany and began to design the Nikolaikirche. He now enlarged his staff, and there were quickly enough of them to drive Scott's family out of the house that they had shared with Scott's practice at 20 Spring Gardens, just southwest of Trafalgar Square. Among the new men was George Edmund Street, who had served a studentship with a provincial architect of no great distinction. Street drew many of the Hamburg competition drawings (now lost), and he seems to have assumed the role of what we would call a project architect for the design. Although he did not make his own first foreign trip until 1850, he also took up the theme of amalgamating "developments" with enthusiasm. Street soon established his reputation as the other principal theorist of the new High Victorian movement.[16]

Germany was not the only foreign port of call for the newly liberated architectural imagination of Scott's office. France also beckoned, particularly the stern, lithic architecture of French early Gothic. In this direction of exploration, Street again played a large role, most notably in making the French-spirited plans for the cathedral at Saint John's, Newfoundland, whose design was begun in 1846 (fig. 4).[17] Street made many of the drawings for the bold and rather austere cathedral; additionally, he was responsible for some of the correspondence with the distant clerk of the works (fig. 5).[18] Street's hand can also be seen in the design for Saint Anne, Alderney (1847–1850), whose stern, buttressed façade and apsidal chancel reflect the ascendance of Gallic taste. In the fall of 1847, just after ground was broken on Alderney, Scott made his first extended excursion in France.

Most of the Newfoundland and Alderney work fell in 1847, and that year Street also produced his first acknowledged independent commission, although he continued to work for Scott until 1849. This was the rugged little church of Saint Mary at

Biscovey (Par), Cornwall, a commission obtained through his sister's chance conversation with a stranger in Bath.[19] Although it quoted some Cornish regionalisms, its general massive bluntness was of the kind that architectural critics were learning to call "Early French." This style proved to be a much more long-lived enthusiasm of the High Victorians than Scott's flirtation with Germany, and indeed it became a hallmark of Street's entire career, stretching from his first church in Cornwall into such midcareer works as his "thorough" restoration of the church at Barford, Oxfordshire, of 1860 (fig. 6) and his great Law Courts on the Strand in London, still abuilding at the time of his death in 1881.

In addition to this French influence, Street also shared his contemporaries' interest in John Ruskin's Italy. Scott had toured there in 1851, and in 1853 Street followed, building his first boldly polychromatic work at Chalfont Saint Peter, Buckinghamshire (now on the western outskirts of Greater London), in the same year (fig. 7). With all of this diverse and exciting architecture to take into account, it is not surprising that in the early 1850s Street began to expand on Scott's notion of development. In February 1852 he

delivered a paper to the more progressive Oxford architectural society on "The True Principles of Architecture and the Possibility of Developement." He told them that it was no longer enough to study Gothic architecture, as wonderfully varied as it was. "That architecture is best," he

6. George Edmund Street, Saint John, Barford Saint John, Oxfordshire, 1860–1861

7. George Edmund Street, Saint Peter, Chalfont Saint Peter, Buckinghamshire, 1853–1854

8. George Gilbert Scott, Saint John the Baptist, Moulsford, Oxfordshire, 1846–1847

9. George Edmund Street, Saint Michael, Sandhurst, Berkshire, 1853–1854

said, "which best combines the verticality of Pointed with the repose of Classic architecture."[20] Fifteen years earlier, such a bold statement in favor of classicism would have reaped a harvest of abuse from the Gothic absolutists, but Scott (and those who thought like him) had so successfully changed the ground rules for the Gothic Revival in the interim that his former assistant could now say the words without criticism and even have them published in the *Ecclesiologist*, the journal of the Ecclesiological Society. That was what Street owed to Scott, while the older architect enjoyed the enormous invigoration Street brought to his designs of the middle and late 1840s.

Of course not everything the Scott office produced during Street's tenure of 1844–1849 fulfilled this bold agenda. A large number of smaller designs continued to follow English models and present a gentler profile to the world, enlivened only by the textures of humble materials and the outward evidences of their plans' inner divisions. Such was the church of Saint John, Moulsford, Oxfordshire (1846–

1847), built of the flint of the home counties and topped by an appropriate timber bell tower (fig. 8). A related phenomenon could be seen in the coeval Christ Church, Ramsgate, where the nave and side aisles were all sheltered by their own peaked roofs, resulting in a softly picturesque straggle across the landscape.[21]

Street may have had a hand in these works, for some of his own first designs were also gently English as, for example, his second independent commission, another Cornish church at Treverbyn of 1848–1850, created while he was still officially with Scott,[22] and the church of 1853–1854 at Sandhurst, with its relaxed profile and unprepossessing wooden spire (fig. 9). But Street's use of the vernacular was usually less innocent, as at East Hanney, Oxfordshire, 1856–1858 (fig. 10). Here the simplicities of village architecture reassembled themselves in a composition of disquieting abstract power, a power that was, at base, what Street was always trying to achieve.

Thus there was very probably another hand behind the gentler, more English

10. George Edmund Street, Saint James the Less, East Hanney, Oxfordshire, 1856–1858

class of Scott's works from the late 1840s, and a good circumstantial case can be made for it being that of William White. He joined Scott's office in 1845, one year later than Street and, like Street, fresh from a period of training under a lackluster provincial architect. Scott's and White's fathers had cared for neighboring parishes in Hertfordshire, and although they disagreed on doctrinal matters (Scott's father had Wesleyan leanings while White's were impeccably High Church), the families had always been friendly.

The first commissions that White undertook when he left Scott's office and moved to Cornwall in 1847 (two years before Street set up for himself), offer the best evidence of his role while an assistant. White's little church of Saint Michael at Baldhu (1847–1848) (fig. 11), with its nave and single aisle each under

11. William White, Saint Michael, Baldhu, Cornwall, 1847–1848

12. William White, Rectory, Saint Columb, Cornwall, 1849–1850

13. George Edmund Street, Rectory, Wantage, Oxfordshire, 1849–1850

its own ridge and the tower topped by a chamfered wooden roof, echoes forms common in Scott's gentler designs from the time that White spent with him. By contrast, the slackness of its composition is very unlike Street's exactly contemporary Cornish work at Biscovey, with its kinship to the Early French side of Scott's practice.

White's largest work from his early Cornish years, a huge rectory at Saint Columb (1849–1850), again reveals a taste unlike Street's (fig. 12). The complexity of its roofline contrasts markedly with the quieter massing of the big rectory that Street designed for William Butler at Wantage in Oxfordshire (also built in 1849–1850; fig. 13). Such juxtapositions help to clarify the

earlier division of responsibility within Scott's office, illuminating the diversity of architectural forms that it produced.

White and Street continued to see a good deal of each other as they launched their independent careers, for Street's own Cornish commissions at Biscovey and Treverbyn often took him to the west. It is evident that they continued to joust artistically and to learn from each other; indeed, despite their sometimes divergent tastes, White supported the campaign Street launched in 1850 to reduce the degree of affected irregularity that had crept into the Gothic Revival.[23] On 22 May 1851 he lectured to the Ecclesiological Society on the same subject, attempting to steer his listeners on the narrow path between monotony and eccentricity. It must be admitted, however, that the most seductive of the illustrations accompanying his lecture (and its subsequent publication) were the irregular buildings that he invented as negative examples.[24]

In White's own work, this continuing exchange of ideas with Street led him to experiment with the muscular Early French forms of which his friend was now enamored. His design of 1855 for Saint Michael's retreat house at Wantage (not far from Street's sturdy rectory) has thick

proportions and quiet surfaces. Indeed, it could be mistaken for a building by Street himself.

At the same time Street's brawny architecture held little lasting interest for White, who much preferred to continue his experiments with a gentler kind of picturesque. His sweet church of Saint Mary at Hawridge, Buckinghamshire, of 1856 could have been built ten years earlier when he was still working with Scott (figs. 14, 8). That idiom persisted throughout his career, although it was sometimes energized by High Victorian polychromy and compositional strength, as can be seen in the contemporary Christ Church at Smannel, Hampshire, of 1856–1857 (fig. 15). Here the regional flint and red brick of southern England are taken up as a theme and contorted strenuously with the vigor of the 1850s; however, the forms are idiosyncratically White's own—notably thinner and more angular than Street's.

In White and Street's long exchange of ideas, White was the net debtor. By Victorian standards White had a relatively small practice. He had "only" some 550 commissions, and most of them were small, requiring no great office establishment. Street's list topped 800, many of them enormous, and his office was correspondingly larger, although there were probably never more than twenty employees. Unlike Scott, Street also saw to it that he touched almost every drawing.[25] This intensity made his office the much

14. William White, Saint Mary, Hawridge, Buckinghamshire, 1856

15. William White, Christ Church, Smannel, Hampshire, 1856–1857

16. George Gilbert Scott, Holy Trinity, Headington Quarry, Oxfordshire, 1848–1849

sought-after training ground for such younger men as Richard Norman Shaw, Philip Webb, William Morris, and John Sedding, the leaders of the generation that would dominate architectural practice in the last quarter of the century, just as Scott's office had groomed the leaders of the third quarter.

Given White's strongly visual architecture, it is surprising to discover that he wrote nearly as much on theoretical matters as Street. Both, in other words, had inherited Scott's commitment to grounding design in philosophy, but whereas Street followed Scott quite faithfully along the path that led from strict historicism to artistic liberty, White, despite his own design idiosyncrasies, was a rule maker. For instance, he was alone among the High Victorians in believing that architectural proportions could be governed by laws, and on that basis he even wrote an appreciative pamphlet about that most geometrical building, the Crystal Palace, after it had been reerected at Sydenham.[26] White also sought to reduce symbolism and the use of color to sciences, arguing doggedly that while they induced instinctive reactions (like proportion), the natural

laws governing those reactions could be understood and exploited by the astute artist.[27] Unfortunately, White wrote and spoke poorly, and his complex message was never very influential. It did reflect, however, the positivist strain that was never far from the surface of even artistic Victorian endeavors. This was part of the matrix of ideas that Scott's office had fostered.

Theory did not concern George Frederick Bodley. Two years younger than White and three junior to Street, he entered Scott's office in 1845 and remained until 1850. Unlike the others, he had no prior training and was taken on as an old-fashioned articled pupil, even living in Scott's house. (Their close relationship stemmed from the wedding of Scott's brother Samuel and Bodley's sister Georgiana.) Because of his junior status, it is impossible to discern much of Bodley's hand in the work of the office, but it is clear what he learned there. In 1848 the design for Holy Trinity, Headington Quarry, near Oxford, was on the boards (fig. 16). White had left by then, and one's suspicion that Street had a hand in such strong forms as the great buttress splitting the west façade is confirmed by a glance at the similar church designed by Street five years later for Milton-under-Wychwood, not far away (fig. 17). Generically called Early French, this was the style Bodley cut his teeth on. Both he and Street are recorded as saying that they had been frustrated by Scott's willingness to dabble with later styles—Street recalled that the office joke was to call their boss's work "'ogee' because we thought it too late in character,"[28] and it is quite clear that they were allies in sustaining the Early French line in the office's practice. After leaving Scott in 1850, Bodley freelanced for a few years, sometimes helping Street, who had landed an appointment as the diocesan architect of Oxfordshire in 1850. He even may have aided Street at Milton, and he had surely watched Street work while they were both with Scott and afterward.

Their relationship is apparent when one turns to Bodley's first independent works, which date from 1854. Begun in that year was Christ Church at Long Grove, Hereford and Worcester, where Bodley shows, particularly in the buttressing of the west, that he was hoeing a Streetian row (fig. 18). But Early French muscularity is here restrained, and the tracery reveals that Bodley was interested in English things, too.

Perhaps under Street's continued influence, that restraint died away in the course of the next few years, and in 1858 Bodley produced a design for a beautiful hillside site at Selsley, Gloucestershire, that summarized his evolved position (fig. 19). The brawn of the Early French (with such Gallic signatures as plate tracery in the apse, the apsidal plan itself, and the saddleback tower) had now cast off its earlier fetters, and the church evinces all of the earthy vigor that it is possible to leave in cut stone. In many ways, Bodley now surpassed Street as a practitioner in this idiom, for Street in the late fifties had his attention divided between France and Italy; at the same time, he was also paying an increased amount of attention to secular buildings in which raw muscle was usually inappropriate.

Scott was not entirely left behind by the artistic adventures of his erstwhile assistants and pupils as they moved rapidly to

17. George Edmund Street, Saints Simon and Jude, Milton-under-Wychwood, Oxfordshire, 1853–1854

18. George Frederick Bodley, Christ Church, Long Grove, Hereford and Worcester, 1854–1856

19. George Frederick Bodley, All Saints, Selsley, Gloucestershire, 1858–1862

the top of the profession. There is abundant evidence that he and his staff kept an eye on their work, and indeed, it was hard to ignore their achievements, including a sensational near sweep of the competition for the Crimean Memorial Church in Istanbul in 1856. Street placed second, Bodley third, and White tied for fifth. William Burges, the winner, later forfeited the commission to Street, who built one of his boldest Early French designs. The influence of such examples is visible in the work of Scott's Spring Gardens office. His church at Leafield, Oxfordshire (1858–1860), is the contemporary of Bodley's church at Selsley, and the short cylindri-

cal columns of its nave and its boldly sculpted octagonal spire are confident if unoriginal expositions of the latest Early French thinking (fig. 20).

This artistic exchange also seems to have flowed in the other direction, and the Scott office, because of its continuing pluralism, served as the incubator for ideas that were subsequently adopted by its alumni. Among the most important accomplishments of the office in the 1850s was the further development of the Middle Pointed English form of the Gothic Revival, even after it was jettisoned by the avant-garde as they rushed abroad in search of new inspirations. This momen-

tarily eclipsed vocabulary defined the active skyline and lush carved ornament and sculpture of what Scott called his best church, the richly endowed All Souls, Haley Hill, Halifax (1855–1859).[29] Such survivals helped to launch the revival of things English that the younger men undertook in the early 1860s, when they began to react against the exaggerated robustness into which their fancies had led them. Some of the first evidences of that revival can be seen in the relaxed, gentle composition of Street's little church at Brightwalton, Berkshire, of 1862–1863, with its delicate and abundant Decorated

tracery (fig. 21). It is also apparent in the soft fen-country profile of spire-cum-crenelated tower that Bodley raised above All Saints, Cambridge, as built in 1863–1870 (fig. 22). To build that design, he abandoned his own proposal of just two years earlier in which a heavily buttressed tower and broached spire bespoke the sterner geometries of the fifties.

The sixties also saw the building of the monuments for which Gilbert Scott is nowadays largely remembered: the Franco-Italian pastiches of the Midland Hotel at Saint Pancras Station (1868–1874) and the Albert Memorial (1863–1872). In

20. George Gilbert Scott, Saint Michael, Leafield, Oxfordshire, 1858–1860

21. George Edmund Street, All Saints, Brightwalton, Berkshire, 1862–1863

22. George Frederick Bodley,
All Saints, Cambridge,
1863–1870

some senses they reflect the climax of the High Victorian "development" of style that Scott and his assistants commenced in the 1840s, but they are also works detached from what those younger men were now doing. They reflect, undoubtedly, the complex interrelationships of another batch of talented junior members of the office, for despite competition from Street's practice, Scott continued to be popular with young men beginning careers in architecture. Among those who followed Street, White, and Bodley in the drafting rooms in Spring Gardens were many of the leaders of the next, that is,

"Queen Anne" generation, whose eclecticism was even more freewheeling. These included Thomas Graham Jackson (with Scott in 1858–1861), Edward Robert Robson (1854–1859), John James Stevenson (1858–1860), and Scott's sons George Gilbert Scott, Jr. (1858–1863) and John Oldrid Scott (1858–1878). As before, they possessed enough talent and exercised it with sufficient freedom to preclude any easy stylistic generalizations. In so doing they established the pattern that has characterized the architecture of large offices ever since.

NOTES

All photographs are by the author except as indicated.

1. This change in office practice has received scant attention, although there are important allusions to the subject in Barrington Kaye, *The Development of the Architectural Profession in Britain: A Sociological Study* (London, 1960); Frank Jenkins, *Architect and Patron: A Survey of Professional Relations and Practice in England from the Sixteenth Century to the Present Day* (London and New York, 1961); John Wilton Ely, "The Rise of the Professional Architect in England," in *The Architect: Chapters in the History of the Profession*, ed. Spiro Kostof (New York, 1977), 180–208; and Andrew Saint, *The Image of the Architect* (New Haven and London, 1983).

2. George Gilbert Scott, *Personal and Professional Recollections*, ed. George Gilbert Scott, Jr. (London, 1879); Gavin Stamp, "Sir Gilbert Scott's Recollections," *Architectural History* 19 (1976), 54–73; David Cole, *The Work of Sir Gilbert Scott* (London, 1980).

3. Arthur Edmund Street, *Memoir of George Edmund Street, 1824–1881* (London, 1888); David B. Brownlee, *The Law Courts: The Architecture of George Edmund Street* (New York; Cambridge, Massachusetts; and London, 1984).

4. Thomas H. Watson, "The Late William White, F.S.A.," *Journal of the Royal Institute of British Architects* 7 (10 February 1900), 145–146; Paul Thompson, "The Writings of William White," in *Concerning Architecture*, ed. John Summerson (London, 1968), 226–237.

5. Edward P. Warren, "The Work of Messrs. G. F. Bodley and T. Garner," *Architectural Review* [Boston] 6 (March 1899), 25–34. Edward P. Warren, "George Frederick Bodley, R.A.," *Architectural Review* [London] 11 (1902), 130–139; Henry Vaughan, "The Late George Frederick Bodley, R.A.," *Architectural Review* [Boston] 14 (October 1907), 213–215; "Obituary: Mr. G. F. Bodley," *Builder* 93 (26 October 1907), 447–448; F. M. Simpson, "George Frederick Bodley, R.A., F.S.A., D.C.L.," *Journal of the Royal Institute of British Architects* 15 (11 January 1908), 145–158; Edward P. Warren, "The Life and Work of George Frederick Bodley," *Journal of the Royal Institute of British Architects* 17 (19 February 1910), 305–340; David Verey, "George Frederick Bodley: Climax of the Gothic Revival," in *Seven Victorian Architects*, ed. Jane Fawcett (University Park, Pennsylvania, 1977), 84–101.

6. Thomas Graham Jackson, *Recollections of Thomas Graham Jackson, 1835–1925*, ed. Basil H. Jackson (London, New York, and Toronto, 1950), 58–59.

7. William R. Lethaby, *Philip Webb and His Work* (Oxford, 1935), 66.

8. Jackson 1950, 59.

9. David Cole, "Some Early Works of George Gilbert Scott," *Architectural Association Journal* 66 (1950–1951), 98–108.

10. James M. Neale, "New Churches," *Ecclesiologist* 1 (February 1842), 52–55. Scott commented on this review (which he had seen before publication) in Scott to Edward Boyce, 31 December 1841 (Royal Institute of British Architects, British Architectural Library [hereafter RIBA/BAL] ScGGS/4/8/1).

11. Scott 1879, 88.

12. Cole 1980, pls. 20–21.

13. The nave was gutted in World War II. F. Stöter, *Geschichte und Beschreibung des St. Nikolai Kirchenbaues in Hamburg* (Hamburg, 1883). Julius Faulwasser, *Die St. Nikolai-Kirche in Hamburg* (Hamburg, 1926).

14. For Scott and the rival Oxford and Cambridge societies, see David B. Brownlee, "The First High Victorians: British Architectural Theory in the 1840s," *Architectura* 15 (1985), 33–46.

15. George Gilbert Scott, "On the Questions of the Selection of a Single Variety of Pointed Architecture for Modern Use, and of Which Variety Has the Strongest Claims on Such Selection," in *A Plea for the Faithful Restoration of Our Ancient Churches* (London and Oxford, 1850), 116. Since the introduction is dated January 1850, it is reasonable to assume that this essay was written in 1849 or earlier. (Another essay in the anthology was first given as a lecture on 27 July 1848.)

16. Brownlee 1984, 20–35.

17. "Saint John's Cathedral, Newfoundland," *Ecclesiologist* 8 (April 1848), 274–279.

18. Most of the correspondence for this important commission was handled by Scott himself, but a letter from Street to William Hay, clerk of works, is mentioned in Hay to Scott, 28 April 1848 (RIBA/BAL, SC/NSJ/39). Street's hand is apparent in the following drawings: RIBA/BAL [119] 19, 20, 21.

19. Illustrated in Roger Dixon and Stefan Muthesius, *Victorian Architecture* (London, 1978), ills. 193–194.

20. George Edmund Street, "The True Principles of Architecture and the Possibility of Developement," *Ecclesiologist* 13 (August 1852), 253.

21. Illustrated in Stefan Muthesius, *The High Victorian Movement in Architecture, 1850–1870* (London and Boston, 1972), ill. 4.

22. Illustrated in Brownlee 1984, fig. 2.

23. George Edmund Street, "On the Proper Characteristics of a Town Church," *Ecclesiologist* 11 (December 1850), 227–233.

24. William White, "Upon Some of the Causes and Points of Failure in Modern Design," *Ecclesiologist* 12 (October 1851), 305–313.

25. Brownlee 1984, 266–273.

26. [William White], *The Palace: An Artistic Sketch of the 10th of June 1854*, 3d ed. (London, [1855]). Attributed on the basis of a review of *The Palace*, *Ecclesiologist* 16 (June 1855), 162–163. See also:

White, "Modern Design," *Ecclesiologist* 14 (October 1853), 313–330; White, "Modern Design—No. III: On Proportion in Architectural Design," *Ecclesiologist* 15 (October 1854), 291–297.

27. William White, "Symbolism: Its Practical Benefits and Uses," *Transactions of the Exeter Diocesan Architectural Society* 4 (1853), 304–322. White, "A Lecture on Polychromy at the Architectural Museum," *Building News* 7 (18 January 1861), 50–51, 55.

28. Street 1888, 106.

29. Dixon and Muthesius 1978, ill. 191.

LARRY D. LUTCHMANSINGH
Bowdoin College

The British Arts and Crafts Workshop between Tradition and Reform

Trust Pindar for the truth of his saying, that to the cunning workman—(and let me solemnly enforce the words by adding, that to him only)—knowledge comes undeceitful.

John Ruskin, *Aratra Pentelici* (1872)

We have to create a psychology for, instead of against, bodily toil—the will to work. Part of this transformation is to be brought about by approaching labour as Art.

William R. Lethaby, "Labour a Manifestation of God" (1928)

If inquiry into the artist's workshop calls attention to structural relations beyond art objects themselves, the workshops and practices of the late nineteenth-century British Arts and Crafts Movement were conspicuously shaped through such relations. But rather than simply being endured as the brute facts of history, the force of those relations was constructed by the craftsmen involved into an elaborate mythology of art and its production in the heyday of industrialization. Perhaps more than any previous movement in the history of art, the Arts and Crafts Movement may be said to have been the institutional and practical outcome of a systematic body of theory, though by no means a monolithic one. That theory addressed the three influences on artistic production that W. G. Constable later noted in *The Painter's Workshop*, namely the artist's changing place in society, his conception of his work, and changes in patronage.[1]

But radically problematizing those principles, the Arts and Crafts Movement located itself at the end of a complicated historical process that had broken established traditions and disabled proven methods of craft work. The sheer scope and intricacy of the movement's theorizing not only attested to a preoccupation with historical conditions, but forecast and epitomized the movements of high modernism, whose creative achievements characteristically would be attended by explanatory manifestos, justifications of intent, and defenses by their adherents, as if every new movement, every radical effort, had sprung out of rupture and crisis. Poised then, as they perceived themselves to be, between disintegrating artistic traditions and overwhelming social changes, the Arts and Crafts Movement sought to define a position that would be at once conservative of beneficent forces from the past and adaptive to the demands of the new. The terrain on which this dual imperative would be most acutely negotiated was the workshop and the productive processes that transpired in it, as well as the very concepts of *art, artist,* and *work.*

These last were among the several institutional and procedural concepts thought to have been unraveled by history; that is, not simply superseded by more effective developments in some progressive and benevolent march of events, but undermined in the course of unequal contests of powers and factional interests. This perceived conflict raises the issue of the movement's tendency to look backward to certain privileged art-historical moments while condemning more recent ones. On the one hand, this retrospective vision has sometimes been dismissed as a futile romantic nostalgia, while on the other, the apparent refusal to acquiesce to the triumphal version of art history has been deemed a limitation of their own vision. There is a further irony in the approximate coincidence of the formative and early phase of the Arts and Crafts Movement with the high moment of Victorian material triumph, that "golden era of capitalist growth."[2] This period, between the early 1850s and 1873, witnessed the Great Exhibition of the Works of Industry of All Nations; the founding of the firm of Morris, Marshall, Faulkner and Company (an early Arts and Crafts organization); influential writings of John Ruskin, such as his essay on "Pre-Raphaelitism," two volumes of *The Stones of Venice*, and *Fors Clavigera*; and the founding of his Guild of Saint George, which provided an important example of work organization.

When the Arts and Crafts Exhibition Society published a series of papers at the end of World War I on the role of the crafts in national reconstruction, one of its members, Henry Wilson (1864–1934), saw fit to recall the contributions to past societies of such great workshops as the Opera del Duomo in Florence, the temple workshops of Egypt, the palace workshops of Knossos, the magisteria of the Middle Ages, and the scriptoria of the Benedictine monasteries. The only comparable modern equivalent he thought were the "studios, workshops, and printing rooms" of William Morris (1834–1896), the "great exemplar" (a reference to the Morris firm).[3] This was not partisan justification as much as severe historical judgment: at a time of international and social crisis, Wilson was concerned, in a manner typical of the Arts and Crafts Movement, to point to a hiatus in the history of art and work between the great traditional workshops and their attempted revival in the nineteenth century. He believed that the intervening decline of artistic traditions was accountable to a host of general fac-

tors, notably the rise of an exchange economy, the decline of communitarian forms of religion and popular celebration, and the industrialization of work and craft. What can be seen on the part of the Arts and Crafts leaders as a perverse resistance to historical progress can also be interpreted as both a critique of the devastation of traditional artistic forms and a concern to salvage valuable productive arrangements and skills and adapt them to modern conditions. The apparent incongruence between such retrievals of the past and the inescapable demands of the present lent some of the movement's ideals and products an air of romantic quaintness, irrelevance even, and contributed to internal tensions; as between a tendency to aestheticism and modernist functionalism on one side, and to a politically sensitive art on the other. The inherent difficulty of their position was well appreciated by members of the movement, as expressed, for example, by William Morris: "The very fact that there is a 'revival' shows that the arts . . . have been sick unto death. In all such changes the first of the new does not appear till there is little or no life in the old, and yet the old, even when it is all but dead, goes on living in corruption, and refuses to get itself quietly put out of the way and decently buried. So that while the revival advances and does some good work, the period of corruption goes on from worse to worse, till it arrives at the point when it can no longer be borne, and disappears."[4]

This was a curious position at a time when generous patronage and popular acclaim ensured eminence and, on occasion, unusual wealth to certain artists and purveyors of eclectic architectural styles, when academies and salons were enjoying great success, and advanced styles such as realism and impressionism were pointing the way to the triumph of an esoteric high culture. But such latter developments either made artistic virtue out of historical necessity, as it were, or remained indifferent to the ravages on artistic traditions, or embraced modernity without dissent.[5]

The fundamental historical change that the Arts and Crafts Movement attempted to counter was the elevation of certain traditional crafts—notably painting, sculpture, and architecture—into highly specialized and autonomous fine arts at the expense of other skills, which had been correspondingly demoted to the mere service of decoration or divorced from the sphere of the aesthetic altogether. Yet in the view of the craftsman Edward Prior, the professional architect emerged from the medieval master-craftsman, and in that of Morris himself, the specialist artist emerged from the handicraftsman. Both developments were seen as harmful.[6] A miscellany of philosophical reflection, historical analysis, and archaeological interpretation led these artists to the general conclusion that traditional art had usually meant the skilled making of necessities and accordingly had been governed by the principle of fitness.

Architect William R. Lethaby (1857–1931), for example, maintained that "a work of art is first of all a well-made thing," a principle governing "all right labour—something like mind and heart embodied in worthy toil." Lethaby's definition correlates with the ideal ascribed to the founders of the Art Workers' Guild by another architect of the movement, Arthur Mackmurdo (1851–1942)—that the arts might be united in a "single devotion to the needs of common human life."[7] Among their contemporaries, the craftsmen found Ruskin to be the most eloquent and persuasive proponent of this utilitarian aesthetic. But the particular inflection they gave that aesthetic was already being expressed as early as 1840, when Sir Francis Palgrave, in a review of Vasari's *Lives*, wrote that the leading lights of the Tuscan Renaissance were not artists in the nineteenth-century sense but artificers trained in a workshop rather than an academy, that painters were to be found in a *bottega* rather than a studio; and that they all worked, like artisans generally, in the preparation of objects of common use.[8] Walter Crane (1845–1915), himself a designer in all the major arts except architecture, found apt illustration of the identity of objects of art and of everyday use in *The Book of Trades, or Library of the Useful Arts* (1806–1811), whose plates depicted the painter, sculptor, and engraver cheek by jowl with the trunkmaker, wheelwright, and ironfounder,

that is, with "no artificial distinction between art and labour."[9] As examples of the ideal polymath, critic William Rosetti recalled Giotto, Verrocchio, Leonardo, Michelangelo, Raphael, and Dürer, whereas he found in his own day copperengravers ignorant of wood, and watercolorists of oils.[10]

The effective implementation of this abstruse aesthetic in an Arts and Crafts workshop may be taken to have been achieved by the early 1860s, as we learn from William Rossetti's response to the London International Exhibition of 1862, at which some of the first products of the newly established firm of Morris, Marshall, Faulkner and Company were on view (including furniture and stained glass). Observing that it was not easy to determine where industrial art ended and fine art began among the exhibits, Rossetti enumerated what were to become central guidelines of the Arts and Crafts Movement:

We conceive the faculty for art throughout its whole range to be essentially the same; being composed, firstly, of a strong perception of character and beauty in the abstract properties of form and colour, and in the actual facts of nature; and, secondly, of a vivid adaptation of these in whatever shape. The painting of a picture, the carving of a statue, the design of a building, the setting of a jewel, are all exemplifications of the faculty of fine art; the right doing of any of these things is the function of an artist, and none but the artist, in the correct sense of the word, can manage it well. We conceive also that the extreme division and subdivision of art in the present day is one of the most baneful features of it—one of those which most cramp the artist, mislead the public, and cripple the powers of art itself . . . . The healthy and progressive periods of art have been those in which an artist for one thing was intrinsically an artist for anything.[11]

The perceived failure of the Great Exhibition of 1851 to point the expected way to reform led one of its organizers, Henry Cole, to particularly regret this situation: "We have no principles, no unity; the architect, the upholsterer, the paper stainer, the weaver, the calico-printer and the potter, run each their independent course; each struggles fruitlessly, each produces in art novelty without beauty or beauty without intelligence."[12]

Reviewing contemporary usage of the word *art*, Raymond Williams corroborates the idea of a comprehensive artistic category, pointing out that between the thirteenth and seventeenth centuries the word denoted, "without predominant specialization," a wide variety of skills, including mathematics, medicine, and even angling, but that thereafter "there was an increasingly common specialized application to a group not hitherto formally represented: painting, drawing, engraving and sculpture."[13] In corresponding fashion, the eighteenth-century Royal Academy, deliberately excluding engravers from its ranks, endorsed the distinction between *artist* and *artisan*, "the latter being specialized to 'skilled manual worker' without 'intellectual' or 'imaginative' or 'creative' purposes."[14] Thus the Arts and Crafts Movement was apparently attempting to undo a bit of history in restoring the unity of fine and useful arts. They thought their crusade was supported not only by the evidence of art history (for example, the unity of the medieval crafts), but also by such emblematic truths as they found in Homer's description of the furniture in Helen's apartment: which they took as announcing to future generations "how nobly and how simply the men of its own day felt and satisfied their needs." Similarly, the scenes of human labor represented by Hephaistos on Achilles' shield suggested "what an industry may be."[15] This latter judgment evoked the stark contrast with nineteenth-century industry, "so broken up, so distributed and magnified, that . . . it passes beyond the ken, the interest, and intelligence of those to whom the lot has fallen to pursue it in some infinitesimal particular."[16] The writer of this passage, Thomas Cobden-Sanderson (1840–1922), was a pioneering reviver of fine bookbinding. Here he was referring to the notorious institution of the division of labor, which was charged with contributing to the loss of traditional craft skills. Adam Smith's widely accepted view that the division of labor resulted in "the greatest improvement in the productive powers of labour, and the greater part of the skill, dexterity, and judgment with which it is anywhere directed,"[17] was memorably rebutted by Ruskin in "The Nature of Gothic" (*The Stones of Venice*, 1853, volume two, chapter five), the single art-historical writing that more than any other shaped the reformatory outlook of the Arts and Crafts Movement.

Artists who shared Ruskin's discouragement with the widespread division of labor in Victorian industry and its effect on modern artistic practice, saw a superior model in traditional work practices, where diverse crafts were practiced by both individual artists and the collective. Not surprisingly, a number of Arts and Crafts workshops not only tried to model themselves on the medieval guild, but took the name as well; for example, the Century Guild (1882), the Guild of Handicraft (1888), the Birmingham Guild of Handicraft (1890), the Artificer's Guild (1901), and the nonproductive Art Workers' Guild (1884). We should be reminded that to many nineteenth-century artists such notions as the unity of the arts and the equation of ornamental and useful crafts were somewhat novel, even abstract. A founder of the Century Guild, designer Selwyn Image (1849–1930), observed as late as 1887 that even then these ideas were relatively unfamiliar.[18] Architect Thomas Graham Jackson (1835–1934) provided personal testimony of this when he recalled how impressed he had been on a trip to Italy by the "close union of the three arts, Architecture, Sculpture, and Painting, in a fashion that of course I had never seen before." He further discovered that all three arts had been "commonly practiced by the same man from the earliest times down to the days of Bramante and Michelangelo, after whom the arts fell apart and the divorce took place which is not yet reconciled."[19] In his later practice, Graham Jackson pointed to the "evil results of the separation of architecture from the sister arts" and urged a "closer association of artists of all kinds" and a "return to the practice of the Middle Ages and earlier Renaissance."[20] Members of the Arts and Crafts Movement were almost unanimous in tracing the disintegration of the Italian Renaissance to the disregard of the late medieval unity of the arts and crafts.[21] The modern factory and the mechanization of production were presumed to have merely completed the disintegration begun with the break-up of the medieval guilds and the exploitation of art for profit.[22]

So radical yet necessary did the idea of the unity of the arts appear that Selwyn Image imagined an inscription above the entrance to the Century Guild workshop in Southampton Street: "Credo in unam Artem, multipartitam, indivisibilem."[23] The first circular of the Arts and Crafts Exhibition of 1888, from which the movement took its name, was titled "The Combined Arts," though the members later settled on its present name, as proposed by Cobden-Sanderson.[24] The revived ideal and practice of the combined arts necessarily endowed those arts, separately and together, with new significances; conversely, the status and function of the newer arts were subjected to severe criticism, especially modern sculpture and easel painting. The structural principle around which the arts and crafts might be reunited and employed in concert was taken to be architectural or environmental, and herein lay the basis of Morris' argument that architecture was the *mistress art*: "It is this union of the arts, mutually helpful and harmoniously subordinated to one another, which I have learned to think of as Architecture."[25] But the movement's artists and architects tended to define architecture in rather wide terms, as embracing, in Morris' words, "the whole external surroundings of the life of man," and "the moulding and altering to human needs of the very face of the earth itself."[26] Reginald Blomfield (1856–1942), another movement architect, qualified this by insisting on the autonomy of architecture on account of its dependence on such abstract qualities as mass, rhythm, and proportion, rather than on "any art external to itself," though he nevertheless called for the careful orchestration of the different arts in building design. He looked to the Greek Doric temple as a model in which "the architect, the sculptor, and the painter worked with complete understanding of each other's limitations and resources." Conversely, he rejected the Certosa at Pavia.[27]

In serving architecture all the arts would be governed by similar considerations of design, fitness, and aesthetic effect, but in particular they would be united in their common basis in craftsmanship and knowledge of materials. On this principle, a sympathetic academic painter, Sir William B. Richmond, could recommend that since the foundations of the three arts were the same, "students of each art should work in the same room and progress together exactly equally, learning the same things, until one finds out he would like to set to painting, another to sculpture, and another to architecture."[28] In this spirit architect Thomas Jackson proposed that "it is in the workshop that the art student, be he architect or what else, will find the readiest stimulus to his fancy and the best antidote for a slavish adherence to precedent."[29] If the arts were, as argued, thus unified, it would follow that they found strength in each other and in their service to architecture, but would suffer when separated to each serve its own end. As early as 1840, Palgrave had perceived a decline in sculpture when it was separated from architecture, for "the first object of its intent and application was lost, and, instead of being a significant and living art, [it] dwindled into the mere minister to the desires of the eye."[30] And it was argued by other Arts and Crafts associates that while the mere carver continued to do decorative work for the architect and builder as best he could, the sculptor specialized in objects "wanting in sympathy with [their] surroundings";[31] that the "practical extermination of the decorative effect" could be illustrated, for example, by the history of the mural, which fell out of favor as the easel painting rose and wallpaper came to be used in its stead; while Ford Madox Brown (1821–1893) claimed, on the basis of distinguished achievement in both fresco and easel painting and close knowledge of German Nazarene practice, that painters who worked in both techniques found themselves to that extent enriched.[32]

To the Arts and Crafts artists, the emergence of easel painting demonstrated directly the problems besetting all the arts since their devolution from the traditional structure. That painting should in some sense have been elevated to a special and autonomous status, "arrogating to herself the role which hitherto the whole company had combined to make successful,"[33] indicated a reductionism at work in the larger artistic enterprise—an attenuation of principles beyond the visual, such as harmony with surroundings, sensitivity to material, and of course, service toward some concrete and larger purpose. To this list some added precedence of truthful representation over beauty of effect. Now that the several arts were dedicated to their distinctive, independent ends, they would all be more vulnerable to distorting influences of popular consumer psychology, market manipulation, and ideological bias. These several arts, and painting in particular, would be annexed to the "expression" of subjective and often private experience.

The concept of a distinctive, and peculiarly modern, phenomenon of "studio" art was proposed: freed from cooperative work with fellow artists, the sculptor had become a "child of the studio," according to Somers Clark, producing a curious kind of object which "may be placed now in a drawing-room, now in a conservatory or a public square, alone and unsheltered."[34] Hence Walter Crane's perception of an homology between the autonomy of the easel painting, with the painter feeling no obligation "to consider anything outside its own dimensions," and "the practice of holding large and mixed picture-shows" of works of every sort without specific connection to each other. For Crane architecture, its furnishing and decoration depended for effect on such factors as coordination, a specific sense of place, spatial arrangement, and light, which the neutral ground of the museum negated.[35] A connection was detected between the production of paintings in the studio and the novel phenomenon of pure exhibitionism, as suggested by architect John Sedding's (1838–1891) ironic distinction between traditional crafts, destined "for the adornment of human life, and to add to the pleasantness of home," and what is seen in a museum, "a place for odds and ends, for things that have drifted, for the flotsam and jetsam of the wrecked homes of humanity."[36] The home itself being absent, the old crafts began to dwell in an abstract space and time, their condition being signified in the artificial homogeneity of a catalogue: in lieu of a customary poetical reflection on humanity and the romance of well-appointed habitation, they offered mere simulacra of those effects.

The principle of *pure* and neutral exhibitionism evoked its counterpart in the concept of a *pure* style, which several of the movement artists took to be central to the definition of modern *fine art*. And if art was no longer answerable to specific and local requirements of place, arrangement, material, and so forth, then it would have become universal. But Lethaby dismissed this as an inauthentic condition merely "suitable for picture exhibitions and . . . for dealers."[37]

This series of unusual distinctions probably lay behind Crane's judgment that English taste of his day was, regrettably, no longer for allegory in painting, but instead for a "realistic form of domestic sentiment or portraiture."[38] However, Lethaby observed that even portraiture betrayed a loss of artistic integrity, for "English people as such have hardly been painted since Holbein; they have been painted as titles, or as property, or fox-hunting, or clothes and fashion," that is, for pure exhibition. Further, he maintained, "The fact is, exhibitionist portraits do not make house portraits, nor gallery pictures room pictures, nor popular success food for human joy. In truth there is an *artificial* standard all along 'the line.' Too many pictures are merely professional products."[39] The accusation of professionalism took on a particular force when applied to architecture, the "mistress art." Indeed, one of the most contentious episodes in the movement's history occurred in 1891 when a number of its members, architects as well as nonarchitects, publicly resisted the move toward professionalization. They rejected the common view that architects' recent achievement of social and professional parity with lawyers and physicians, which made them "secure and respected in the Victorian social hierarchy," was a sign of progress.[40] They maintained that the qualities required for artistic success could not be tested and regulated, and that far more important was preservation of architecture's ties to painting, sculpture, and the decorative arts, which they thought would be difficult with professionalization.[41] Again, the argument centered around the alleged transformation of the traditional, integral craft into a pursuit of style for its own sake, or for the sake of exhibition.

Lethaby and others distinguished between contemporary architects who, in more traditional manner, directly involved themselves in building, its processes and materials, and those moderns, more or less distanced from the process of construction, who dealt in "imitation, style 'effects,' paper designs, and exhibition": the former made true working drawings, the latter cultivated a hard style and the "brilliant trick 'draughtsmanship' which wins competitions."[42] With many members of the movement trained as architects, stories circulated regarding the vagaries of well-known architectural offices. Thomas Jackson, for example, told of training in Sir George Gilbert Scott's office, where the large staff of twenty-seven included eighteen pupils drawing in three rooms. But Scott "was up to the eyes in engagements and it was hard to get him to look at our work"; indeed, it was alleged that he had only a slight acquaintance with much of what came out of his office.[43] Jackson also pointed out at an 1888 congress of artists in Liverpool that none of the nominal architects of certain prominent buildings in that city had done a single drawing for them, the work being done by surrogate designers or *ghosts*.[44] The practice of ghost-designing was illustrated in Prior's notorious report of an architect who entered a national competition with a set of drawings commissioned for four hundred pounds from a ghost who, it was later discovered, had in turn commissioned them from another ghost![45]

Such was the general state of affairs that led several men to give up architecture. Morris left Street's office because, he informed Philip Webb, "he found he could not get into close contact with it, it had to be done at second hand"; John Emmet (1828–1898) told Lethaby that, "having come to understand the old art of building, [he] gave up the modern practice of the profession"; and Arthur Mackmurdo (1851–1942) confessed that he, too, abandoned architecture for decorative design (after several outstanding buildings) in

search of "a more spontaneous method."[46] These critics also lamented the separation of the designer from actual craftsmanship and construction. Lethaby made the colorful distinction between "soft" and "hard" methods, the former based on style, imitation, paper design, and exhibition (as noted above), the latter on actual building, workmanship, materials, and experimentation. George Scott was taken to exemplify the former, William Butterfield (1814–1900) the latter.[47] Sir Reginald Blomfield reiterated the central architectural tenets of the movement in recalling Lethaby's position:

He wanted art to come down into the street and the market-place, divest itself of all trappings, and devote its energies to the simpler, nearest and dearest realisation of the purpose in hand. His first idea had been that an architect should take a much more active part in the execution of the work than is done in modern practice. . . . He suggested that the right thing for an architect to do was to be a craftsman himself, and to associate with him not thirty draughtsmen in a back office, but a group of associates and assistants in the building itself.[48]

Sympathetic as he was to this position, Blomfield added that Lethaby must have realized in time that "under modern conditions, this was impracticable."[49] Yet it is necessary to understand what appeared— regrettably, in the eyes of an artist like Lethaby—to be passing away before the irresistible progress of modernization. What modern artistic self-consciousness and stylistic pluralism signified to him and many other members of the Arts and Crafts Movement may perhaps be inferred from a letter written in the mid-1820s by George Wightwick (who had been an assistant to John Soane), distinguishing between the "Architect" and the "ordinary *Builder*," the former being necessary for "the superadded graces of correct design and suitable decoration."[50]

From this confused situation, it was but a few steps to the "battle of the styles," and even the Gothic, so uncritically identified with the Arts and Crafts Movement, would be put into question by architects of the movement such as Lethaby, Blomfield, and, interestingly, Webb (1831– 1915), who was reported to have left

Street's office in 1858 "because he saw that modern medievalism was an open contradiction." He therefore "resolved to try whether it was not possible to make the buildings of our own day pleasant without pretences of style."[51] This impulse permeated the greater part of Arts and Crafts theory and practice, and inspired the seemingly simple style which the artists sought to derive from such considerations as technical process, material, and purpose. Their reiterated insistence on the *spirit* rather than the *letter* of Gothic was meant to suggest its source in these latter principles. To Webb, Gothic meant *barbaric*, a stage to be found in all architecture, and denoting a "direct expressiveness, before consciousness of attractive detail."[52] This individualizing and supervening consciousness was later seen as the coordinate of professional specialization and the sense of autonomy which would predispose the nineteenth-century manipulation of historical styles. Richard Krautheimer has traced the trajectory sketched by theorists of the Arts and Crafts Movement more fully, detecting

even in the thirteenth century "a gradual process of draining the edifice of its *content*," to reach "a peak in the late 19th and early 20th centuries," when architectural patterns are "used regardless of their original significance."[53]

The determination of a sort of unconscious style, then, by the immediate demands of technique, function, material, and appropriate decoration, was taken to mark all traditional arts and crafts, and constituted the final argument for their reunification. Lethaby's ideal may be seen expressed in three designs reproduced here. The directness and clarity of his Eagle Insurance Building, Birmingham, of 1902 (fig. 1) relate to the structural elements—the horizontal of reinforced concrete and the vertical of steel—and the ornamental effects, like the band of lettering across the top of the ground wall, being closely integrated into the whole. The interior view of his All Saints Church, Brockhampton, of 1902 (fig. 2), shows three pointed arches of rough stone supporting a concrete roof, which is covered on the exterior by thatch, giving the building a traditional aspect but in fact serving as thermal insulation for the concrete structure. In 1902 Lethaby, four architects, a sculptor, and a stained-glass artist collaborated in submitting to the Liverpool Cathedral competition a re-

1. William R. Lethaby, Eagle Insurance Building, Colmore Row, Birmingham, 1902

2. William R. Lethaby, All Saints Church, Brockhampton, Herefordshire, 1902, interior

3. William R. Lethaby et al., Liverpool Cathedral competition design, 1902, perspective view super-imposed on photograph
Victoria and Albert Museum, London

markable design for a massive edifice of concrete (fig. 3), whose structural stability was expressed in the corrugated roof and a series of buttressing semicylindrical chapels—the unusual match of form, material, and structure pointing in a quite new direction.

II

The actual measures that the Arts and Crafts Movement took to reform art and its production would be unintelligible without consideration of at least some of their historical and theoretical concerns as outlined above. Something of this is indicated in Charles Ashbee's proposition that the movement was convinced of "the fundamental need for the reconstruction of the workshop before the flower of Art can be fulfilled."[54] The statement locates the artist in an uncertain present, powerless to create until a lost ideal from the past has been restored, but hopeful of future success. Ashbee implied that, given the decline of a major artistic tradition, the workshop acquired new significance as

more than the site of production: here ancient and proven skills were to be rejuvenated, a concern with craft processes, material, fitness, and utility was to be rekindled, and beauty as the romance of humankind's habitation of the earth was to be restored. These artists' sense of what harmonious design had been in the past and the spirit of what they needed to strive for can be glimpsed in two reactions to the interiors depicted in the *Saint Jerome in His Study* of Dürer and Antonello da Messina (the latter just then acquired by the National Gallery in London and misattributed to Giovanni Bellini). Lethaby urged his reader to compare Antonello's interior, with its "dignity of serene and satisfying order," with the most beautiful room he knew, to learn "how vulgar our *good taste* appears and how foreign to the end of culture—Peace."[55] The observation of Halsey Ricardo (1854–1928) that Antonello da Messina's saint "gets all that he can properly want, and he gets over and above—the addition born of his denial—the look of peace in his room, that can so seldom be found with us" has broad ethical implications for the period.[56]

Inspiration of this reflective and nostalgic sort, expressed by Lethaby and Ricardo, accompanied by discontent over the prevailing conditions of artistic work and the plight of industrial workers, helped to shape the Arts and Crafts Movement. Although the first organization to implement what were to become distinctive Arts and Crafts ideals was Morris, Marshall, Faulkner and Company, founded in 1861, several previous attempts had been made. In 1847 Henry Cole brought a number of artists together in *Summerly's Art-Manufactures*, "directed towards improving contemporary industrial products."[57] Mackmurdo recorded the founding of several craft organizations in the 1840s and 1850s. For example, Thomas Seddon, an associate of the Pre-Raphaelites, established a school of design for craftsmen in his family's furniture workshop, with Ford Madox Brown as an instructor. In 1854 the Reverend Frederick D. Maurice and his Christian Socialists founded the Working Men's College, whose instructors included Ruskin, Dante Rossetti, Ford Madox Brown, and Edward Burne-Jones; Mackmurdo commented that "the work carried on here was a real start in the emancipation of the crafts." Around the same time Benjamin Woodward also participated and was noted as "the first architect to gather round him a group of artists and craftsmen to design and execute the decoration of his buildings." And Mackmurdo recalled that as early as the year of their founding (1848), members of the Pre-Raphaelite Brotherhood were thinking of designing for decoration.[58] The involvement of Rossetti, Morris, Burne-Jones, and others in the decoration of the octagonal hall of Benjamin Woodward's new Union Society in Oxford, some nine years later, was a largely failed implementation of that aim. Nonetheless, it seems to have directed them toward the next major steps in decorative design, the construction and furnishing, to Webb's design, of Morris' Red House in 1859–1860, and the foundation of the Morris firm in 1861.[59]

William Rossetti's later and not entirely reliable memory of the founding of Morris' firm conveys a valuable poetical truth in suggesting the inspiration that the founding group of friends derived from the thought of "the way in which artists did all kinds of things in olden times, designed every kind of decoration and most kinds of furniture...."[60] The subtitle of the firm was Fine Art Workmen in Painting, Carving, Furniture, and the Metals. Its prospectus was characteristically polemical, claiming that the country's architecture called for the services of "artists of reputation"; for it needed "that artistic supervision, which can alone bring about harmony between the various parts of a successful work," but which was costly on account of the necessity of taking individual artists away from their main work. The firm's association of artists proposed to resolve this problem, and they advertised their readiness to "undertake any species of decoration, mural or otherwise, from pictures, properly so called, down to the consideration of the smallest work susceptible of art and beauty." They were accordingly ready to produce either by themselves or under their supervision, in one workshop, a variety of decorative work and furnishings, including mural decoration (in pictures, pattern-work, or simple color arrangement); architectural carving; stained glass ("especially with reference to its harmony with Mural Decoration"); metalwork and jewelry; furniture, plain with applied materials, or painted with figure and pattern; embroidery; stamped leather; and "ornamental work in other such materials, besides every article necessary for domestic use."[61] The list does not include wallpaper, but Morris and Webb designed one in 1862 and manufactured another in 1864.

The firm's first headquarters were at Red Lion Square, London, and what they lacked in business sense in the early years they apparently possessed in enthusiasm. Morris' official biographer believed that the firm represented not so much a business or manufacturing enterprise as "a definite agreement for cooperation and common work among friends who were also artists."[62] At this time Ford Madox Brown, already a practitioner of several crafts, and Rossetti, poet-painter and organizer of the Oxford Union decoration,

4. King René's Honeymoon Cabinet, designed by John P. Seddon, painted by William Morris, Ford Madox Brown, Dante Rossetti, Edward Burne-Jones, and others, 1861, oak and inlaid woods
Victoria and Albert Museum, London

were apparently the major initiators; Morris, also a poet and painter, had done some carving, illumination, and embroidery. The other members of the firm included Edward Burne-Jones (1833–1898), painter and stained-glass designer, and Webb, architect and designer for furniture. At the outset and later, the firm also employed a number of remarkable craftswomen, some of them trained by Morris himself, including Kate Faulkner, Georgiana Burne-Jones, and Morris' daughter May, an outstanding designer in her own right. Designs for commissioned work, at first chiefly ecclesiastical stained glass, were made by these artists and others outside the firm such as Albert Moore (1841–1893) and Simeon Solomon (1840–1905); they were all executed either by the firm's workmen on the premises, or by firms such as James Powell and Sons Glassworks of Whitefriars.[63] Among early commissions were the more comprehensive schemes for the Green Dining Room in the South Kensington (now Victoria and Albert) Museum and the Armoury and Tapestry Rooms of Saint James's Palace in 1867. These awards must have been at least partially the result of the favorable impression created by the firm's early work, including its public debut at the Medieval Court of the 1862 International Exhibition. The firm

won two medals and the following citation from the jury: "Messrs. Morris & Company have exhibited several pieces of furniture, tapestries &c in the style of the Middle Ages. The general forms of the furniture, the arrangement of the tapestry, and the character of the details are satisfying to the archaeologist from the exactness of the imitation, at the same time that the general finish is excellent."[64] But seven stained-glass panels by Rossetti were unjustly suspected of being original medieval glass merely touched up.[65]

One unusual work exhibited in 1862, the oak King René's Honeymoon Cabinet (fig. 4), may be taken to exemplify certain central ideals of the firm as well as the later Arts and Crafts Movement. Designed with the assistance of his pupil, William Burges, by the architect John P. Seddon (1827–1906), who himself had "a passionate belief in the unity of the arts,"[66] it was probably built in the Seddon family furniture workshop, of oak with colored inlaid woods and metal hinges, and submitted to the Morris firm for decoration with subjects illustrative of painting, sculpture, architecture, and music.[67] Here was a signal occasion to combine several crafts in a cooperative enterprise of decoration in the presumably medieval manner, and their approach was instructive. Ford Madox

Brown suggested illustrating scenes of artistic activity in the life of the fifteenth-century monarch, René of Anjou, who had appeared in Sir Walter Scott's 1829 novel, *Anne of Geierstein*, as an ineffectual monarch but also an example of Rossetti's many-talented artist of bygone times. In a setting of four compartments with cusped arches, decorated spandrels, and gilded backgrounds designed by Morris, King René was represented as architect (by Brown), painter and sculptor (by Burne-Jones), and musician (by Rossetti), embodying the many-sided artist, while six smaller panels at the top represented scenes of everyday work, namely gardening (by Rossetti), weaving (by Burne-Jones), glass-blowing, metalwork, and embroidery (by Valentine Prinsep), and pottery by another, unknown artist. In its conception, manufacture, and narrative depiction of the romance of the royal artist, King René's Honeymoon Cabinet embodied several levels of symbolic significance. The very principle of richly painted furniture (the firm as well as William Burges having several other pieces to their credit at this time) alluded to the traditional practice that employed decorative painting on useful objects before the emergence of autonomous easel painting.

The emblematic elevation of the arts—through practice by the monarch—and the dignity accorded the crafts through association with them gave expression to central ideals of the artists, as of the larger movement to follow. It also demonstrated the belief, as Seddon expressed it, *"that in the unity and fellowship of the several arts lies their power."*[68] Sensitive to the importance of the careful coordination of the artists' efforts, and in particular to Morris' unifying structural scheme, which made the whole into a "work of art truly decorative, and not merely a collection of misplaced paintings," Seddon recalled one critic's comparison of their cooperation to that of Jacopo della Quercia, Ghiberti, and Donatello on the Baptistery font in Siena.[69]

A series of commissions from colleges at Cambridge directed the artists and workshops of the Morris firm to larger decorative schemes. The first of these came with their involvement in the restoration of Queen's College chapel and hall from 1862 to 1864. Morris, Rossetti, Brown, and Burne-Jones designed a set of inlaid tiles for an alabaster panel above the fireplace; for this again they chose a traditional motif, the labors of the months, probably based on a thirteenth-century manuscript or a sixteenth-century almanac, while Webb designed a frieze of eleven coats of arms below.[70] Their fireplace panels, roof decoration, and George Bodley's stone and tile floor have been said to make this "one of the most sumptuous interiors in the country."[71] In 1866 the firm undertook the decoration of Jesus College's chapel roof; designed by Morris and Webb, it was executed by Morris and his workmen, with a Cambridge assistant, Frederick R. Leach, reputed to have been Morris' "favourite decorator."[72] The antechapel stained-glass windows, also entrusted to the firm, were designed by Burne-Jones, Brown, and Morris.

Their production of stained glass reveals the organization of one of the firm's major enterprises. They benefited from Webb's previous experience in matching stained glass to architecture (under Street), and from the expertise of such craftsmen as George Campfield, Fairfax Murray, and Charles Holloway, although Webb himself later complained that not manufacturing their own glass and not having draftsmen sufficiently capable of translating drawings compromised the firm's products in this medium.[73] Morris seldom made complete designs, but relied on the painters Rossetti, Brown, and especially Burne-Jones, for figures; on Webb for layout, animals, architectural details, and lettering; and reserving backgrounds and foliage to himself.[74] When the subject and layout of a decorative scheme had been decided, and measured cartoons commissioned and received from the artists, Morris himself usually supervised the interpretation of designs by the craftsmen, the more able ones being assigned faces and hands. He then determined the color scheme of a window, after which the glass would be distributed and painted under his direction, burned and leaded up, and the final product examined. According to the firm's manager, "If any part did not satisfy him, new glass was cut and that piece of the window done again."[75] Probably more than any other factor, Morris' close supervision and coordination ensured that the designs of so many different artists produced a distinctive style that harmonized with the setting. Indeed, the firm's best stained glass was produced in the 1860s, under these conditions, and quality suffered whenever Morris was called elsewhere.

Morris, Marshall, Faulkner and Company, reorganized in 1875 as Morris and Company, enjoyed success on many fronts, not least in seeming to consolidate the scattered currents of reform in the decorative and building crafts, and inspiring other artists, architects, and craftsmen to similar organization in the late 1870s and early 1880s. The first of these was the Century Guild, established in 1882 by Arthur H. Mackmurdo—architect and designer of wallpaper, furniture, and fabric, and later a social theorist—and Selwyn Image, graphic artist and designer of mosaics and stained glass. Its members included Herbert Horne (1864–1916)—designer of fabric, metalwork, and wallpaper—and Clement Heaton (1861–1940)—designer and craftsman in stained glass and metalwork. Mackmurdo's personal concern over the plight of the worker in industry bears testimony to a swelling current of opinion at this time against ill treatment at the hands of manufacturers and tradesmen, and one practice in particular elicited attempts at redress. As Mackmurdo put it, "In the stress of . . . competition it became a trade policy to conceal the authorship of designs that were considered successful: from this point of view, then, the designers became mere instruments of a very degenerate and artless commercial system."[76] The Century Guild's approach to this problem was, in the words of its program, "to render all branches of art the sphere no longer of the tradesman but of the artist," and echoing the prospectus of the Morris firm, they proposed to "restore building, decoration, glass-painting, pottery, wood-carving and metal to their right place beside painting and sculpture."[77] Anticipating later attempts by the Arts and Crafts Movement, Mackmurdo made the condition of his participation in an 1883 exhibition at Enfield the due acknowledgment of the executant alongside the designer.[78] By contrast, the guild's own practice seems to have been different; they presented their work as the result of cooperative endeavor, so it became difficult to establish individual contributions.[79]

The single artist of the Arts and Crafts Movement who can be said more than any other to have developed a systematic theory of the reformed workshop (if not an entirely clear workshop practice) was Charles R. Ashbee (1863–1942), who founded the Guild and School of Handicraft in 1888. These organizations brought together most of the diverse currents of the Arts and Crafts Movement, and gave particular emphasis to two problems which would be more effectively dealt with in Germany, namely the connection between craft reform and industry, and the related issue of education. Ruskin's maxim, "Life without industry is guilt, and industry without art is brutality," inscribed on a beam for the inauguration of the guild, clearly indicated Ashbee's orientation.[80] Indeed, the guild and school grew both out of classes Ashbee conducted "for the study of design & the reading of Ruskin" at Toynbee Hall in London's East End in 1886–1887, and out of the need felt for a practical application.[81] The guild or productive unit was conceived as a cooperative workshop, managed by a worker-elected committee, with annual profits shared in proportion to wages received. The workshop was intended to produce and offer for sale, "Furniture, metal work, gold and silver work, jewellery, leather work, gesso and decorative painting, and such things as conveniently group themselves under the direction of architecture."[82] Ashbee's conviction that the problems of art and industry, which had so engaged previous reformers and had been practically addressed by the Arts and Crafts workshops, needed to be dealt with at the root, gave rise to the School of Handicraft attached to the guild. In its classes, held evenings, Ashbee and the guild craftsmen taught men and boys what he termed "the life of Workmanship," with the expectation that once trained, pupils would choose to join the guild. Ashbee intended

5. Guild of Handicraft, Chipping Campden, cabinet workshop, c. 1901
Victoria and Albert Museum, London

6. Third Arts and Crafts Exhibition, London, 1890, showing Kenton and Company furniture. From left to right: circular rosewood table by William R. Lethaby, corner cabinet by Reginald Blomfield, fall-front oak cabinet by Ernest Gimson, and walnut cupboard by William R. Lethaby (chest of drawers at extreme left by Ford Madox Brown, not a member of the company)

this experiment (adapting the medieval guild idea) to solve the problems caused in contemporary industry by rampant competition, exploitation, and militant trade unionism:

The traditions of the past, under which good work throve, were, broadly, two, the tradition of the Guild and the tradition of the Workshop. The tradition of the Guild implied a cooperative and exclusive system, and a corporate responsibility among the producers to the community for the goodness of the work produced. The tradition of the Workshop implied a strong handing down, from generation to generation, of old methods of workmanship, in small workshops, every craftsman's direct interest in the work of his own hands and his personal responsibility to the Guild for it. It followed necessarily from this, that technical and artistic education, in our sense of the word, was implied in the workshop teaching; there was no educational difficulty outside the workshop, and divorced from it.[83]

We may infer from this and other similar statements that what Ashbee learned from medieval industry did not concern primarily craftsmanship and stylistic integrity, but the nature of work, its contribution to the well-being of the worker and community, and the condition of the

individual craftsman. Ashbee, more than any other member of the Arts and Crafts Movement, gave serious consideration to the inroads machinery had made into contemporary crafts and industry. And though he approached the problem in general terms, his concern was specifically

7. Pinbury workshop, c. 1895. From left to right, music chest and workbox by Ernest Barnsley, plaster friezes by Ernest Gimson (at rear), two ends of an oak chest by Sidney Barnsley, and a turned ladder-back chair by Ernest Gimson
Edward Barnsley Educational Trust, Cheltenham, England

with the worker's experience in the craft process. Hence he recommended that the first concern in using machinery ought to be mitigating the onerousness and tedium of work, but not its pleasure.[84] Ashbee maintained that in the workshop "a sharp distinction . . . be drawn between what is produced by machinery and the direct work of man's hands."[85] This Morrisian elevation of the worker's experience rather than that of the consumer or the public would have conflicted with Lethaby's functionalist aesthetic, which embraced the machine to the extent of regarding the modern steamship and locomotive as models. Not surprisingly, in the guild workshop where handwork reigned supreme (fig. 5), Ashbee was content to accept standards short of excellence so long as the work experience had an improving effect on craftsmen and apprentices and gave hope of future industrial benefit (although he reserved the right as head designer to exert some control over guild production).[86]

Extreme marginalization of the machine characterized several furniture workshops in the period between 1890 and World War I. A lecture titled "Carpenter's Furniture," which Lethaby delivered to the Arts and Crafts Exhibition Society in 1889,

suggests the orientation of the artists involved, most of whom were trained as architects. Lethaby himself was one of five architects to form Kenton and Company in London in 1890, the others being Blomfield, Mervin MacCartney (1853–1932), Ernest Gimson (1864–1919), and Sidney Barnsley (1865–1926) (fig. 6). An element of dissatisfaction with current architectural practice and the promise of a more direct, unhampered approach to a vernacular, "unconscious" style via furniture seem to have inspired this venture. Other concerns included the responsibility of the designer to supervise the manufacture of his own work, the obligations of the shared venture, and the recognition by name, stamped on each item produced, of the designer, the executant, and the firm.[87] After the early demise of the company, Gimson, Barnsley, and the latter's brother, Ernest Barnsley (1863–1926), also an architect, established the Pinbury workshop in the Cotswolds region. They were still attached to the ideals of a fellowship of craftsmen and a vernacular idiom, but now also desired a country setting. With this and the move by Ashbee's Guild of Handicraft to nearby Chipping Campden, the Arts and Crafts workshop widened its interest to encompass a way of life lived close to the earth and devoted to handicraft. A photograph of the Pinbury workshop about 1895 (fig. 7) gives evidence of the group spirit with which their furniture was produced. Various items are seen in the course of manufacture, from left to right, a music cabinet and workbox by Ernest Barnsley, some plaster panels by Ernest Gimson, parts of an oak chest by Sidney Barnsley, and a turned ladder-back chair by Gimson. Collaboration extended even to single designs, as in five 1902 drawings for furniture by Gimson and Ernest Barnsley, one of which (fig. 8), signed and dated "B & G. May 17 1902," is for an oak washstand. The use of machinery was kept to a minimum, although Sidney Barnsley did use a large circular saw while executing his designs in his own workshop. The time-consuming nature of this kind of work probably accounts for the relative scarcity of drawings by him.[88] The furniture of these workshops generally achieved a forward-looking simplic-

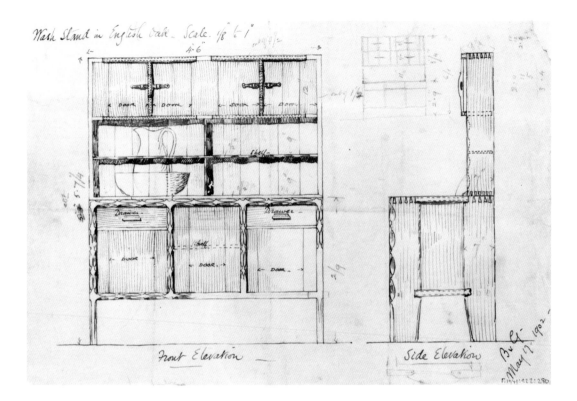

Front Elevation — Side Elevation

ity, its character determined largely by the nature of the materials, the absence of applied ornament, and the principles of construction (such as frequent visible dovetailing and surface treatment). So radical were their designs that an 1896 reviewer ascribed to them a "primitive character."[89]

By the end of World War I the major force of the Arts and Crafts Movement appears to have been spent, though its spokesmen might have remained convinced of the relevance of their message to the tasks of reconstruction, insisting that the aim of art ought still to be "to do things in the right way" and to instill a "pride of the spirit in good honest craftsmanship."[90] But the quaint sound of this, even its seeming anachronism, was a symptom of the inroads already made into the popular consciousness by the inexorable progress of the machine, the appropriation of art by the market economy, and the isolation of the fine arts, now more specialized than ever, from public and popular concerns. It may be understandable, therefore, that critic Arthur Symons should write in his review, "The Decay of Craftsmanship in England," that

"it is certain that we have outlived the age of the craftsman, the age in which beauty was the natural attendant on use."[91] Symons was true to the Arts and Crafts ideal and regretted its failure to take root in an inhospitable soil. Lethaby and other members of the Arts and Crafts Movement recognized that new steps toward realizing the ideals of the movement were being taken in Germany, where workshop reform and the related issues of education and industry were being tackled by the Werkbund and the Bauhaus. Yet even there public events would limit and overturn advances. The conviction of a recent writer that "the search for an alternative architecture through a renaissance of the minor arts" is precisely the way out of the ruins of modernism, and the parallels between the dilemmas of the 1880s and the 1980s suggest that the agenda of the Arts and Crafts Movement remains urgent.[92]

8. Ernest Gimson and Ernest Barnsley, design for an oak washstand, signed and dated B & G, May 17, 1902, drawing in ink on tracing paper
Cheltenham Art Gallery and Museums, England

NOTES

1. W. G. Constable, *The Painter's Workshop* (Boston, 1963), 6.

2. E. J. Hobsbawm, *The Age of Capital, 1848–1875* (New York, 1979), 30.

3. Henry Wilson, "The Crafts and Reconstruction," in *Handicrafts and Reconstruction: Notes by Members of the Arts and Crafts Exhibition Society* (London, 1919), 13–14. See also Wilson, "Introduction: The Crafts and Modern Life," in *Problems of Reconstruction: Lectures and Addresses* (London, 1918), 211–220.

4. William Morris, "Preface," *Arts and Crafts Essays by Members of the Arts and Crafts Movement* (London, 1893), v–vi.

5. But note the "similarity of tenor" that one recent critic, in an incisive study, detects between the Arts and Crafts Movement and postimpressionism and early modernism, a crusading outlook, the use of a religious type of language, and the adoption of converts. See S. K. Tillyard, "Early Modernism and the Arts and Crafts Movement," *The Impact of Modernism, 1900–1920: Early Modernism and the Arts and Crafts in Edwardian England* (London and New York, 1988), 47–80.

6. Edward S. Prior, "The Ghosts of the Profession," in *Architecture: A Profession or an Art*, ed. R. Norman Shaw and Thomas G. Jackson (London, 1892), 102; William Morris, "The Lesser Arts," in *Collected Works*, 24 vols. (London, 1910–1915), 22:9.

7. William Lethaby, *Form in Civilization: Collected Papers on Art and Labour* (London, New York, and Toronto, 1957), 66, and Arthur H. Mackmurdo, "History of the Arts and Crafts Movement," unpublished manuscript, with irregular pagination (William Morris Gallery, Walthamstow), chap. 10:5. See also William R. Lethaby, "Labour a Manifestation of God," *Hibbert Journal* 27 (1928), 48, and Frank A. Walker, "William Lethaby and His 'Scientific Outlook,'" *Architectural Association Quarterly* 9 (1977), 45–53.

8. Francis Palgrave, "The Fine Arts in Florence," *Quarterly Review* 66 (1840), 322–323. See also John Ruskin, Lecture 4, "The Relation of Art to Use," *Library Edition of the Works of John Ruskin*, ed. E. W. Cook and A. Wedderburn, 39 vols. (London, 1903–1912), 20:95–97; "Aratra Pentelici," 20:200–203; and "On the Old Road," 34:353–354.

9. Walter Crane, *The Claims of Decorative Art* (London, 1892), 57.

10. William M. Rossetti, *Fine Art, Chiefly Contemporary* (New York, 1970), 127.

11. Rossetti 1970, 128.

12. Henry Cole, cited in Mary Comino, *Gimson and the Barnsleys* (London, 1980), 23.

13. Raymond Williams, *Keywords: A Vocabulary of Culture and Society* (New York, 1976), 33.

14. Williams 1976, 33.

15. Thomas Cobden-Sanderson, "On Art and Life," *Art and Life, and the Building and Decoration of Cities*, Arts and Crafts Exhibition Society (London, 1897), 10.

16. Thomas Cobden-Sanderson 1897, 23.

17. Adam Smith, *An Inquiry into the Nature and Causes of the Wealth of Nations* (New York, 1965), 3.

18. Selwyn Image, "On the Unity of Art," *Century Guild Hobby Horse* 2 (1887), 3.

19. Basil H. Jackson, ed., *Recollections of Thomas Graham Jackson* (London, 1950), 101.

20. Jackson 1950, 121–122.

21. Prior, "Ghosts," 102–103.

22. Wilson 1918, 218–219. See also Jackson 1950, 53; John R. Clayton, "The Isolation of 'Professional' Architecture," in Shaw and Jackson 1892, 682; and Gerald Horsley, "The Unity of Art," in Shaw and Jackson 1892, 685; Reginald Blomfield, "The Artist and the Community," in *The Touchstone of Architecture* (Oxford, 1925), 208–210; and "Architecture and the Craftsman," in *The Mistress Art* (London, 1908), 79–113; William Burges, cited in J. Mordaunt-Crook, *William Burgess and the High Victorian Dream* (Chicago, 1981), 137; George E. Street, cited in Stefan Muthesius, *The High Victorian Movement in Architecture, 1859–1870* (London and Boston, 1972), 154; Image 1887, 2–3; Morris, "The Lesser Arts," in Morris 1910–1915, 22:3–27; "The History of Pattern Designing," in Morris 1910–1915, 22:206–234; "The Revival of Handicraft," in Morris 1910–1915, 22:331–334; and "The Arts and Crafts Today," in Morris 1910–1915, 22:356–374; and John Harvey, *Mediaeval Craftsmen* (London and Sydney, 1975), 85, 159.

23. Image 1887, 3.

24. Walter Crane, *An Artist's Reminiscences* (London, 1907), 298.

25. Morris 1910–1915, 22:119; see also 73–74 and 240–241.

26. Morris 1910–1915, 22:119.

27. Blomfield 1925, 202–206. Blomfield's judgment is surprising. It is possible that most members of the movement, following Ruskin, would have held the opposite view, though rejecting the Greek temple on grounds other than that of artistic unity. John Harvey agrees in general with this position, noting that "it is impossible to draw any hard and fast line between the construction and the enrichment of mediaeval buildings. Their art and craftsmanship were united and produced a single whole incorporating structural and aesthetic elements": Harvey 1975, 159.

28. William B. Richmond, "Thoughts on Three Arts and the Training for Them," in Shaw and Jackson 1892, 189.

29. Thomas G. Jackson, "The Presidential Address," in *Transactions of the National Association for the Advancement of Art in Industry, 1890* (London,

1891), 86. John Harvey notes similarly that in the original late medieval situation "there is no clearcut frontier between the art that is fine and that which is applied." Harvey 1975, 85.

30. Palgrave 1840, 349.

31. Somers Clark, "Stone and Wood Carving," in *Arts and Crafts Essays*, 83. See also Crane 1892, 31 and *Line and Form* (London, 1900), 198.

32. Blomfield 1925, 218; Walter Crane, "Of Wall Papers," in *Arts and Crafts Essays*, 52–53; and Ford Madox Brown, "Of Mural Painting," in *Arts and Crafts Essays*, 159.

33. Edward S. Prior, "Furniture and the Room," in *Arts and Crafts Essays*, 266.

34. Clark, "Stone and Wood Carving," 83.

35. Walter Crane, "Of Decorative Painting and Design," in *Arts and Crafts Essays*, 42, 44. Crane explained this phenomenon in a later essay as follows: "The Modern picture-exhibitions—I mean big shows like that of the Royal Academy—have perhaps done more to destroy the decorative relationship of the easel picture than anything. An analogous effect is produced on the mind by the sight of so many pictures of so many different sorts, subjects, and scales, and treatments crowded together, to that produced by a surfeit of ornament, and pattern on pattern, in internal decoration. This seems to point to the fact that true decoration lies rather in the sense of proportion and arrangement or distribution than in the use of particular units of ornament, styles, colours, or materials, and that one may destroy decorative effect by the very means of decoration." Crane, "The Relationship of the Easel Picture to Decorative Art," in *Ideals in Art: Papers Theoretical, Practical, Critical* (London, 1905), 266–267.

36. John D. Sedding, *Art and Handicraft* (London, 1893), 57.

37. Lethaby 1957, 126. On this aspect of the Victorian collection see Larry D. Lutchmansingh, "Commodity Exhibitionism at the London Great Exhibition of 1851," *Annals of Scholarship* 7 (1990), 203–216.

38. Crane, cited in Irwin Macdonald, "An Afternoon with Walter Crane: His Views on the Artistic, Social, and Industrial Conditions Prevailing in England Today," *The Craftsman* 17 (October 1909), 40.

39. Lethaby 1957, 140, 144 (emphasis added).

40. See Frank Jenkins, "The Victorian Architectural Profession," in *Victorian Architecture*, ed. P. Ferriday (Philadelphia and New York, 1964), 39.

41. Jackson, 1950, 212–213. The protest against the move for professionalization is recorded in Shaw and Jackson 1892, xxxii–xxxv; a deposition to the president and council of the Royal Institute of British Architects is reprinted on page xxxiv of this document, and includes the following paragraph: "Architecture has for some time been less constantly associated with the sister arts of Painting and Sculpture than, in our opinion, is desirable, and we think

that examinations and diplomas, by raising artificial barriers, would have a tendency still further to alienate these branches of art." Robert Macleod, examining the controversy, was of the opinion that "there can be little doubt that [the] insistence on, and success in achieving a formal professional structure encouraged an increasing isolation from developments in the visual arts on the one hand, and from the building industry on the other, during the first quarter of the twentieth century." Macleod, *Style and Society: Architectural Ideology in Britain, 1835–1914* (London, 1971), 126–127. Stefan Muthesius notes that as early as 1857, George Edmund Street had warned that "we architects are in great danger of endorsing the popular idea that we are 'professional men' and not artists!" Muthesius 1972, 157 and 159.

42. William R. Lethaby, *Philip Webb and His Work* (London, 1935), 67, 79. Lethaby's observation was remarkably similar to that of the designer, Lewis F. Day: "You may take it . . . as a general rule that highly finished and elaborate drawings are got up for show, 'finished for exhibition' as they say . . . and that drawings completed only so far as necessary, precise in their details, disfigured by notes in writing, sections, and so on, are at least genuine workaday drawings." Lewis F. Day, "Of Design and Working Drawings," in *Arts and Crafts Essays*, 251.

43. Jackson 1950, 315–316.

44. Jackson 1891, 88.

45. Prior, in Shaw and Jackson 1892, 109.

46. Lethaby 1935, 122; Emmett, in Lethaby 1935, 84: Mackmurdo, "Autobiographical Notes," unpublished, irregularly paginated manuscript (William Morris Gallery, Walthamstow). See also for Morris, Nikolaus Pevsner, "Architecture and William Morris," *Journal of the Royal Institute of British Architects* 64 (March 1957), 172–175.

47. Macleod 1971, 69.

48. Reginald Blomfield, "W. R. Lethaby: An Impression and Tribute," *Journal of the Royal Institute of British Architects* 39 (February 1932), 301–302.

49. Blomfield 1932, 302.

50. Wightwick, cited in Barrington Kaye, *The Development of the Architectural Profession* (London, 1960), 54 (emphasis in original). Kaye adds amusingly to this that "country houses of the period were transformed from buildings into architecture simply by the addition of a large Ionic portico" (56).

51. Webb, cited in Kaye 1960, 124. Lethaby was close to Webb in defining style as "a museum name for a phase of past art" and "a means of classifying what is dead and done," and in calling for "an active art of building which will take its 'style' for granted, as does naval architecture." Lethaby 1957, 9. See also Lethaby, "The Modern Position," in *Architecture* (London and New York, 1922), chap. 15.

52. Webb, cited in Lethaby 1935, 132. See also "The Handicrafts in Old Days," in Sedding 1893; and William R. Lethaby, "The Builder's Art and the

Craftsman," in Shaw and Jackson 1892, 151–172.

53. Richard Krautheimer, "Introduction to an 'Iconography' of Mediaeval Architecture," *Journal of the Warburg and Courtauld Institutes* 5 (1942), 20. See also Nikolaus Pevsner, "The Term 'Architect' in the Middle Ages," *Speculum* 17 (October 1942), 549–562; Spiro Kostoff, "The Architect in the Middle Ages, East and West," and Leopold D. Ettlinger, "The Emergence of the Italian Architect during the Fifteenth Century," in *The Architect: Chapters in the History of the Profession*, ed. Spiro Kostoff (New York and Oxford, 1977), chaps. 3, 4; and Martin S. Briggs, "The Middle Ages" and "The Nineteenth Century in England," in *The Architect in History* (Oxford, 1927), chaps. 4, 8.

54. Charles R. Ashbee, *A Few Chapters in Workshop Reconstruction and Citizenship* (London, 1894), 22.

55. William R. Lethaby, "Carpenter's Furniture," in *Arts and Crafts Essays*, 307.

56. Halsey Ricardo, "Of the Room and Furniture," in *Arts and Crafts Essays*, 282.

57. Alf Bøe, *From Gothic Revival to Functional Form* (Oslo and Oxford, 1957), 50.

58. Mackmurdo, "Autobiographical Notes," chap. 2:31, 32; chap. 3:57; chap. 4:25.

59. Rossetti's version of the Oxford mural project is given in *Letters of Dante Gabriel Rossetti*, ed. O. Doughty and R. J. Wahl, 4 vols. (Oxford, 1967), 2:404–408. The building of Red House is detailed in W. J. Mackail, *The Life of William Morris*, 2 vols. (London, 1922), 1:143–49.

60. Rossetti, cited in Theodore Watts-Dunton, "Mr. William Morris," *The Athenaeum* 3598 (10 October 1896), 498.

61. Mackail 1922, 1:155–56.

62. Mackail 1922, 1:149.

63. Paul Thompson, *The Work of William Morris* (New York, 1967), 16.

64. Cited in Philip Henderson, *William Morris: His Life, Work, and Friends* (Harmondsworth, Middlesex, 1973), 93–94.

65. Henderson 1973, 93.

66. Michael Darby, *John Pollard Seddon* (London, 1983), 14.

67. The issue of construction is not entirely clear, several writers suggesting that the cabinet was made by the Morris firm. In one account, "The King René's Honeymoon Cabinet," *Magazine of Art* 20 (November 1896–April 1897), 323, Seddon himself said only that the Morris firm "undertook the commission to paint for it the four large panels of the lower part . . . and the six small panels of the upper part. . . ." In another account, however, Seddon wrote that the cabinet, "having left the hands of the cabinet-makers, may be said to have been completed as far as had been usual to that date"; but "as the author was seeking further decorative treatment," he submitted it to the Morris firm. John P. Seddon,

King René's Honeymoon Cabinet (London, 1898), 4. Burges' involvement is mentioned on page 2 of the latter work.

68. Seddon 1898, viii (emphasis in original).

69. Seddon 1898, 5, vii.

70. Duncan Robinson and Stephen Wildman, *Morris and Company in Cambridge* (London, 1980), 27–28.

71. Robinson and Wildman 1980, 27.

72. Thompson 1967, 30.

73. Philip Webb, cited in A. Charles Sewter, *The Stained Glass of William Morris and His Circle*, 2 vols. (New Haven and London, 1974), 1:89. See also Webb, 1:19; Martin Harrison, *Victorian Stained Glass* (London, 1980), 40; and Thompson 1967, 119.

74. Mackail 1922, 2:44; Thompson 1967, 120.

75. George Wardle, cited in Mackail 1922, 2:45.

76. Mackmurdo, "Autobiographical Notes," chap. 10:14.

77. Cited in *Victorian and Edwardian Decorative Arts* [exh. cat., Victoria and Albert Museum] (London, 1952), 58.

78. Mackmurdo, "Autobiographical Notes," chap. 10:14.

79. *Victorian and Edwardian Decorative Arts*, 1952, 58.

80. Alan Crawford, *C. R. Ashbee: Architect, Designer, and Romantic Socialist* (New Haven and London, 1985), 30.

81. Charles R. Ashbee, *An Endeavour towards the Teaching of John Ruskin and William Morris* (London, 1901), 1–2.

82. Charles R. Ashbee, ed., *Manual of the Guild and School of Handicraft* (London, 1892), 16.

83. Ashbee 1894, 90–91.

84. Ashbee 1894, 16; and Ashbee 1901, 47–48.

85. Ashbee 1894, 16. See also Ashbee 1908, 31–32.

86. Ashbee 1901, 19–20.

87. Comino 1980, 54–55.

88. *"Good Citizen's Furniture": The Work of Ernest and Sidney Barnsley* [exh. cat., Cheltenham Art Gallery and Museum] (Cheltenham, 1976), n.p.

89. Comino 1980, 86.

90. Halsey Ricardo, "Tradition in Its Bearing on Modern Art," and Thomas Okey, "Art Schools and Crafts Workshops," in *Problems of Reconstruction*, 233, 257.

91. Arthur Symons, *Studies in Seven Arts* (London, 1924), 125.

92. Mordaunt-Crook 1981, 137.

Craftsman," in Shaw and Jackson 1892, 151–172.

53. Richard Krautheimer, "Introduction to an 'Iconography' of Mediaeval Architecture," *Journal of the Warburg and Courtauld Institutes* 5 (1942), 20. See also Nikolaus Pevsner, "The Term 'Architect' in the Middle Ages," *Speculum* 17 (October 1942), 549–562; Spiro Kostoff, "The Architect in the Middle Ages, East and West," and Leopold D. Ettlinger, "The Emergence of the Italian Architect during the Fifteenth Century," in *The Architect: Chapters in the History of the Profession*, ed. Spiro Kostoff (New York and Oxford, 1977), chaps. 3, 4; and Martin S. Briggs, "The Middle Ages" and "The Nineteenth Century in England," in *The Architect in History* (Oxford, 1927), chaps. 4, 8.

54. Charles R. Ashbee, *A Few Chapters in Workshop Reconstruction and Citizenship* (London, 1894), 22.

55. William R. Lethaby, "Carpenter's Furniture," in *Arts and Crafts Essays*, 307.

56. Halsey Ricardo, "Of the Room and Furniture," in *Arts and Crafts Essays*, 282.

57. Alf Bøe, *From Gothic Revival to Functional Form* (Oslo and Oxford, 1957), 50.

58. Mackmurdo, "Autobiographical Notes," chap. 2:31, 32; chap. 3:57; chap. 4:25.

59. Rossetti's version of the Oxford mural project is given in *Letters of Dante Gabriel Rossetti*, ed. O. Doughty and R. J. Wahl, 4 vols. (Oxford, 1967), 2:404–408. The building of Red House is detailed in W. J. Mackail, *The Life of William Morris*, 2 vols. (London, 1922), 1:143–49.

60. Rossetti, cited in Theodore Watts-Dunton, "Mr. William Morris," *The Athenaeum* 3598 (10 October 1896), 498.

61. Mackail 1922, 1:155–56.

62. Mackail 1922, 1:149.

63. Paul Thompson, *The Work of William Morris* (New York, 1967), 16.

64. Cited in Philip Henderson, *William Morris: His Life, Work, and Friends* (Harmondsworth, Middlesex, 1973), 93–94.

65. Henderson 1973, 93.

66. Michael Darby, *John Pollard Seddon* (London, 1983), 14.

67. The issue of construction is not entirely clear, several writers suggesting that the cabinet was made by the Morris firm. In one account, "The King René's Honeymoon Cabinet," *Magazine of Art* 20 (November 1896–April 1897), 323, Seddon himself said only that the Morris firm "undertook the commission to paint for it the four large panels of the lower part . . . and the six small panels of the upper part. . . ." In another account, however, Seddon wrote that the cabinet, "having left the hands of the cabinet-makers, may be said to have been completed as far as had been usual to that date"; but "as the author was seeking further decorative treatment," he submitted it to the Morris firm. John P. Seddon,

King René's Honeymoon Cabinet (London, 1898), 4. Burges' involvement is mentioned on page 2 of the latter work.

68. Seddon 1898, viii (emphasis in original).

69. Seddon 1898, 5, vii.

70. Duncan Robinson and Stephen Wildman, *Morris and Company in Cambridge* (London, 1980), 27–28.

71. Robinson and Wildman 1980, 27.

72. Thompson 1967, 30.

73. Philip Webb, cited in A. Charles Sewter, *The Stained Glass of William Morris and His Circle*, 2 vols. (New Haven and London, 1974), 1:89. See also Webb, 1:19; Martin Harrison, *Victorian Stained Glass* (London, 1980), 40; and Thompson 1967, 119.

74. Mackail 1922, 2:44; Thompson 1967, 120.

75. George Wardle, cited in Mackail 1922, 2:45.

76. Mackmurdo, "Autobiographical Notes," chap. 10:14.

77. Cited in *Victorian and Edwardian Decorative Arts* [exh. cat., Victoria and Albert Museum] (London, 1952), 58.

78. Mackmurdo, "Autobiographical Notes," chap. 10:14.

79. *Victorian and Edwardian Decorative Arts*, 1952, 58.

80. Alan Crawford, *C. R. Ashbee: Architect, Designer, and Romantic Socialist* (New Haven and London, 1985), 30.

81. Charles R. Ashbee, *An Endeavour towards the Teaching of John Ruskin and William Morris* (London, 1901), 1–2.

82. Charles R. Ashbee, ed., *Manual of the Guild and School of Handicraft* (London, 1892), 16.

83. Ashbee 1894, 90–91.

84. Ashbee 1894, 16; and Ashbee 1901, 47–48.

85. Ashbee 1894, 16. See also Ashbee 1908, 31–32.

86. Ashbee 1901, 19–20.

87. Comino 1980, 54–55.

88. *"Good Citizen's Furniture": The Work of Ernest and Sidney Barnsley* [exh. cat., Cheltenham Art Gallery and Museum] (Cheltenham, 1976), n.p.

89. Comino 1980, 86.

90. Halsey Ricardo, "Tradition in Its Bearing on Modern Art," and Thomas Okey, "Art Schools and Crafts Workshops," in *Problems of Reconstruction*, 233, 257.

91. Arthur Symons, *Studies in Seven Arts* (London, 1924), 125.

92. Mordaunt-Crook 1981, 137.

Contributors

David B. Brownlee teaches in the department of the history of art at the University of Pennsylvania. He is the author of *The Law Courts: The Architecture of George Edmund Street* and several articles on British Victorian architecture. His other publications include *Friedrich Weinbrenner: Architect of Karlsruhe; Building the City Beautiful: The Benjamin Franklin Parkway and the Philadelphia Museum of Art;* and (with David G. De Long) *Louis I. Kahn: In the Realm of Architecture.*

Gail Feigenbaum received her doctorate from Princeton University and is currently curator of academic programs at the National Gallery of Art. Coauthor with John Rupert Martin of *Van Dyck as Religious Artist* (1979), she has also written articles on sixteenth- and seventeenth-century Italian painting and drawing. Her monograph and catalogue raisonné of Lodovico Carracci's paintings and related drawings is forthcoming.

Mojmír S. Frinta is professor of medieval and early Renaissance art at the State University of New York at Albany. His research aims to bridge the gap between art-historical and art-technological investigations. In this spirit his book *The Genius of Robert Campin* (The Hague, 1966) and numerous articles on Italian and Central European painting were conceived. His comprehensive catalogue of punch shapes in late medieval panel and miniature painting is ready for publication in Prague, and the companion volume of interpretive text is near completion.

Hellmut Hager is Distinguished Professor of Art History and department head at Pennsylvania State University. He has published widely in the field of Italian late baroque architecture with emphasis on the followers of Bernini, especially Carlo Fontana. His doctoral degree is from the University of Bonn (1959), and before coming to this country (1971) he served as assistant to the director of the Bibliotheca Hertziana in Rome, where he spent many years doing research.

Peter M. Lukehart is director of the Trout Gallery and teaches art history at Dickinson College. With Craig Hugh Smyth he is working on a history of the teaching of art history in the United States.

Larry D. Lutchmansingh, associate professor of art history at Bowdoin College, is a Fulbright Fellow of the Graduate Institute of Art History, National Taiwan University, for 1991–1993. He has published in the areas of late nineteenth-century British art and design and twentieth-century art and is preparing a book on William Morris in relation to the Arts and Crafts Movement.

John M. Rosenfield is Abby Aldrich Rockefeller Professor Emeritus of East Asian Art at Harvard University. He received his doctorate from Harvard in Indian and Central Asian Buddhist art and extended his studies to medieval Japanese Buddhist art; he has also done much work in Japanese art of the Early Modern era. At Harvard he has served as chair of the Department of Fine Arts, acting director of the Art Museums, and delegate to the board of trustees, Museum of Fine Arts, Boston. His major publications include *Dynastic Arts of the Kushans, Traditions of Japanese Art, Courtly Tradition in Japanese Art and Literature,* and *Masters of Japanese Calligraphy.*

Marianna Shreve Simpson is curator of Islamic Near Eastern art at the Freer Gallery of Art and Arthur M. Sackler Gallery, Smithsonian Institution. From 1980 to 1992 she served as associate dean at the Center for Advanced Study in the Visual Arts, National Gallery of Art. Her primary area of research is the art of the Islamic book, and her publications treat illustrated manuscripts and paintings, narrative imagery, and related topics.